Raúl Castro and
the New Cuba

D1250132

DATE DUE

WEST CAMPUS

GAYLORD

Raúl Castro and the New Cuba

A Close-Up View of Change

HARLAN ABRAHAMS *and*
ARTURO LOPEZ-LEVY

McFarland & Company, Inc., Publishers
Jefferson, North Carolina, and London

LIBRARY OF CONGRESS ONLINE CATALOG DATA

Abrahams, Harlan.
    Raúl Castro and the new Cuba : a close-up view of change /
Harlan Abrahams and Arturo Lopez-Levy.
      p.   cm.
    Includes bibliographical references and index.

    ISBN 978-0-7864-6527-9
    softcover : 50# alkaline paper ∞

  1. Castro Ruz, Raúl, 1930–
  2. Castro Ruz, Raúl, 1930– — Political and social views.
  3. Presidents — Cuba.
  4. Social change — Cuba.
  5. One-party systems — Cuba.
  6. Rule of law — Cuba.
  7. Cuba — Politics and government —1990–
  8. Cuba — Economic conditions —1990–
  9. Cuba — Economic policy.
10. Cuba — Social conditions, 1959–
I. Title.   II. Lopez-Levy, Arturo.
    F1788.22.C32   2011   2011035281

BRITISH LIBRARY CATALOGUING DATA ARE AVAILABLE

© 2011 Harlan Abrahams and Arturo Lopez-Levy. All rights reserved

*No part of this book may be reproduced or transmitted in any form
or by any means, electronic or mechanical, including photocopying
or recording, or by any information storage and retrieval system,
without permission in writing from the publisher.*

On the cover: (inset) Raúl Castro; (background) A Ford Consul
passes in front of the Great Theatre of Havana (Brian S. Nelson)

Manufactured in the United States of America

*McFarland & Company, Inc., Publishers
  Box 611, Jefferson, North Carolina 28640
  www.mcfarlandpub.com*

For Carolyn,
who made this book possible
— Harlan

and

To the memory of my mother,
Gilda Sara,
who taught me to love Cuba
and the United States
— Arturo

Table of Contents

Preface

Harlan Abrahams

Cuba — the forbidden island — is a place of wondrous enchantment. It is also a land of deep contradictions, misunderstandings, and mythologies. I first traveled to Cuba in the summer of 1998 to research a novel I was writing. What better backdrop for a thriller than contemporary Havana? Think of the possibilities as characters collide with "hot" Latin culture and "cold" communism. It appealed greatly to the fiction writer in me.

But my academic self saw something different. As a former professor of law — constitutional law in particular — I had increasingly been viewing the solution to real-world problems as residing not in any single discipline, but rather in the intersections or interactions among the multiple disciplines. I saw current events as being largely driven by three great forces: economics, politics, and law. In the international context, these three great forces found expression in globalization, sovereignty, and the rule of law.

This book tells the story of the economic, political, legal, and social changes happening in Cuba under Raúl Castro Ruz, the younger brother of Fidel Castro, and the first new president the nation has seen in nearly five decades. This subject is tremendously instructive when it comes to real politics (both domestic and international), economics in the wake of the Great Recession of 2008–2009, and law as the official mediator between the two. Cuba has historically occupied a disproportionately large amount of public space not simply since Fidel took power in 1959, but since Europeans first came to the Americas five centuries ago. Look no further than the impact of the Cuban American exile community in Florida on national elections in the United States to confirm that Cuba's importance to America and to the world remains unusually strong.

And what more exotic and enchanting place could there be to study the interactions among economics, politics, and law than a nearby island nation, whose history has long been tied to ours, now emerging from decades of com-

1

munism? Cuba becomes a case study about the ways in which the United States responds to nations formerly viewed as "rogues" or "failed states."

So this book is the culmination of my dozen years of traveling to Cuba — all of the personal visits, the people I have met there, the experiences I have shared, and, of course, over ten years of study and research. But it is much more than that. This book is also the story — and the analysis and experiences and insights — of my coauthor Arturo Lopez-Levy. No tourist or even repeat traveler to the island can ever hope to see it "for real" without the guidance of someone who is deeply involved in its past, present, and future.

Our experiences — mine in traveling to the island, Arturo's in living there for the first three decades of his life — have given us the narrative bones for the stories of real Cubans experiencing real changes in real time. We attempt to focus on the present and the future, generally leaving histories and arguments about the past to other authors. And we also try to keep our focus on the younger Castro — the "little brother" — rather than on his older brother, the icon who still lives. Many others have written about Fidel and we believe our contribution lies elsewhere.

Nevertheless, we have included a handful of historic episodes from the past — not to dwell on them, but to provide background, context, and especially character. When weaving together the narrative stories we tell with the analysis of the issues these stories raise, we employ a considerable amount of dialogue. In most cases, this dialogue is derived either from actual conversations in which Arturo or I (or both of us) took part or from previously published sources, which are duly cited. When it comes to conversations in which Arturo or I took part, we have reproduced dialogue to the best of our memories and, in many cases, working from the contemporary notes we took during our interviews over the past two years. We did record some interviews as well, though our most crucial recording was drowned out by loud salsa music playing in a nearby park.

Of course, in addition to our own experiences and interviews, we did years of research into the literature about Cuba and the issues we decided to cover. My own perspective as a law professor and lecturer on public policy fit nicely with Arturo's perspective as a former political analyst for the Cuban government, a student of global economics and foreign affairs, and a Ph.D. candidate at the Josef Korbel School of International Relations at Denver University.

In Chapter Three we discuss several of the more recent books on Cuba, including Dan Erikson's fine book, *The Cuba Wars: Fidel Castro, the United States, and the Next Revolution* (2008), and Brian Latell's *After Fidel: Raul Castro and the Future of Cuba's Revolution* (2005). To those we should add *Cuba: What Everyone Needs to Know* (2009), by Julia Sweig of the Council of

Foreign Relations, and *Without Fidel: A Death Foretold in Miami, Havana, and Washington* (2009), by veteran journalist and Cuba watcher Louise Ann Bardach.

Our book differs from these books in three significant ways. First, despite what their titles might suggest, all of these books tend to focus far more on past events and past arguments than on the present or future of Cuba. By contrast, we pay close attention to the current situation and future prospects for the island. Second, these books all focus far more on the role of Fidel Castro than on the role of Raúl Castro, the younger brother and Cuba's current president. However, we pay close attention to Raúl and his ongoing presidency. And third — perhaps most importantly — none of these other books come with the voice of a native Cuban. Arturo's contributions to this book give it an authenticity I could not have achieved on my own.

We wish to thank all of the people who gave us interviews, hosted us, talked to us, and taught us about current life on the island. Those whose names we can use freely are identified in the text. Notable among them are Carlos Alzugaray, one of the most sophisticated Cuban analysts I have ever met; Monsignor Carlos Manuel de Céspedes, the general secretary of the Bishop's Council in Cuba; the staff of the fine Catholic lay publication *Espacio Laical*; the artists Adrián Pellegrini and Pedro García Espinosa; and, of course, Arturo's father, Arturo Lopez-Calleja.

We add a special thanks to Gloria Johnston and *Swing Vote Magazine*, which published an earlier version of this book online, in fourteen weekly installments, during the spring and summer of 2010.

I also wish to thank Arturo, my coauthor. One of the finest works of narrative nonfiction I have read comes from prize-winning journalist Dexter Filkins. His book *The Forever War* (2008) has been an inspiration. On page 343, Filkins says, "The writing of any book is a journey." I am privileged to have taken the journey of writing this book with Arturo. And I am honored to call him my friend.

Preface

Arturo Lopez-Levy

When Harlan Abrahams proposed that we write a book about the way Raúl Castro might change the lives of millions of Cubans and Cuba's relations with the United States in a different way from his brother Fidel, I couldn't say no. As a recent immigrant from Cuba and a doctoral candidate, I have a schedule that's far too busy for extra projects, but I couldn't miss the opportunity to discuss this issue as I see it.

I lived in Cuba for my first thirty-three years, with half of my family living in the United States. Pro-Castro, anti–Castro, or non-political — all of us were in some way traumatized in our innermost character by the choices of the generation that preceded us.

Harlan always insists on thanking me for the inside knowledge I bring from my experience of living in Cuba. He is right. I have had the experience of living in four different provinces. I've lived in a *batey* near a sugar factory, where my father worked as an engineer; in Santa Clara, where I grew up and where most of my family is from; in Havana, a city I learned to love after I moved there when I was seventeen; and in Guantánamo, where I went as a punishment and had my "man-up" experience.

At the same time, my participation in this book is the result of a deep love and admiration for the United States. This love has not been an easy affair. Like most Cubans on the island, I have suffered from the separation from relatives who left the country and settled in the United States and from a U.S. policy of sanctions that targeted not only the government but also the whole population of our country. There was a lot of what is proudly called in Cuba "anti-imperialist" propaganda. When it is sophisticated, it is against the American government; when it is not, it is anti–American, plain and simple.

I was lucky my mother had lived for a year in the United States before returning to Cuba in 1958. As an idealist and a revolutionary, she had very critical views about things America fought against in the 1960s, especially issues like racism and anti–Semitism. At the same time, she would remember her American friends, and the kindness of American people in the Miami she knew before Castro took power and it became the capital of the Cuban exiles. This was a testimony to the importance of contacts from people to people. The more people from Cuba and the United States can interact with each other, the easier it will be to undermine hostility and stereotypes about each other.

The United States was also where my grandparents and many of my relatives lived. It was a tragedy that until my mother died in 1994, when I was 25, I was able to see my relatives (grandparents, uncles, cousins) on the other side of the Straits only four times for one or two weeks. This is not normal among my American friends. Fifty years of a political war between Cuba and the United States is "easy said," but the emotional toll it has taken on many families is immense. My grandmother Chicha asked my brothers and me to write letters to our relatives in America, but at the same time we weren't supposed to tell other people, because such warm relations with people living outside were not well seen by the state.

Between 1995 and 2001, while unable to have a professional job in Cuba because of my open and sincere disagreement with many of Castro's policies, I dedicated a large part of my time to developing my Jewish identity. For years I was in charge of commenting on the weekly Torah reading at the Patronato, the synagogue in Havana I went to with my brothers. I could not be grateful enough to G-d for the community I got. In the terrible crisis years of the 1990s, when electricity was on and off, and food was scarce, and life was really difficult, we had a community of brothers and sisters in faith.

In those difficult times, the American Jewish community couldn't have been more supportive of their brothers and sisters in Cuba. Through BJ Synagogue in New York and the missions of the American Jewish Joint Distribution Committee, I met several Jewish American friends who went to Cuba and became very active in supporting what was clearly a religious and institutional revival of our congregations across the island, including my hometown of Santa Clara.

I must mention my great friend Walter Scheuer, the most generous *mensch* I have ever known, a *tzadik*. Wally and his family have been extremely kind to me since we met. Through his friend Reuben Hazak and his wife Nira, Wally ensured that I had a soft landing in Israel, where I went after I left Cuba (since every time I had asked the Cuban authorities to leave for the United States, my exit visa was denied). Wally made sure that Reuben showed me the north and south, and the east and west of Israel, and of course Jerusalem, land we love as our ancestors and religion taught us to do from generation to generation.

After I came to New York, the Scheuer family helped me to study, to manage the language, to have friends in the city, to feel part of America. When I arrived in NYC, after September 11, Wally, a veteran of World War II, showed me the strength and wisdom of a true patriot. I had met him in the middle of the Elián González crisis. After he returned to America, he sent me many American history books. He wanted me to know about the glory of American values and how, despite the wrong American policies toward Cuba — he agreed with me on that from the first time we discussed the issue — I must understand how American democracy was a force for good in the world. Later he would laugh every time I told him something about American history he didn't already know.

In Cuba I met other Americans who made a difference since I came to the States. Rose Glazer, a force of passion if there is one, pushed my application to Columbia University even when I was not sure I could be accepted. There are also Sherryl Gold and Rochelle Wolf, in whom I always see the image of the American friends my mother used to tell me about — warm, generous, cosmopolitan, loving Cuban culture but at the same time critical. Sherryl introduced me to Jackie Lewinson, whose home has been "mi casa" in Washington for several years. Jackie loves Cuba but she has not been able to visit Santa Clara due to the travel ban. She was my main support in the fall of 2006 when my grandmother in Cuba was sick just before her one hundredth birthday. My family in Cuba already loves Jackie but they have never been able to reciprocate her friendship. Paul Dean, "my amigo Pablo," as I like to call him, has been a brother since we met. Despite our age differences, Paul and I are buddies. He introduced me to Steve Berman, whose clothes I have literally worn and who, together with his wife Elaine, made me a Coloradan.

When my friend Harlan asked me to write this book with him, I had many other responsibilities, among them to write my doctoral dissertation, but writing this couldn't be postponed. It was an opportunity to give back just a little to those Cubans and Americans who made me love and feel passionately for my two countries, so that I miss them wherever I am not on the Cuban beaches or in the Colorado mountains, and also to the two people from whom I learned to speak passionately, and move my arms, as a Cuban, in addition to searching for common ground and compromise when there is a good deal in sight, saying as a good American: "I can live with that."

Part I

Two New Presidents

Chapter One
Arturo and Raúl

I arrived in Havana on the night of Barack Obama's inauguration. I had watched in the Denver airport as Chief Justice Roberts and the new president stumbled over the oath of office — and it hadn't spoiled a thing. I wept anyway and so did many others gathered around the flat-screen monitor tuned to CNN.

Five hours later I watched Obama's inaugural address on my netbook in Cancún, drinking a margarita and reading the text alongside the streaming video image. How many times have I explained that going to Cuba through Mexico is a mere convenience? It's not about legality. U.S. citizens can travel legally to Cuba, but they cannot spend money there. That violates the Trading with the Enemy Act — unless you get a license from the Treasury Department. And that's why I had bothered to get a "specific license" to travel to the island and spend money there — so long as I did it to research this book.

At 11:15 P.M. I cleared Customs and took a battered white taxi to Nuevo Vedado. When my driver — a man of sixty with stubble on his chin and grey in his hair — realized I was not going to a tourist hotel, he launched into a tirade about conditions on the island. Thus were illustrated the four "big" truths that stamped themselves on everything during that visit to the Pearl of the Antilles: (1) taxi drivers, no matter where they are, can always find something to bitch about; (2) older people in Cuba continue to cling to their ideologies more than younger people, just like in America; (3) the reforms I was going to witness in Cuba were not yet trickling down to the poorest people; and (4) the more I wanted to talk to people about their new president, Raúl Castro Ruz, the younger brother of their icon Fidel Castro, the more they wanted to talk to me about Obama.

These four truths show how much Americans have in common with Cubans. They also show why the dance that is unfolding between the leaders in Washington and the leaders in Havana will result in a gradual dismantling of the American embargo of Cuba, coupled with greater openings for business and political participation on the island.

It seems inevitable. The great forces of global economics, international politics, and the rule of law are busy in Cuba. Professors Daniel Deudney of Johns Hopkins and John Ikenberry of Princeton wrote in 2009 about the ways in which these three great forces interact.[1] First, they said, rising standards of living made possible by capitalism create a middle class whose interests often challenge those of authoritarian leaders. Stated differently, greater levels of wealth and education lead naturally to demands for greater political participation and more accountability. Second, there is a link between capitalist property systems and the rule of law. Under capitalism, means of production are held as private property and transactions occur through contracts. For capitalist economies to function, "the enforcement of contracts and the adjudication of business disputes require court systems and the rule of law." Private economic rights and the institutions that enforce them necessarily constrain state power and, over time, generate demands for more political rights. Third, development resulting from capitalism leads to a proliferation of interests. Modern capitalist societies grow increasingly complex. Vocations become specialized. Plurality proliferates. Diversity of interests leads to demands for real elections among competing parties.

That all sounds pretty theoretical, but it applies directly to the experience of the Cuban people today. Despite the widespread bashing of America's brand of capitalism — "market fundamentalism" — in the aftermath of the recession of 2009, Cuba is struggling to maintain its socialist identity while doing real business in the real world, a world of markets and globalization mending from serious wounds.

The taxi driver pulled off Ave 26 onto Calle 33, and immediately it was dark.

We were on a little-traveled residential street, lined with shade trees, motor bikes, and rusty cars. The driver slowed to a crawl toward the middle of the block. In the twin headlight beams, a slender man with silver hair and black eyeglasses was caught walking his dog. The man looked vaguely familiar, though I knew I had never seen him before. The dog was a sleek Siberian Husky — far sleeker than any Cuban dog has any right to be.

The man came to the taxi, looked inside, and the driver rolled down his window. The man spoke to me in heavily accented English, "Who are you looking for?"

"Arturo Lopez-Levy," I said.

The man said, "I am his father. Come with me."

Arturo's story begins with Antonio Enrique Lussón, a real guerrilla's guerrilla.[2] During the Revolution, Comandante Lussón fought with Raúl Castro on the Second Front, where he had led Column No. 17, called "Abel

Santamaría." In January 1959, Raúl assigned Lussón the task of organizing Fidel's victory caravan from Santiago de Cuba to Havana. Lussón was with Fidel when Cuban revolutionary troops and militias repelled the CIA's invaders at the Bay of Pigs. Today, almost five decades later, he serves his country as Cuba's minister of transportation.

In the summer of 1966, however, Comandante Lussón was leading a cadre of youngsters on a march from the Sierra Maestra in southeast Cuba to the Sierra Cristal in the northeast. The march was meant to relive Raúl's creation of the Second Front as separate from Fidel's First Front. It was meant for those who were too young to fight seven years before. There were thousands making the march, all recent graduates from major universities.

During the march Comandante Lussón was approached by a young man named Arturo Lopez-Calleja Hiort-Lorenzen and a young woman named Gilda Sara Fernandez-Levy. They were both mechanical engineers who had just graduated from the University in Santa Clara. They said they wanted to get married at the end of the march.

Comandante Lussón studied the young man. He was tall for a Cuban, tall enough to be a basketball player. In fact, he would later play on the national team. He got his height from his Danish blood, for while the Lopez-Calleja family had been on the island for many decades, the Hiort-Lorenzen family had not. Notably pale skin, a long nose, and a thin physique completed the young man's image.

The Comandante turned his gaze upon the young woman. She was very pretty: brown hair, olive skin, and hazel eyes, as well as a long nose. And, said many, a sweet disposition that showed in her quiet laughter and her "Jewish smile." Her mother Sara was called the "Mora," like the Moors, so people called her "Sarita" or "Morita."

That night Comandante Lussón reported the couple's request to Raúl Castro, the leader of all the cadres. Raúl laughed with good nature and declared he wanted to be the best man. This was a major honor, for the best man is very important in Cuban culture. He's the person who arranges the couple's honeymoon, and indeed Raúl would later send the newlyweds to the sunny beaches of Varadero and the romantic city of Santiago de Cuba to celebrate their marriage. Raúl's wife, Vilma Espin, a celebrated revolutionary icon in her own right, would be their matron of honor. The wedding would be held at the end of the march in the small village of Micara, near the secret headquarters of the Second Front.

The lovers each had Jewish blood but neither was religious. So they married in a civil ceremony. Everyone enjoyed the beautiful setting. The place was surrounded by groves of tall jucaro trees, similar to aspens. The mountains were filled with the greens of summer. Colorful flowers bloomed everywhere. No pavement was in sight, for the only access was by dirt track.

Raúl Castro (far right, in hat) at the wedding of Arturo's parents (far left) in 1966 (Arturo Lopez-Levy collection).

And that's how Raúl Castro became the best man at Arturo and Sara's wedding. Two years later, they would have a son and name him Arturo. Fifteen years later, Raúl's first daughter Deborah would marry the younger Arturo's cousin, Luís Rodríguez Lopez-Calleja, who is today the chief executive officer of Grupo GAESA, the branch of the military that supervises "military enterprises"— the business of Cuba's economy.

And then there's Uncle Guillermo, the father of Luís, an even bigger general.

"There has always been a connection between our families," explains the younger Arturo, coauthor of this book. "I was born in 1968, a year after Che was killed, in the ninth year of the Revolution, while the Soviets were crushing Prague. My parents met in college. My mother's family came from Turkey in 1912. My great-grandfather was the first to be buried in the Jewish cemetery of Santa Clara."

The link began with Guillermo, Arturo's father's brother-in-law, who lived with the family. He was a major leader of the underground July 26 movement in Las Villas. The family suffered from living with a rebel. Batista's men would come often and search their home, removing everything from each of the rooms and leaving it strewn about.

"My father tells the story," Arturo recalls, "how he was once arrested by the police because he went to the house of Orlando Bosch to pick up a pair of basketball shoes that my aunt Cristina had sent him from Miami through Bosch's first wife. Bosch later became a notorious terrorist, but at the time, he was fighting against Batista side by side with my Uncle Guillermo. My father still believes that he was saved by one of his classmates' fathers, an officer who recognized him as simply a fourteen-year-old boy, despite his unusual height, with no direct involvement in the rebellion."

By 1960, however, Fidel had chased Batista from the island, and Arturo's parents were old enough to join Cuba's new literacy campaign. Arturo's mother used to tell him that joining the literacy campaign was a decisive moment in her life. Her parents had already left Cuba and she had been planning to join them in the States. But the literacy campaign gave her the opportunity to teach and help poor people, so she decided to stay and join the Revolution.

Arturo and Sara arrived at the university in 1961. Sara was the first woman in Cuba to graduate as a mechanical engineer. By 1966 her parents were living in Miami. Also, her husband's brother was living in Chicago. He had left Cuba after seeing all his family's property confiscated and had been mistreated at the airport by the communists.

Sara's father wanted to send them a car. It would open opportunities in the brave new Cuba. But he couldn't buy one in Miami: too costly and too politically difficult. It was easy, however, to buy one in Canada and have it shipped to Cuba. And it would be even easier if Arturo's uncle would go from Chicago to Canada to buy it.

So Sara's father telephoned Arturo's uncle and said he would give the uncle the money so that he could buy the car in Canada and have it shipped to Cuba. But the uncle flatly refused. He wouldn't touch it. When Sara's father asked for a reason, the uncle declared he would not do business in Cuba — or have anything to do with the island — as long as Fidel Castro held power.

So Sara's father traveled to Canada, bought the car there, and sent it to Sara and Arturo in Santa Clara. It was a white Volkswagen Beetle. Its heater worked fine, but it had no air conditioner. Everyone called it "La Cucarachita"— the little cockroach.

Young Arturo recalls how the family would pour into that little car. It got tighter and tighter as three brothers were added over the next few years. Still, the Volkswagen distinguished the family because transportation did indeed bring opportunities. By the mid–1970s the Russians were handing out their boxy little Ladas like candy, but by then the family had gotten its head start. They lived well by Cuban standards.

At 6 or 7, young Arturo began to note things about his family that were different. "We had a very close family that supported each other," he recalls, "even among those who had left the island. This was not common. And it certainly wasn't the policy of the Cuban government."

Maintaining close ties with those who had gone to America cost those who had stayed in Cuba. When Arturo's mother applied for party membership, she was asked whether she kept in contact with her parents and brother who lived in the United States.

"Yes," answered Sara truthfully.

She was then asked if she was such a committed revolutionary, how could she consider these people — these *gusanos!*— these worms — to be her family?

Again Sara answered truthfully: First, her parents and brother had left the island before Castro took power. Second, and more important, it wasn't that she *considered* them to be family; they *were* her family. This was a fact. She wouldn't deny it.

Sara's honesty delayed her acceptance into the Communist Party. And when Arturo was 9, something else happened. His father left for 18 months. Arturo explains: "In 1975 my uncle — then an officer in the Armed Forces Medical Services — was sent to Angola on some kind of mission, in secrecy. He traveled on a commercial ship that was ordered to land at Luanda as soon as independence was declared. In 1977 my father went there to help to create a system of higher education after decolonization. Like many Cubans who contributed to Angola's independence and the defeat of apartheid in South Africa, my father has always been very proud of his time teaching at the University of Luanda."

In 1975, Sara became a delegate to the 1st Party Congress. Others in the family continued to climb the party ladder. And while young Arturo was realizing his family was both politically involved and also different from many others, he became aware of a further complication: the Jewish issue.

Arturo had Jewish blood on both sides of his family. He began becoming more aware of it. His mother had always been called Morita because her family had come from Turkey and she had dark olive skin. To Cubans, anyone from North Africa, Turkey or the Middle East was "Moorish" or "Turkish," whether Christian, Muslim or Jew.

He says, "There was a black friend of the family named Lando, who came from the Monteagudos, who used to sing a song to my mother that goes, 'From Syria comes the Moorish, so beautiful her eyes, an enchantress!'[3] Well, that was my mother. To be conscious of our Jewish identity made us more tolerant. There was still a lot of racism in Cuba but our best friends in the neighborhood were 'Abuela Nila' from the Monteagudos and another black family, the Hernandez-Moyas, who lived next door. As I got older I noticed my mother kept copies of *Exodus* and Anne Frank's diary on the bookshelves for anyone to see. I read *Exodus* and it changed the way I saw my Jewish identity."

Under these conflicting influences — the party line, the family reality, the father who was often away, and that nagging Jewish issue — Arturo began acting out. He started running with a rough crowd. "My brothers and I were rebellious," he says in a casual, matter-of-fact way. "We threw stones and eggs at buses. That sort of thing."

When his father learned of his antics, he sent Arturo to the military high school in Santa Clara to straighten him out. "Every Friday," recalls Arturo, "we would march and learn guerrilla warfare. They taught us how to make Molotov Cocktails and how to shoot rifles using bolt-action carbines and AK-47s, which we called 'AKs' — as in 'aka.' I was still in high school when my cousin Luís married Raúl's daughter Deborah. Now this was a very big thing for our family. It was the summer of 1983. I was nearly fifteen years old."

Arturo had been in the presence of Fidel and Raúl before, but never so closely. He looked forward to the big celebration after the wedding. It was held at the home of his Aunt Cristina in the swanky neighborhood called Kohly, east of the Río Almandares, just off Calle 23 near Miramar. This was a very pretty neighborhood, with a nice park and forest used by the party elite.

A cry went forth from those on the porch: "Fidel is coming! Fidel is coming!"

Three shiny black Mercedes rolled up the street. It stopped and Fidel sprang out, wearing his trademark green fatigues. The wedding guests cheered. He was a celebrity.

Fidel spent a lot of time talking to Arturo's grandmother, Eva, better known as "Abuelita Lula," who was ill with kidney disease. Since her parents were an Austrian Jew from Cracow and a Dane, Lula was always a smiling European in the tropics, sweltering in the heat. Fidel saw she needed fans to cool down. And a couple of days later, two boxes of electric fans arrived at the house.

"Fidel was the legend," says Arturo, "but Raúl was the guy in the family photo."

The father of the bride wore a fine *guayabera* that day. He made a point of talking to everyone personally, one by one. He paid special attention to Arturo's father.

By then Arturo had already grown an inch taller than his father, so Raúl gave him the nickname "Pancho El Largo" — the tall fellow. Raúl would laugh and say, "Pancho! You are too tall!" Or he might order young Arturo about: "Pancho, come here!"

Finally Arturo stood face to face with Raúl for his one-on-one talk. Raúl asked, "What high school do you go to?"

"Camilo Cienfuegos Military School," answered Arturo.

Raúl laughed his good-natured laugh. Then, with the hardened heel of his hand, he punched Arturo square in the chest and declared, "This makes me very proud for you. It is a very great thing you are doing for your country."

The punch surprised Arturo but didn't hurt. He knew Raúl could have made it hurt if he had wanted to. You didn't get to be head of the Revolutionary Armed Forces — the FAR — by being soft. Arturo looked down, feeling embarrassed.

"What's wrong?" asked Raúl.

"I just don't know if I can be a good soldier," answered Arturo.

"Why not?"

"Because I am asthmatic."

Raúl laughed and punched Arturo in the chest again. "That's no problem!" he exclaimed, sharing his smile with Arturo's three younger brothers. "Che had asthma too! But he was still the best fighter we ever had!"

A few years later Arturo sat before a scowling Captain Olga. Her work with military counterintelligence was to monitor the students at the Higher Institute for International Relations, the diplomatic academy in Havana. And though they were all hand-picked and vetted, she didn't wear kid gloves. It wasn't her job to be their friend.

Exasperated with Arturo's intransigence — who did this arrogant kid think he was? — she stated the latest charges against him: "You are too critical of our Soviet friends."

Arturo calculated his response, measuring Captain Olga with his clear blue eyes. She was a big woman — almost as tall as his mother — and wore her thick black hair clipped short. She always looked well put together in her starched and creased uniform, but she didn't know much about international relations. So the students all called her "Olguita" despite her size and her overbearing manner, which had to be deliberate.

When Arturo didn't respond fast enough, she snapped, "You should be proud of being pro–Soviet. I am pro–Soviet. And our minister Raúl has said that he is pro–Soviet."

"I am proud," Arturo said a bit too quickly, "of being pro–Cuban."

The captain frowned. She was no psychologist and didn't appreciate his attitude. Rather, she was a simple functionary assigned by the military to keep his mind intact. And their sessions had grown contentious, degenerating into cliché. Arturo believed Captain Olga was typical of the kind of communist that's always challenging your bona fides as a revolutionary and always attacking "the enemies" of the movement.

For her part, Captain Olga believed Arturo had problems in his thinking because he had so much family living in the United States. She was frustrated she could not get Arturo to adopt this view. She tried a different angle: "I've heard you are a great admirer of Che."

Now this was no big secret. Arturo had grown up in Santa Clara, near the mountains where Che had fought some of the most important battles in the Revolution. As a youth Arturo had spent many solitary hours hiking in the very same mountains where Che had hidden in Caballete de Casas. The members of his family who had stayed on the island were committed to the Revolution.

"Yes," he said.

He decided not to add anything. His antennae were twitching. He knew what had brought him to this place. It began at the wedding of Luís and Deborah. Arturo's parents had stayed in touch with Raúl and Vilma. A few months after the wedding, Sara, then a professor of mechanical engineering in Santa Clara, was given a promotion. She would be the rector at the new Higher Institute of Industrial Design in Havana. The family moved and Arturo transferred high schools. He joined the Young Communist League.

"I was sixteen," he says. "It was 1985 and people were saying Reagan was getting ready to invade the island. I started getting interested in international relations. Foreign affairs. Anything and everything political. I talked my parents into letting me apply to the Higher Institute of International Relations, the diplomatic academy in Havana, which was connected to the university and the Ministry of Foreign Affairs."

Arturo wasn't training to be a spy or diplomat. He was going to be an analyst. He soon gained access to a wealth of information published outside Cuba. He would spend many hours in the library reading books, magazines and articles that could never be read by everyday citizens. Writings very different from the ideological norm.

He recalls, "Havana was more cosmopolitan than Santa Clara. There were many foreign influences in Havana beyond the Soviets. I had professors at the Institute who had been in the Foreign Service and had lived abroad."

One professor, named Miguel Alfonso, was married to a Jewish American journalist named Portia Siegelbaum from New York. Professor Alfonso would listen, and recommend that his students should listen, to world news on shortwave radios. Broadcasts from the Netherlands and BBC brought abstract ideas into the real world. Arturo gained a more global perspective. He saw many shades of color in addition to black and white. The world was not all about us-versus-them. He started to be attracted to the less dogmatic ways of the Social Democratic Parties.

"I began to question some of the policies of my government. I thought this was consistent with my training as an analyst. I was, after all, being told to think for myself. It was also the time of *glasnost* and *perestroika*. Kids from revolutionary families all over the world were questioning the wisdom of their elders. I became active in student federation politics. And I participated in discussion groups about non-orthodox and democratic forms of socialism."

Many students said they would like to democratize the system. They wanted to see more than one candidate stand for high party positions. They weren't questioning socialism but rather the way things got decided. So they kept their groups small. They knew they were walking a thin line. They would read foreign books and articles in class and bring controversial ideas to their discussions. Arturo read more and more, and soon began speaking out.

At the same time, the Jewish issue sprouted anew. After reading *Exodus* again, Arturo visited the library at the Patronato, the Conservative Jewish Community Center built during the 1950s. It houses one of the largest libraries of Judaica in Latin America. He met Adela Dworin, the head of the library. She and Jose Miller, the president of the Jewish community, introduced him to the history of the Cuban Jews and some important Zionist publications.

A few months later, Arturo was taking a class with Professor Domingo Amuchastegui about the Middle East. Arturo says, "His book provided a good survey of the history of Asia and Africa, but it was so critical of Israel that it bordered on being anti–Semitic. There were thirty students there. It was 1990. Professor Amuchastegui was rattling on and on about Israel in a very negative way."

Finally, Arturo interrupted the professor and asked why, when all other nations had the right to self-determination, was the creation of a Jewish State being presented as some sort of plot by the United States — especially since other nationalist movements in other postcolonial places, like Africa, were being presented in such a positive light?

The professor responded, "The Arabs and Jews lived together for many decades in Palestine before the Zionists came to chase the Arabs out...."

But it was too late for Arturo to accept the orthodox response. He was moving toward more independent thinking. At that time he was working as an intern for the Americas Department of the Central Committee, in the section that was charged with analyzing Peru. He also mingled with students from other universities. And MININT — the Ministry of the Interior — began following him.

One day, after he criticized the views of a lieutenant colonel at an international conference on sociology, MININT agents approached Arturo, asking his name and work. The next thing he knew, he was sitting before Captain Olga, who was smirking at him while grilling and pumping him for information: "Do you think your *engreido* attitudes — challenging your professors and those in authority — and your criticism of our allies abroad — especially our Soviet friends — would be what Che would want for you?"

Arturo wouldn't yield: "Yes, yes! Because I have read his writings and in them he says very clearly that our minds should never become slaves of the official thinking."

Captain Olga muttered something about "Jews ... Zionists ... leftist deviations."

Again Arturo couldn't help himself: "We should have a more balanced view!"

"You have no idea what you are talking about," said Captain Olga, jotting down some notes about her problem case. She carefully straightened the papers on which she had made them, squared their edges, and slipped them into the file. Then she brusquely terminated the meeting.

Arturo went about his business until a few months later, when Saddam Hussein invaded Kuwait. At a presentation on current affairs, he spoke out: "Saddam has invaded his neighbor — a sovereign country! — in violation of international law. Perhaps we should join in common cause with the Americans in expelling the Iraqis from Kuwait. This could create some problems for those Cuban exiles who are trying to prevent any cooperation between Cuba and the United States."

People were shocked. Some jeered. Afterward, he left with his close friend Alejandro, who was the president of the student federation at the Institute. They were getting on their Russian-made bicycles when Alejandro leaned close and said, "Arturo, you had better watch how you are saying things. You are shooting your mouth off in places where you don't know who is listening."

Arturo didn't take the hint. His good friend Alejandro could be exaggerating.

But two weeks later, Arturo was summoned to the Ministry of Armed Forces. He was led to the back of a building that faced Revolution Square. He entered a back door and was taken to a plain little office where two women in uniform waited for him. One was a lieutenant colonel named Ada and the other was a major named Marta.

Ada affected a formal attitude, like a mother about to scold her child. Marta was fatter and tougher and coarser. The good cop and the bad. The bad one cut to the chase: "You are being expelled from the Institute because your ideas are incompatible with what the FAR expects of its members." Arturo opened his mouth to ask why, but the good cop cut him off: "This matter has already been discussed with your uncle."

Arturo's heart sank. Uncle Guillermo, the father of Luís, had given his okay. Guillermo was known as the "Gallo Ronco," the rooster with the gravelly voice. Arturo admired him. Now he could just imagine that gravelly voice saying, perhaps with a hint of genuine regret, "Do what you must."

Arturo argued, "I feel I am a good revolutionary. I am committed. I could have made mistakes, but I do not see this as a correct decision — that you are expelling me."

The bad cop insisted the decision had already been made.

The good cop told Arturo that the military expected him to remedy his mistakes. She warned him against strutting about acting like he was more important than the party.

So Arturo ran home to tell his parents. His mother went ballistic. "We must appeal this injustice!" she exclaimed. She wrote letters to Raúl and even went to see Arturo's cousin Luís in person. Arturo's father took a different route. He called in a debt.

"Recall," says Arturo, "my mother was the first woman to become the rector of a Cuban institution of higher learning. She uncovered great corruption and abuse of power in the office of the man who ran the National Office of Industrial Design. The problem was that the man was Ivan Espin, the brother of Vilma Espin, wife of Raúl. My mother went to Vilma and denounced his corruption. Vilma was furious at my mother and protective of her brother. It cost my mother her job."

A parade of professors, workers and students from the Higher Institute of Industrial Design came to Arturo's house to express solidarity with his mother. During their summer vacation in Varadero, Arturo's cousin Luís and his wife Deborah also came to visit. They told Arturo's mother and father that they had opposed Vilma's protection of her brother's behavior. Deborah even claimed that she had argued strongly with her mother when Vilma had said that Arturo's mother was too naïve.

Not long after Sara was forced to resign her deanship, Arturo was sitting on a bench in the living room on the second floor of his aunt and uncle's house in Kohly, where Luís and Deborah lived for a time. He was listening to the family discussion, called by his aunt and uncle, that was occurring outside on the balcony.

Raúl — who had come without Vilma — was sitting next to Arturo's father across the porch, but within easy earshot. Raúl had been making small talk: "How are you? And how is the family?" Then he said, "I always respected your wife for taking the stand she took. I know she was made to resign but she has my respect."

Arturo didn't hear his father's response. But he did hear what Raúl said next: "That brother-in-law of mine is a piece of shit! I owe you one."

As it turned out, Arturo was the one. Raúl intervened and Arturo was sent to Guantánamo as a soldier to keep an eye on the Americans who had a naval base across the minefields. A year later, Arturo was called back to Havana, where he finished his education and graduated from the Institute.

His political slate was wiped clean. He went back to the FAR, this time as a lieutenant, assigned to a tank brigade at Managua, outside Havana. It was a big step up from Guantánamo.

In May, Arturo took off his uniform and put on his *guayabera* for another party at the Kohly home of his aunt and uncle. Sure enough, there was Raúl, seated with a group of men. When he spotted Arturo, he called out, "Pancho! You're back!"

Arturo smiled and waved politely. He was gratified the general remembered the nickname he had bestowed years before. Arturo waited patiently for his one-on-one chat.

When his turn came, they spoke for about 20 minutes. Raúl recalled not only the nickname but also the drama. He asked, "So, Pancho, how was Guantánamo?"

Arturo answered, "It was a very good experience for me."

"What did you think of your fellow soldiers?"

"They were very nice to work with."

"Did you make any mates — any friends — in the army?"

"Oh, yes," said Arturo, "I made many friends."

"What about your unit?" pressed the general. "Was there any misbehavior?"

"No, sir," answered Arturo.

"Were the soldiers treated correctly?"

"Yes, sir." Arturo realized Raúl was checking on the mood of the troops, garnering feedback from the bottom up. By this time Cuba was beginning to enter the so-called Special Period of Austerity caused by the collapse of the Soviet Union. A third of the island's economy had dried up as subsidies from the Soviets suddenly disappeared. Discontent was rampant. Dissent was on the rise.

Arturo played it cool. He gave politically correct answers.

Raúl said, "Congratulations on your service at Guantánamo. You've witnessed what it is like to be on the lines. It's very good for your patriotic spirit. I think every young leader should spend some time in Guantánamo."

Arturo nodded his agreement.

Raúl concluded, "It is good, Pancho, this unfortunate incident is behind you."

Arturo smiled and departed. Luís intercepted him and led him to a private room. Luís closed the door and said, "You did very well. Now be mature — in how you think and what you say. Don't let opportunities go by. Don't speak out of place."

A month later, in June 1993, Arturo was transferred to MININT, where he went to a school inside the ministry to finish his training as an intelligence analyst. A year later, he was assigned to the Department of Analysis, Section of the United States. He was finally getting to do exactly what he had been recruited to do in the first place.

But it only lasted a few months. By the end of 1994, he had decided to resign from the military. In March his mother died an untimely death at 49, a few months after he began working as an intelligence analyst. Arturo was devastated. His family had always been so close. He says, "When my grandmother and uncle came from the United States after the funeral, I wanted to spend time with them. But MININT policy required that I ask permission to see them. It caused a big problem for me. I knew I had never really wanted to stay in the military anyway. I had figured it was better to go into the army and spend my time at Guantánamo than accept my expulsion from the Institute. But now I could no longer reconcile my work with my convictions. My family issues provoked this situation, but it had been coming for a long time."

Headquarters of Cuba's Ministry of the Interior, in the Plaza of the Revolution; note the iconic steel sculpture of Che Guevara built on to the side of the building (Arturo Lopez-Levy collection).

So in December 1994 he submitted his resignation to the chief of the intelligence services, Colonel Eduardo Delgado. The colonel refused to accept it. He handed it back to Arturo and said, "Think it over. You have a good career here. Do not throw it away."

Arturo thought it over. Then he re-submitted his resignation in February 1995. This time no one handed it back. But it was not immediately accepted, either. You don't extricate yourself from MININT overnight. It dragged on for a year. Meanwhile, Arturo was taken out of his sensitive position and sent to work in the fields outside Havana. For three days a week he would toil in agriculture, most often picking tomatoes. And for two days he would work as a librarian in a small library for officers of the state.

Again Arturo had fallen. And again the Jewish issue raised its head. For while he waited for his resignation to be accepted, Arturo again started frequenting the library at the Patronato. When finally his resignation was accepted and he started looking for jobs — there were no jobs! Not for him.

Unemployed, he searched for alternatives. Carleton University from Ottawa was running a program in Havana, so from September 1996 to December 1997 he enrolled in that program and earned his master's degree in economics. He also attended services every Saturday at the Patronato, growing more deeply involved in Jewish life.

Arturo met a lot of people at the synagogue, including Americans who were allowed to go to the island for "humanitarian reasons." Nature took its course and he began driving Jewish visitors around, serving as their tour guide. He met a Jewish doctor from New York and began dating her. She stayed in Cuba to study "green medicine."

Near the end of 1999, Arturo grew anxious. It was almost 5 years since he had left MININT and he had to go 5 years without access to secret information before he could travel abroad. He had been accepted into a Ph.D. program at Emory University in Atlanta and was hoping the 5 years would run from when he first tried to resign, or at worst a few months later. He certainly had been given no access to secret information while he was picking tomatoes in the fields outside Havana.

Relations with the United States were, however, strained at the time due to the raging disputes over Elián González. Arturo's future hung in the balance — both his romance with the American doctor and his program at Emory, an extraordinary opportunity.

MININT denied him an exit visa. Though 5 years had passed, he wasn't allowed to leave the island. He lost his woman and his Ph.D. He was stuck in Havana giving tours to B'nai B'rith groups from Canada and the States.

And that's how I met him. It was the morning of December 3, 1999. I was covering the Latin American Film Festival for *Raygun* magazine and researching a novel set in contemporary Havana. My wife Carolyn and our friends Dan and Tonda were traveling with me. My novel was set in Cuba's tiny Jewish community, so we searched in the hot winter sun, along narrow steaming streets, for Adath Israel, the little synagogue in La Habana Vieja, near Acosta and Picota. When we finally found it, we were shocked. A giant black tour bus, smelling of diesel and venting cold steam from the air conditioning inside, was sitting in front of it, idling in the street.

We went inside. Dan and I donned yarmulkes. We dropped our voices. Tonda, in her loud Midwestern tones, and Carolyn, in her louder Long Island ones, continued to jabber. Until we entered the sanctuary and beheld a handsome young Cuban man, his thick long hair tied in a ponytail, lecturing a group of little old ladies.

"He's cute," squealed Tonda as we slid into the pews, listening to the lecture.

"...and Calle Muralla was once the 'Jewish Appian Way' because it was the main street of the neighborhood for thousands of Jewish refugees. There were over 20,000. These were not the old Spanish Jews — the *conversos* or *marranos*—who came during the Conquest and practiced their Judaism secretly. These were Sephardic Jews who came from the Ottoman Empire and Ashkenazim from Eastern Europe. Many spoke Yiddish. They were called *Polacos* by the locals because so many of them came from Poland."

The young man spoke in heavily accented but educated English: long sentences punctuated with florid gestures and flashing blue eyes. The little old ladies were mesmerized, hanging on every syllable. Later, Carolyn gave a dozen boxes of Chanukah candles to the elderly caretaker of the synagogue. She asked, "Who were those ladies?"

"B'nai B'rith," he said. "From the city of Phoenix, in Arizona. They are here for the tour."

"The tour?"

"*Sí, sí*— the Jewish tour." He explained that although there were only 1,500 Jews left in Cuba, each year about 15,000 Americans came to visit them. He laughed and said, "We can't afford a rabbi, but we always have plenty of candles for Chanukah."

Every morning after that, we noticed the same handsome young man in the grand lobby of the Hotel Nacional, gathering up his charges for that day's tour. He began to acknowledge our existence with a nod or a smile.

One day, after lunch, Carolyn and I were standing at the top of the low cliff behind the Nacional, overlooking the Malecón. We saw a crowd of young adults dressed in light khaki trousers and white button-up shirts, running up the Malecón.

Their numbers swelled. We wondered what was going on. A convoy of

The historic Hotel Nacional, site of many adventures in Havana (Harlan Abrahams collection).

buses arrived near the intersection of La Rampa and the Malecón, letting off more crowds, many of them teenagers dressed in orange trousers and white shirts. Then came more buses with more youngsters. They all began marching up the Malecón.

"We've got to go down there and see what's happening," I said.

"You bet," said Carolyn. So we flew down the cliff to the Malecón.

"What's going on?" asked Carolyn of some of the youths who were rushing by us.

"It's a *manifestación*," said one of the youths, slowing up. "A demonstration."

"A demonstration?"

"*Sí*—a spontaneous demonstration. A protest."

Spontaneous demonstration? There was nothing spontaneous about it. Convoys were rolling up the Malecón, hauling people in from the countryside. Signs were appearing from nowhere — placards and posters — revealing the subject of the protest: Elián González.

I had forgotten about the 5-year-old plucked from the sea by fishermen, 3 miles off Ft. Lauderdale, on November 25, Thanksgiving Day. Elián's mother and 11 others had drowned trying to come to America. The boy had been released to the custody of his uncle in Miami. The Cuban government had sent a note to the United States asking for his return. Elián's father had also filed a complaint with the United Nations to protest the delays in returning the boy to him. The State Department had left the matter to the Florida courts.

Then, on December 7, Carolyn and I found ourselves in the middle of the first spontaneous demonstration to protest the continued refusal of the United States to return Elián to his father, who seemed to be a good fellow even if he was a communist. We followed the crowd to a place a few blocks up the Malecón. It was the wide concrete expanse — you couldn't have called it a plaza — just outside the U.S. Interests Section.

Since the United States had no diplomatic relations with Cuba, it had no official embassy or ambassador in Havana. The Interests Section housed the faux diplomats who dealt with the faux problems that did arise between the two nations. A stark boxy building, five stories tall, with mirrored blue windows, its entrance was on Calle Calzada and it was guarded 24-7 by chain fences topped with razor wire and armed U.S. Marines.

Milling about with the crowds, we took more photos. Spontaneously, a sturdy stage complete with microphones and speakers arose outside the Interests Section. Cuban flags flew from its frame. Huge scrims that displayed the iconic image of Che Guevara fell from the ledges of apartment houses around the square. Cheers went up from the crowd.

"He's going to give a speech," someone said, meaning Fidel. We waited for an hour, but he didn't come and we grew tired of waiting. It was getting hot under the sun. And the only thing that was happening was an occasional burst of patriotic music from the speakers mounted on the stage or an occasional chant: "Elián! Elián!"

Finally Carolyn and I abandoned our adventure. Of course, only 70 minutes later Fidel showed up and spoke. And only seven months later the United States would send the boy back to Cuba with his father. And only seven years later Raúl Castro, dressed in his olive uniform, would sit in for his ailing brother at Elián's 13th birthday party in Cardenas.

By the time Elián would join the Young Communist Union in June 2008 at the age of fourteen, Raúl would be president of Cuba. And Elián would pledge that he would never let down either of the Castro brothers.

A few years after marching for the boy's release, I took a call from the woman of Cuban descent who ran Denver University's adult enrichment program. I was teaching a class for her and another at the Institute for Public Policy Studies. She reminded me that I had met a young Cuban man at an IPPS lecture the week before. "He's a Ph.D. candidate in international relations," she said. "He grew up in Havana. He has two masters — one from Carleton and one from Columbia. He's heard you're the guru on Cuba and —"

"I'm hardly a guru," I protested, though I rather liked the sound of it.

"Whatever," she said. "This guy wants to meet you." She paused, then added, "It's a good idea. We're trying to build better relations with other departments and..."

Three days later I sat at a coffee shop on Evans near the university. Soon the man I met at the party opened the door, swept inside, and looked around, his chin held high in a vaguely aristocratic manner. He spotted me and smiled, then warmly shook my hand.

"Professor," he said, "I am Arturo Lopez-Levy." His accent was heavily Cuban.

"I'm not a professor," I said. I was the sort of academic snob who would never call myself a professor unless I was on a faculty full-time. "Call me Harlan."

Arturo stared at me. There was something familiar about him, something more than our brief encounter the week before. I looked hard at him, running his face through my memory banks. I observed his manner and stature. Where had I seen him before?

I blurted out, "Is it possible that in December of 1999 you were giving lectures to little old ladies from Phoenix at Adath Israel in Havana?"

Surprised by the question, he answered, "Why, yes — I was doing that then..."

And that's all it took to connect the dots. I was sitting face to face with the same young man who had sported a ponytail back in the days of the Elián protests. Since that meeting at the coffee shop in Denver, we have taught several classes together, written a few articles together, and worked with Wellington Webb, the former three-term mayor of Denver, to add Colorado to the list of other states that sell agricultural products to Cuba under an exemption from the embargo.

If you are a liberal or libertarian, you should want the embargo to go away so you can exercise your constitutional right to travel to Cuba. And if you are a conservative, you should want the embargo to go away so you can flood Cuba with goods and services and let nature take its course. For you, capitalism comes naturally. It is inevitable. Or as Pulitzer Prize–winning journalist Thomas Friedman says, "Inexorable."[4]

Indeed, globalization — the spread of market-based or capitalist economics — is one of the three great forces that drive today's events. It has become fashionable to argue that globalization is dead, especially since the recession of 2009. But try looking at the world's biggest nation — the People's Republic of China — and proclaiming the death of globalization.

Globalization is most certainly not dead, though it has entered a whole new phase. David Sanger of the *New York Times* has described this new phase as follows:

> China has managed to turn the forces of globalization into the most successful antipoverty project the world has ever seen. So how does one explain the fact that when the latest round of global trade negotiations blew up for good, it was China with a hand on the detonator?
>
> The answer has a lot to do with how the world — and China in particular — has changed, and how the Chinese see the world that's coming....
>
> It is not that the Chinese think the great era of globalization is over. Far from it.... But the era in which free trade is organized around rules set in the West — with developing nations following along — definitely appears over.
>
> The system is being rethought in China and India and other countries that spent the 1990s trying to become integrated into the global trading system by accepting the West's rules. They applied to join the World Trade Organization, using its mandates to speed up reforms at home and pump out cheap exports. But now they are done with that phase. When the Chinese finally took the so-called Doha round of trade talks off of life support ... it was about a fundamental shift in power that the United States is just beginning to appreciate.[5]

Stunning as it seems, Thomas Friedman has observed, "China [is really] not a Communist country anymore — it may now be the world's *most capitalist* country."[6]

Still, economics is only one of the three forces that drive today's events. The two others are politics and law. And when it comes to international politics, the concept of "sovereignty" still reigns. Of course, sovereignty also faces big challenges in the new millennium. The conditions attached to International Monetary Fund and World Bank loans often reduce the borrower's sovereignty. The proliferation of trans-sovereign organizations (like the International Criminal Court), and global nongovernmental organizations (like Amnesty International) modifies the very premise of sovereignty as the central organizing principle of the international structure. The "flattening"[7] of the world through modern technology, especially the Internet, decreases the borders of sovereignty. And the spread of armed militia like the Janjaweed and mercenaries like Blackwater defiles the very idea.

In other words, the system of international politics that has governed the world since the Treaty of Westphalia in 1648 is getting long in the tooth. Sovereignty posits a world of individual nation-states with geographic borders, populations that live within those borders, governments that rule those populations, and international recognition.[8] When recognized by other nation-states, the government holds a monopoly on force within its borders, and the actions of the government within its borders go without challenge — unless they so overstep the boundaries of conscience that they are labeled "criminal" by the international community.

That limitation is critical to understanding sovereignty in the 21st century. As the Nuremberg trials showed, and the International Criminal Court demands, the government that today commits genocide or crimes against humanity can most definitely be held accountable by the international community. These violations trigger the "rule of law," the third great force that drives today's events.

The "rule of law" — generally expressed in written constitutions — provides rules or standards for governing society. They include procedural rules and substantive rules. These often conflict with the economic interests of business when they regulate it, and they often conflict with the political interests of the state when they limit its reach. Indeed, the rule of law challenges globalization by imposing norms on the marketplace, and it inevitably challenges sovereignty by limiting the legitimate actions of the state.

What's important is this: Economics, politics and law are constantly messing with each other. Their intersections hold the key to solving today's global problems. And the future of Cuba will spring from these forces.

Arturo and I believe that history will show Raúl Castro, the little brother of Fidel, as the central figure in Cuba's transition from the past to the future. His role will be seen as pivotal, however long his presidency may last. I traveled to Cuba on the day of Barack Obama's inauguration to witness the changes Raúl was bringing to the island.

Already he had initiated a number of changes seen as important by many Cubans. The government was distributing land for people to work privately for their own profit. It was allowing greater access to modern consumer goods like DVD players, cell phones and computers. There was greater access to the Internet, too. Raúl was also allowing ordinary Cubans to start "going upstairs" in the tourist hotels, something forbidden to them under his big brother. Farmers were permitted to make extra money by selling their excess crops for their own accounts. Limits on government wages were being lifted. And Raúl's daughter Mariela had begun to champion the cause of gay rights.

State TV had even broadcast *Brokeback Mountain*!

Change was coming to Cuba.

Chapter Two
Pedro, Carlos and Raúl

The day after Barack Obama's inauguration, Arturo and I walked the streets of Nuevo Vedado so he could show me his old neighborhood. This is one of the better residential areas in Havana. It lies just south of Vedado and across the Almendares River from Miramar. It's where Arturo lived from 1985, when his family moved to Havana from Santa Clara, until he left for Israel and America 15 years later.

My study of the transition of power from Fidel to Raúl would go from theory to reality during the next week. I had seen Cuba many times before, but I had never seen it through Arturo's "Cuban eyes." And they made all the difference.

We stopped for coffee and a pastry at Dulcinea on Calle 26. A young man was selling bootleg DVDs and Arturo studied them. I mentioned the asphyxiating fumes I had smelled on the walk and Arturo said casually, "It's true. There is more pollution. They have gotten rid of the old camels"— the big double-humped buses used for decades by the people —"and gotten these new Chinese buses. Public transportation is better now. But the pollution is much worse."

He'd been trying all morning to get me to see the little things. There were letters to the editor in the newspapers, something not allowed under Fidel. A Protestant pastor had published a memoir about the discrimination against and internment of religious people under the communists. There were many small changes in the works.

After coffee we headed for Arturo's old house, a few blocks off the main streets. We soon ran into a middle-aged auto mechanic working on several old Fiats. César had a full head of dark wavy hair and wore a jumpsuit smudged with grease.

He was happy to see Arturo: "Tury! Tury! You're home for a visit!"

César's father had been an Italian communist who had come to Cuba to support the Revolution but left because he did not agree with Fidel's rubber-stamp of the Soviets' aggression in Czechoslovakia. César immediately reported that everyone on the island was excited about Obama's inauguration. They were looking forward to big change.

The world media had widely reported that Fidel had watched the U.S. inauguration on television and the next day told Argentina's president Cristina Fernandez that Obama seemed "like a man who is absolutely sincere."[1] Fernandez had said, "Fidel believes in Obama." And Raúl had added that Obama "seems like a good man."

But who knew?

After talking to César a few minutes longer, Arturo and I walked further down the street and stood before his old home. He began speaking in rapid-fire Spanish with an elderly medium-sized man standing on the porch next door. The man had freshly shaved cheeks that were rosy translucent pink. He wore a dark denim jacket over faded blue jeans and a baseball cap over white hair. Soon we were standing with him on his porch. And then he led us inside his home.

His name was Pedro García Espinosa, and he was a fairly well-known painter and filmmaker. He proudly showed us his paintings, lining every wall of his living room, hallway, and studio, often three or four deep, sized from small — roughly 5 by 7 inches — to large — roughly 4 by 5 feet. One of the larger paintings was called "Rupture" and it showed a broken bridge etched in black, with the orange light of hope shining on its wreckage from behind.

Modern Cuban painting, unlike most Latin American art, has very little indigenous influence. That's because the Spaniards killed off most of Cuba's indigenous population in the decades after the Conquest, so there were no natives to influence its art. As a result, Cuban modern art leans heavily toward European abstract expressionism and African influences.

Another of Pedro's paintings, "Brain Drain," showed a tree with

The Cuban artist Pedro García Espinosa at his home in Nuevo Vedado (Arturo Lopez-Levy collection).

The cluttered living room of Pedro García Espinosa (Arturo Lopez-Levy collection).

extravagant roots and branches. This was a large, striking canvas. Pedro said its theme was immigration, separating people from their land, a theme repeated in many of his works. The painting used a red-white-and-blue American dollar in the upper right-hand corner to symbolize capitalist greed, another image repeated in many of his pieces.

By the time we settled on chairs in Pedro's living room and sipped the flat orange soda his diminutive, bespectacled wife served us, we were talking politics. A worldly man who had studied and worked in Italy, and still shows his art in that country, Pedro began by declaring, "I am a Marxist." This, I have learned, is a statement often made by older Cubans at the beginnings of their conversations. Just to keep the record straight, and their ideology intact.

Next we talked about Obama's inauguration and Pedro's hopes for real change, mostly on America's part. Then we turned to change on Cuba's part. I argued that Cuba had already been forced, by virtue of globalization, however tattered in 2009, to engage in market-based trade with many other nations, since it imported a great deal from abroad. Was it not inevitable, I asked Pedro, that Cuba would soon turn to the Chinese model: allowing more and more economic openings — capitalism, if you will — while still maintaining a one-party political system?

Pedro didn't need a primer on the subject or the language. As a well-educated ideologue he knew all the jargon. I assumed Arturo's translation was totally accurate and pressed on: Wasn't it a good thing that Raúl — some already called him the Chinaman — was bringing reform to the island? Pedro didn't disagree. In fact, he seemed to view the Chinese model in a fairly positive light.

At this time it was two and a half years after the intestinal surgery that had prompted Fidel to cede power temporarily to Raúl in the summer of 2006, and a year since Fidel had formally stepped aside, prompting Cuba's legislative branch to officially elect Raúl as Cuba's new president. He had already initiated economic and political change.

"Shouldn't more be expected?" I asked.

That's when Pedro went off on the Cuban Five. If Obama wanted to make a genuine goodwill gesture to Cuba, he said, then Obama should release the Cuban Five, and do so immediately.

I realized he was invoking the latest cause célèbre among the Cuban people.

I asked, "In exchange for Cuba's release of its dissidents from jail?"

"No," Pedro scoffed at my presumption.

Then he explained: The Cuban Five — five Cubans convicted in U.S. federal courts for espionage and conspiracy to commit murder — were an important symbol to many Cubans. Hadn't I seen the billboards all over the island? And what they did wasn't so bad, according to Pedro. Mostly, he argued, they just spied on right-wing Cuban American groups in Miami and only tangentially brushed against U.S. government information, none of which was classified. Their convictions were unjust and their sentences were too long. Obama should release them. Now!

But, I replied, they were tied to the shooting down of the Brothers to the Rescue, and that made them more than trifling interlopers in the view of the United States.

"No," he corrected me in an unusually stern voice, "it is only more than trifling to right-wing Cuban Americans."

"But what about all the dissidents your regime has jailed? From our perspective, they've been put away for expressing their views and exercising free speech. They have not provoked any real violence against your country. They should be let go, too."

"No," insisted Pedro, adamant. And then he said something truly astonishing: "It's not just that the dissidents were thinking differently. They were breaking our laws."

A billboard in support of the Cuban Five (Arturo Lopez-Levy collection).

I pounced on the faulty syllogism. "You can't have it both ways," I protested. "This is not a style of argument that works." I acted more frustrated than I felt, but we were having good sport with each other. I argued, "You can't say the dissidents violated your laws and belong in jail and then turn around and say the Cuban Five should be released from American jails even though they violated our laws. That's a double standard. It only works if you minimize American values and maximize Cuban values. And that's inconsistent with the degree of sovereignty both of our nations require."

Caught in the act, Pedro smiled. Arturo observed that neither the trials of the dissidents in Cuba nor the trials of the Cuban Five in Miami were truly fair and impartial. This perception, he pointed out, was widely shared by Amnesty International and the United Nations organization that tracks arbitrary detentions. Soon we were discussing the initiative by American actors, dancers, and other artists to establish a Department of Culture, something the United States has never had. Pedro thought it was "weird" that Americans could be so rich and not have a Ministry of Culture. All great nations have them.

But we realized, of course, that it could not be at the top of Obama's agenda. He'd been in office for only a day and already he was faced with the biggest economic crisis in decades, renewed violence in the Middle East, and unfinished business in Iraq and Afghanistan. We realized the implications. The huge challenges facing America's new president also meant that improvement in U.S. relations with Cuba could not be at the top of his agenda. Silence fell over us.

Our visit was drawing to a close.

Pedro pulled out a stack of small paintings, each done by hand, signed, and framed in black with a simple cardboard mat. He gave one to Arturo and one to me. Mine has bold strokes of black over a dark brown and white background. It shows a parent figure holding two smaller child figures in its arms. It reminds me of my daughters.

Later that day, Arturo and I drove with his younger brother Ernesto, visiting from Buenos Aires with his wife and toddler daughter, to the El Canal neighborhood in the town of El Cerro, one of the very poorest neighborhoods in Havana. Here was another lesson in Cuban contradictions: There was widespread poverty throughout the island, but virtually no homelessness. Close geographically to upscale Nuevo Vedado, the El Canal neighborhood has more cracks in its streets than most Cuban streets, if that is possible. Hardened mud mixes with crumbling concrete to form an uncertain surface.

Ernesto pulled his aging white Peugeot sedan to the curb across from a row of tenements that bore no resemblance to each other from floor to floor or side to side. Squalid housing like this can be seen in the backstreets of Old Havana and neighboring El Centro, but in El Cerro the smells seemed stronger, the skins seemed darker, even the eyes seemed wearier, the dogs scrawnier, and the cars fewer and farther between.

Arturo and Ernesto had come to give money to the family of a friend who was living in California. I was there only to watch. The family knew no English and Arturo and Ernesto spoke to them in such rapid-fire Cuban Spanish that I could not follow.

I could only imagine what was being said. But later when I asked Arturo if my imagination was correct, he affirmed it. So I listened to the chatter and scanned the living room, which opened onto a dining room, then onto a kitchen and small outdoor space. The place was cluttered and unclean, despite the efforts of a flabby middle-aged woman to mop the floors, using a bucket with water and a little soap. Another older woman, the mother of the first and obvious matriarch of the family, sat in a chair across from me, while Arturo and Ernesto sat to one side. The fourth wall was occupied by a Santería shrine.

Santería is an Afro-Cuban religion often likened, incorrectly, to voodoo. When the slaves from Africa—many of whom came from the Yoruba regions of Nigeria—were forced by their owners to convert to Catholicism, many found they could continue to practice their native religion secretly if they

"There was widespread poverty throughout the island, but virtually no homelessness." Here are some apartments on the Prado, between Old Havana and El Centro (Harlan Abrahams collection).

submerged their deities behind the saints. Prayers to saints were really prayers to one of the Orishas, or gods. This was a ruse not unlike those used by the crypto–Jews who came with the Spaniards to the New World during the Conquest.

Santería is widespread and growing in Cuba. The shrine in the home in which I was sitting was built around the skull of what looked like a goat. A fine Cuban cigar sat in front of the skull as an offering. The skull was festooned with colorful beaded strips. And a little bronze bell sat to the side. It was not as elaborate as many Santería shrines I've seen. There in El Canal there was poverty even among the gods.

Midway through the conversation a pretty adolescent girl came into the room and gave everyone, including me, a soft kiss on the cheek. No one needed to tell her why we had come. Gratitude dripped from her. And throughout the visit, the door remained open and a man or two would stop by to say hello. But mostly it was just Arturo, Ernesto and me with the matriarch, the girl, and her aunt, a daughter of the matriarch.

I let my eyes wander from the shrine to the faces of the three females and to the several photos on the walls, repetitious in angle but in various sizes, of some waterfall unknown to me. All three of the females had the same black features and same bad teeth. The girl and her grandmother were much thinner, however, than the aunt.

The matriarch and, to a lesser extent, the aunt complained bitterly during most of the visit. The girl remained silent. She was the daughter of the friend who was living in California and she had not spoken to her father in many months. The man had not called, had not written, had not sent money for a very long time. And though his photo appeared on the wall amid all the pictures of the waterfall, the anger directed at him was fierce.

The girl wanted her father to send for her so she could go live with him in California, but he wanted her to learn English first. There was always some excuse. Arturo later told me the father was the only member of the family who had left the island, which is typical of many black families. Though a dear friend, he did tend to squander his money on gambling and other frivolous activities, always hoping for the big score.

Yet despite all the anger and poverty, these people showed us great hospitality. They were greatly appreciative of the money Arturo and Ernesto brought, which was for them a considerable amount. And they, like every other Cuban I've ever encountered, insisted on serving us a beverage, in this case thick coffee filled with bitter grounds.

In this room, with these people, in El Cerro, there was no talk of Raúl or Obama. It was all about the family: The wayward son and brother and father in California who had not called, written or sent money in so very long. And the relative in Cuba who was planning to open a private barbershop, but was waiting for the cousin in California to send some money for his initial investment.

The reforms and changes had not yet reached down to them.

Finally, we said our good-byes. We drove back to Nuevo Vedado and the mood in the Peugeot was somber. I remember thinking that in the space of just one day I had been introduced to the four big truths that would guide me on this entire trip. From the taxi driver to the artsy ideologue, the Fiat mechanic to the family in El Cerro, I'd sampled the essence of what tied Cubans to Americans: the universality of their experience.

I awoke the next morning and took my walk. Obama had announced he was closing Guantánamo.

Thumbing on my iPod, I heard Aaron Neville crooning the Sam Cooke classic: "It's been a long, long time coming, but I know a change gonna come — yes it will!"

Discontent and poverty still plague Cuba. The Communist Party still controls. The socialist nature of the Revolution still dominates policy. But things *are* changing. Consumer rights have expanded. And consumer rights lead to economic rights, like those given to the farmers and those lifting the limits on government wages. Eventually economic rights lead to political rights and legal rights — perhaps even democracy.

When it comes to Cuba, material advancement toward the "rule of law" will mean a seismic shift from a system based on ideology, and the charisma of the leader of that ideology, to a system based on the people. Fidel's power to shape the lives of everyday Cubans will be gone. Already it wanes.

Once, there were no big public displays of Fidel's image in Cuba. Che, Camilo and Martí, of course, but never Fidel himself. It was all part of the leader's mystique. Now, when Fidel is not ruling the country, his image is popping up all over. By joining the pantheon of Cuban heroes, he makes way for his little brother.

Raúl Castro, however long his presidency may last, will play a pivotal role in leading Cuba to its future. He is already bringing change to the island but, like his American counterpart, he operates in an environment shaped by the three great forces that drive current events: *economics,* especially globalization, spreading capitalist markets everywhere; *politics,* especially the idea of sovereignty, defining the reach of the modern nation-state; and the *rule of law,* especially the assertion of constitutional rights, human rights and civil liberties throughout the world.

Cuba's experience in facing these forces will be similar to, but not the same as, other countries that emerged from communism in the late twentieth century. That's because the Cuban Revolution has always had a dual character. In addition to the Leninist project embodied in the Communist Party, the triumph of January 1, 1959, represented the victory of a *nationalist* revolution. This perspective envisions Cuba not as a surviving outlier among the Eastern European communist regimes, but closer to the communist countries of East Asia, where the Communist Party presented itself as the embodiment of nationalism. Although the communist project has failed in Cuba as it did elsewhere, the politics of the last five decades consolidated a nationalist narrative as the last reservoir of legitimacy today's Cuban rulers can tap.

Many say Cuba will follow the example of China by liberalizing its markets economically while keeping the Communist Party in control politically. But that's only the beginning. Even in China, there is more democracy and law than ever.

People should not, however, be fooled by those who call Raúl the "Chinaman"— it's actually a nickname that predates his fascination with the Chinese model, which we will explore later in this book. In fact, the nickname refers to his vaguely Asian eyes, which distinguish him as much from his older brother as his smaller stature and more reserved nature.

Whatever direction the Chinaman takes in Cuba, it's sure to provoke a response from the United States. How soon will the Americans dismantle their embargo? How will Cuba's changes affect its relations with other nations and political movements? These questions demand attention. For decades U.S. relations with Cuba have enjoyed a prominence in American politics disproportionate to the size and strength of the island. It's a remnant of the Cold War — a feud — perpetuated by an aging exile generation.

How the United States deals with Cuba's new realities says a lot about how the United States deals with nations it calls "rogues." And that tells us a lot about America's mind-set in the posthegemonic, multipolar world where the violence of a "no state" or a "failed state" could be much worse than having a "rogue" in the backyard.[2]

Carlos Alzugaray, vice director of the Center for U.S. and Hemispheric Studies, lives in one of the most modern houses I've seen in Cuba. On the Saturday afternoon following Obama's inauguration, he greeted Arturo and me at his front door. He said, "It's too loud out here," referring to the pounding salsa music blaring from loudspeakers across the street in the park. "Let's talk out back on my patio." So he led us through his house, over polished wood floors and past sleek surfaces and stainless steel appliances.

Putting the house between us and the music did little to dampen its decibels. Big bass notes rattled the house and its neighbors. Still, we pressed on. There was plainly a real fondness between Arturo and his former professor that went beyond mere respect. Dr. Alzugaray appeared to be a healthy, vibrant man somewhere in his sixties, with a full head of silver hair. He wore a brown tattersall shirt with a button-down collar over dark blue jeans and loafers. He served us a beverage and started by saying, "I am a Marxist."

I thought, "Here we go again."

But Dr. Alzugaray—though not without his ideology—was no mere ideologue. He did not mind being recorded, though the pulsating salsa from the nearby park wreaked havoc with my little digital recorder. And unlike Pedro García Espinosa, Dr. Alzugaray spoke with us in flawless English. Also unlike the painter and filmmaker, the diplomat and educator did not believe the release of the Cuban Five should be at the top of Obama's agenda toward Cuba. Removing Cuba from the list of countries that sponsor terrorism would be much more meaningful, he said, from a foreign relations perspective.

Dr. Alzugaray is astonishingly well read and very articulate. He has bachelor's, master's and doctorate degrees. His dissertation concerned President Eisenhower's policy toward the Cuban Revolution. He has served the Cuban Foreign Service as a diplomat in various capacities in Japan, Bulgaria, Argentina, Colombia, Canada, Kenya, Ethiopia, South Africa, and Belgium. He regularly teaches classes on foreign relations at the University of Havana and lectures on international affairs, European politics, and U.S.-Cuban relations at the National Defense College. He has lectured at universities in Mexico, Venezuela, Nicaragua, Canada, the United States, Belgium, Luxembourg, Spain, Great Britain, Italy, and Switzerland.

Dr. Alzugaray is one sophisticated guy. He has a very organized mind. He said the United States under Obama faces four big changes: (1) changes in class relations, caused mostly by the continuing influx of immigrants and continuing income inequality between the rich and the poor; (2) changes in the structure of the new upper class, which will be a technology-driven class that rules the new economy; (3) changes in the ways politics are practiced, caused by the impact of the new technology and its ability to mobilize people from the "bottom up" instead of the "top down"—a topic we discuss in Part II of this book; and (4) changes in ideology, caused by the collapse of "market fundamentalism," as seen in the crash of 2008 and recession of 2009, and the rebirth of liberalism, as seen in the writings of Nobel Laureate Paul Krugman of Princeton and the *New York Times*.

Whew!

Dr. Alzugaray pressed on: These four big changes will cause three big crises in America: (1) economic "mis-spending" throughout the "empire of consumption," plus (2) military and diplomatic "over-reach," since the United States continues to fight two wars it "cannot win," plus (3) political restructuring, as the United States goes from conservative, unregulated markets and laws to liberal, more regulated markets and laws.

Now this was music to my ears — and far more powerful than the pounding salsa. Dr. Alzugaray was focusing on the intersections among politics, economics, and law. So he was speaking my language. He started ticking off the many things Barack Obama has in common with Raúl Castro. First, and most important, both believe it is imperative to talk to your adversaries. For them, talking to someone does not legitimate them or accept their ideology. This is "powerful stuff," according to Dr. Alzugaray. It's a major change for both the United States and Cuba. "We have to start thinking the unthinkable," he said.

Second, Obama and Raúl share a lot of the same rhetoric. It's not just the slogan (*"Sí se puede!" "Yes, we can!"*), which Raúl first began using in the 1990s. But to the extent that such words and phrases can guide and determine specific economic, political, and legal policies and consequences, this new style of rhetoric can be very significant.

Third, they share a similar style of decision-making. Fidel, said Dr. Alzugaray, would always study an issue in depth by himself, then he would form an opinion or an idea or a decision, and then he would test it out with others. This approach tended to validate decisions made unilaterally by Fidel. By contrast, Obama and Raúl start by gathering the best advice they can from the best and brightest they keep around them. "Bring me the options," as Dr. Alzugaray characterized it. Then, based on their full appraisal of those options, they decide. This approach tends to open the decision-making process to a broader range of alternatives and opinions.

Finally, our host explained, Obama and Raúl are both hard-working family men. Michelle Obama is a bright and accomplished woman in her own right, and most certainly talks things over with Barack. That's similar to the relationship between Raúl and his wife Vilma Espin when she was alive. Vilma was a well-known revolutionary figure and a vocal advocate for women's rights. There was constant debate in her household over this and other issues. "They were always arguing among themselves," said Dr. Alzugaray. No doubt their daughter Mariela's outspoken advocacy of gay rights was influenced by the style of family interaction she grew up with.

I was impressed with the orderliness of it all: the four big changes, the three big crises, and the four commonalities. We turned to the countries in Latin America that Dr. Alzugaray predicted would influence Cuba the most in the future. He thought the influence of Venezuela over Cuba was mostly just a function of Hugo Chávez and his cheap oil — the Old Left and Old Energy. Further, he believed the rise of Brazil as the "New Hegemon of the South" represented a more important alternative for Cuba.

That statement triggered a detour into one of my favorite subjects: the link between Brazil's former minister of strategic planning and America's new president. Brazil is the fifth largest and most populous country in the world and the fourth largest democracy. It has a vibrant market-based economy — the tenth largest in the world — and appears to have weathered the 2008–2009 recession better than most of the emerging and developed nations. Its growing influence, especially among the southern nations of Latin America, makes it America's biggest competitor in the region.

Brazil has become a player through experimentation. It started decades ago. Responding to the Arab oil embargo in the mid–1970s, it launched a national program to produce ethanol from sugarcane — which is far more efficient than corn-based ethanol — to make itself less dependent on imported oil. Today, Brazil does not have to import crude oil. It has learned the value of vision.

Enter Roberto Mangabeira Unger, a professor at Harvard Law School, where a young Barack Obama was his student. From 2007 to 2009, Unger took a leave from Harvard and served as head of the Long-Term Planning Secretariat in his native Brazil. Eccentric, exuberant, and prolific, he first went to Harvard for his master of laws degree in the 1970s. Recognizing his precocious genius, the faculty plucked him from his peers and made him a professor.

I audited Unger's legendary jurisprudence class in 1974 while I earned my own advanced law degree at Harvard. Back then Unger would prowl the stages of the biggest classrooms at the law school, wearing a simple dark suit over a clean white shirt and plain dark tie, his eyes magnified behind his glasses, delivering intricate lectures in clear, precise sentences and structured paragraphs. He drew enthusiastic crowds from across the campus.

Today Unger is associated with the so-called New Left in Latin America. But he disavows the dualistic thinking that polarizes the world into liberals and conservatives, left and right, communists and capitalists. And his two-year stint in Brazil gave him the platform to put his grand experiments into practice.

Here's one example from his book *Democracy Realized*: Unger recognizes the advantages of a three-branch constitutional system with separated powers, fully checked and balanced, but also advocates the need to "quicken democratic experimentalism" by (1) widely accepting "the conventional body of contract and corporate law as the basic framework for the self-organization of civil society," while (2) creating "a [new] branch of government responsible for localized intervention in organizations or practices corrupted by entrenched forms of social exclusion or subjugation."[3]

The idea of creating whole new branches of government may sound radical, but these are times that demand radical solutions to problems made increasingly difficult by the world's deep interconnectedness. Unger explains, "*The conflict between statism and privatism is dying and being replaced by a contest among alternative institutional forms of political, social, and economic pluralism.* Representative democracy, free civil society, and the market economy can all take forms different from those they now assume in the North Atlantic world."[4]

Over the years, Unger has had a major impact on many of his students, including President Obama and me. At the time of his inauguration the new president had already consulted with his former professor from law school. And when I talked with Dr. Alzugaray about Unger and his influence on the future, the Cuban Marxist agreed he needed to take another look into the writings of the Brazilian pragmatist.

That salsa music was unrelenting, however. I couldn't imagine what it was doing to the eardrums of those who were close to the speakers. And Dr. Alzugaray had family visiting from out of town. So we began wrapping up our interview, leaving our detour behind and returning to less tangential matters. I could tell he was choosing his words carefully now, aware that his last impressions would be his most lasting impressions.

"He's slick," I thought, in the most complimentary sense.

"Cuba is moving," he said, "in a more democratic, more tolerant direction." Pause for effect. "But we will do it on our own terms."

Now this was a more political statement than I had been expecting. Plenty of Cubans talk about economics. But politics is more sacred ground. Gingerly, Dr. Alzugaray steered our final moments toward that delicate geography. He began talking about politics in relation to political parties. It seemed an extension of a topic we had glossed over earlier — the ability of the Republican Party in the United States to reinvent itself after the 2008 election by allowing for a greater diversity of views under its umbrella.

Presently Dr. Alzugaray asked the same question of his own one-party system. "I'm not sure how it will go," he said. I noted his statement assumed it was going to go somewhere. He replied by questioning whether Cuba will need more than one party in the future. Will there be enough room for clashing views inside the single party in the one-party system or will Cuba need more than one party to accommodate all those views?

The source and nature of these questions impressed me, like his orderly mind. Arturo had brought me to interview a highly intelligent man, a forward-thinking figure who had written insightfully about many of the topics we discussed.

"Political parties may not be necessary," ventured Dr. Alzugaray. Then his tone became lighter, he shrugged and added, "But I may be wrong."

The Capitolio in Havana, ironically modeled after the U.S. Capitol in Washington, D.C. How do two countries, once so close, reconcile after five decades of estrangement? (Harlan Abrahams collection).

I was learning a lot about the transition of power from Fidel to Raúl, and from Bush to Obama, for that matter, but I wasn't learning more about the *character* of Raúl. For that, I was still relying on Arturo's stories and an interview we had conducted a few months before on the west side of Denver. That interview brought us face to face with "someone who was there." His story began on December 10, 1955.

That was the date when Fidel, after a major fundraising trip to Miami, returned to Mexico City. He wore a mustache but no beard, dark glasses but no fatigues. He used, according to Latin custom, the title "Doctor" due to his law degree. And he brought with him a compact man of 22 named Miguel Sanchez.

Born in Cuba "but lured by adventure," Sanchez had enlisted in the U.S. Army and fought in Korea. Known to be good with weapons and familiar with American methods of training, he had been recruited by Fidel to help run a boot camp for his little band of rebels at the ranch they had rented outside the city.

They burst into the apartment of María Antonia González, a Cuban woman married to a Mexican wrestler, whose home had become the informal headquarters for the rebels. "This is El Coreano!" exclaimed Fidel, slapping Sanchez on the shoulder. "He is a soldier! He fought in the Korean War and he is going to train us!"

A handful of rebels, including Raúl, were gathered in the small parlor.

Raúl took one look at Sanchez and immediately objected: "So, we are going to be trained by a Yanqui invader?"

"Just a second," said El Coreano, not afraid to speak for himself. "America did not invade Korea. The North invaded the South."

When Raúl opened his mouth to respond, Fidel cut him off: "*¡Cuba Primero!*" — Cuba First! But from that moment on, Raúl took a dislike to El Coreano.

Today Miguel Sanchez runs a driving school in the Hispanic section of Denver, on the near west side. "It was a big mistake," he says, "taking on Raúl that day. Now let me tell you how it happened...."[5]

In September 1954, a young physician from Argentina arrived in Mexico City. He was a Marxist and a revolutionary, but he was not yet Che. The place was a sprawling hotbed of radical activity and had been since the 1930s. Indeed, in 1940 Leon Trotsky had been assassinated in his home in the Coyoacán district by an NKVD agent who drove the pick of an ice axe into his skull. The city was also a center of artistic expression. Frida Kahlo and Diego Rivera were among its cultural elite. Movies made locally were launching the careers of Mexican actors like Cantinflas.

Ernesto Guevara fit right in. His on-again-off-again romance with Hilda Gadea, whom he later married, was on. He was volunteering at the general hospital. A Cuban named Ñico López came to the hospital one day with a friend who was suffering from an allergy attack. Ernesto had met Ñico in Guatemala and they were quick to renew their acquaintance. Ñico told Ernesto all about the rebellion brewing in Cuba. He predicted the firebrand, Fidel Castro, would soon be released from prison, with his brother Raúl and others who had tried to spark an uprising by attacking an army barracks at Moncada.

Ernesto couldn't wait to meet these heroes, already soldiers for the cause. Followers of Fidel were beginning to trickle into the city. Ñico said this was the place where Fidel would organize and train an insurrectionary force that would oust Batista once and for all. The Cuban took the Argentine to an apartment at 49 Calle Emparán, where María Antonia González lived. The apartment had become a magnet for Cubans waiting for Fidel. Ernesto became a regular.

When Batista did grant a general amnesty, and the Castro brothers were released, Raúl was the first to come to Mexico City. In June 1955 Fidel had created the radical July 26 movement, police repression had escalated, bombs had ripped through Havana, and Raúl had been accused. Fidel told his little brother he'd better leave for Mexico.

Raúl came with a mission: to prepare for Fidel's arrival. Jon Lee Anderson, Che's leading biographer, says Raúl "went straight to María Antonia's house. Among those waiting to meet him was Ernesto Guevara.... [T]he two hit it off immediately."[6] Raúl had already joined the Young Communist League and visited the Soviet Bloc. Hilda also liked Raúl. Despite his youthful appearance, she said, "blond and beardless and looking like a university student, his ideas were very clear as to how the revolution was to be made and, more important, for what purpose and for whom."[7]

By the time Fidel arrived a short time later, Raúl had already "run into" a prior Soviet acquaintance named Nikolai Leonov, now an official with the Foreign Ministry. Throughout his long career, Raúl has always been the one to deal with the Russians.

July 7, 1955, was the date Fidel landed in Mexico City. A few days later Raúl introduced him to Ernesto at María Antonia's apartment. They talked into the night. Ernesto joined Fidel's movement without hesitation.

Safe houses were established all over the city for the cells of rebels who would launch the Revolution. A "one-eyed, Cuban-born Spanish Civil War veteran and military adventurer [named] General Alberto Bayo" was hired to oversee their training camp.[8] They rented a place called Rancho San Miguel, a large spread east of the city near Chalco, for that purpose. Fidel left for a fundraising tour in the United States. That's where he found El Coreano.

In September 2008, before Barack Obama won the White House, Arturo and I drove to Federal Boulevard to interview Miguel Sanchez, then in his mid-seventies. We parked around the corner from his driving school and entered the modest outer lobby. Three or four early students lounged in plastic chairs. As we told the woman behind the desk who we were, a slender, compact man sprang from an inner office down the hall.

El Coreano cut a striking figure. He looked ten years younger than his age, tight and fit despite the tiny belly he allowed himself. He retained a military bearing, though his dress was anything but: alligator cowboy boots, brown pleated trousers, lizard-skin belt, black shirt, and narrow-brimmed hat. His windowless office was packed with memorabilia, including photos from his days with the U.S. Army, photos from his days in Mexico City with the Cuban rebels, photos from his later years when he worked for the tyrannical regime of Rafael Trujillo in the Dominican Republic, and photos of his children and grandchildren.

He seemed anxious to establish his bona fides. He addressed both Arturo and me as "Professor," though I was no longer one, and Arturo wasn't quite one yet. He gave us photocopies of pictures of María Antonia González, holding a cigarette in her apartment; a photo of Fidel's birthday party in 1956, with Fidel sitting at a large table in a dark shirt, thick mustache and dark glasses, while Raúl leaned over the table that held the birthday cake and eighteen others — including El Coreano — pressed close; and a receipt from a Mexico City bookstore where Fidel charged books by Hitler, Lenin and Disraeli.

We were not allowed to record the voice of El Coreano, however. He maintains strict limits, he explained. It's still a dangerous place out there, he insisted. Then he showed us the loaded pistol he kept in a classic carved-out book on his desk. And he pointed with great pride at the brief passage in the Jon Lee Anderson biography of Che that mentions him by name: "On March 17, Miguel 'El Coreano' Sánchez — a U.S. Army Korean War veteran enlisted by Fidel in Miami to become his force's shooting instructor — summed up Guevara's performance on the firing range. 'Ernesto Guevara attended 20 regular shooting lessons, an excellent shooter with approximately 650 bullets [fired]. Excellent discipline, excellent leadership abilities, physical endurance excellent. Some disciplinary press-ups for small errors at interpreting orders and faint smiles.'"[9]

But he smelled, El Coreano confided to Arturo and me. Che may well have loved his wife — by then he had married Hilda — and especially the daughter she bore him, but nevertheless he smelled like a pig. By then, some had started calling him "Che," but many still simply called him "the Argentine."

"You are," El Coreano asked us, "writing a biography? Or perhaps a history?"

No, we explained, we were writing a book about Raúl's presidency and the changes he is bringing to Cuba. But first we wanted to get a handle on his character. We didn't talk about the insights Arturo already had due to his personal contacts with Raúl and his mastery of his country's history. We wanted to hear from someone who knew the man before all that.

"His character?" said El Coreano. He thought for a moment, then answered, "Raúl was an excellent administrator. Fidel was able to stay in power for so many years thanks to him. He was a brave man, too. He had excellent manners. He was a leader."

We prompted him for more.

"I had a lot of contact with him," said El Coreano. "And, yes, he disliked me at first but over time we grew to be friendly. He was always close to Che. He wanted to be a bull fighter and would pose in the mirror but wouldn't allow anyone to see him naked. He was very dedicated and good at his training. And he was always one hundred percent behind his big brother."

This wasn't what we were looking for. I wanted to explain we were looking for stories: Who did what? Who said what? Where did it happen? What did it look like? For I believe in the truth written by F. Scott Fitzgerald: "Action is character."

I asked, "Are there any stories you can tell us that show us what you mean?"

"Ah," said El Coreano. "I see what you are getting at..."

Then he told us a story that was eerily similar to tales told previously about trials and executions that took place at the ranch outside Mexico City. But the story we heard was different enough from those earlier accounts that Arturo and I were left wondering if we had heard an alternate version of an old story or something entirely new. Either way, it was creepy. And it revealed character galore.

The narrative was so vivid, so dramatic, that I visualized it with the immediacy of the present, filling in many of the details in my mind. It was almost like watching a film:

Early morning sunlight streams through the single window of a squalid tenement room on Ave. Chapulte in Mexico City. An old-fashioned black rotary telephone on the desk rings twice. El Coreano, a trim young man in boxer shorts and thin-ribbed T-shirt, picks up the receiver. He sounds sleepy: "Digame."

Through the receiver he hears the voice of Fidel. And Fidel sounds agitated: "Coreano! We'll pick you up at eight! Bring your pistol and two clips!"

"Click," goes the telephone. El Coreano reaches for his pistol and its holster.

An hour later, an old black sedan pulls onto Ave. Chapulte and screeches to a halt outside the squalid tenement building. El Coreano is waiting at the curb, dressed in trousers and a short-sleeved shirt. The shirt is not tucked in and a slight bulge appears near the waist. The rear passenger's door of the sedan swings open.

Without a word El Coreano gets inside and settles into the backseat. The old black sedan is spacious but its upholstery is torn. Fidel sits in the front passenger's seat, wearing dark sunglasses, and Raúl sits in the driver's seat, gripping the wheel so tightly that his knuckles are turning white.

Fidel draws a 9 mm. semi-automatic pistol from under his shirt. Handing the gun across the seat, he says, "Coreano, give me your pistol. And here, you take mine."

As ordered, El Coreano exchanges pistols with Fidel. Then he asks, "What the hell is going on? Where are we going?"

Raúl, glancing over his shoulder, replies tersely, "We're going to the ranch. We've got a problem. There is a traitor."

Fidel spits, "There is an insurgent inside the insurgency!"

Now El Coreano has seen Fidel angry before. The man has a pretty hot temper. But this morning his words drip with molten rage.

Raúl declares, "We're going to weed him out."

And Fidel decrees, "His health is going to be modified!"

At this point in the story Arturo shot me a wary glance. He later told me that the last two quotations were not ringing true for him. He didn't think that Fidel and Raúl would phrase things the way El Coreano said they did. And he questioned whether the later enmity between El Coreano and Fidel was coloring the telling of the tale.

El Coreano was oblivious, however, to Arturo's concerns. He continued:

The old black sedan has left the outskirts of Mexico City and bumps along rutted roads in a rugged countryside. Snow-covered volcanic peaks can be seen in the distance. The sun is rising high overhead. The air is getting hotter.

The sedan stops in a cloud of dust in front of a row of barracks built like flimsy wooden shanties. Fidel, Raúl and El Coreano pile out of the sedan, each brandishing a semi-automatic pistol, locking and loading with grim expressions. Fidel barks, "Coreano! Call your men out. Put them in formation."

El Coreano takes a plastic whistle from his pocket and blows three sharp blasts. The doors to the barracks burst open and sixty men pour out, hastily pulling on their shirts and boots. They look nervous when they see Fidel standing next to El Coreano. There is no inspection scheduled that morning. They line up in four rows facing Fidel, Raúl and El Coreano. Audibly, so all of them can hear, Fidel says to his little brother and the drill instructor, "If any of them try to run, shoot them. And shoot to kill."

El Coreano says, "As you say, Comandante." Then, "Attention, men!"

Fidel, his face flushed with anger, addresses his men: "There is a spy among us! I want to know who he is! I want to know who is responsible for this insurgency ... against Cuba! And against me!"

The sixty guerrillas-in-training shuffle their feet in the dust. Some look down. Some look sideways. They all look nervous. No one speaks up. The moment wears on. The sun beats down. Then suddenly a tall, skinny mulatto in the second row raises his hand and starts shouting: "Fidel! Fidel!"

The dark man's comrades step away from him. They know he's a little touched in the head. All week long he has been complaining about the food at the camp and ranting that he needs to speak with Fidel. No one believes for a moment that the man is really a spy for Batista or anyone else. And they certainly don't think he is confessing.

But before anyone can try to stop him, Fidel points his pistol — El Coreano's pistol — directly at the dark mulatto and shoots him four times, nearly point blank in the chest. Blood flies everywhere. The dark mulatto falls to the ground.

Fidel delivers two more shots to his head.

The trainees recoil in fear.

Within seconds red ants begin to swarm around the dead man's head. Soon the pools of dark red blood are crawling with dark red ants.

Fidel snarls at the sixty men cowering before him, "Does anyone else want to apply for the job? No?"

Of course, none of them dares to speak up. Fidel then launches into one of his long-winded orations. El Coreano tunes most of it out, hearing only snatches of words: "...Cuban ... traitor..." And a few murmurs. But it is clear to everyone that Fidel is very emotional. His emotions are peppered with politics and platitudes.

Later that night, at one of their many safe houses scattered around Mexico City, Fidel tells Che about the incident at the ranch. Raúl sits to the right of his older brother, their elbows nearly touching. El Coreano sits next to Che. All four are hunched over a low wooden table, speaking in low, confidential tones. Che is smoking a cigar — it is thick and smelly and burned down to a stub — and his expression is blank, unreadable.

Fidel ends his description with a wave of his hand and a simple declaration: "So I shot him on the spot!"

Che looks around the table.

Neither Raúl nor El Coreano has anything to add.

Che asks, "What did you do with the body?"

"We threw him in the ditch at the side of the road!"

"What about his ID?"

"I told Raúl to take his ID and lose it in the forest."

Che pauses and again looks nervously around the table. Then he says, "But if they find his body, they might still be able to identify him."

Raúl chimes in: "I told the men to move his body and bury it in the ravine."

"Still," says Che, "a lot of men saw it happen."

Raúl frowns and says, "No one is going to tell anyone else. Those who are not totally committed to the cause are all too afraid."

"Well," says Che, licking his lips, "this is what I think we should do..."

Two hours later the old black sedan bumps along the same rutted roads in the same rugged countryside. But this time it takes a turn to the left and drives deep into woods so thick that the limbs of the trees brush the fenders of the car. And this time it is dark overhead. There is no moon tonight. The only illumination comes from the stars twinkling in the sky and the twin yellow beams from the old black sedan. Everything else is washed in lurid shades of blue. Soon the old black sedan pulls out of the woods and stops along a dry ravine.

The yellow beams of the headlights find a mound of loose dirt that barely conceals the body of the skinny mulatto. The engine stops but the headlights stay on, trained on the mound of dirt. Raúl, Che and El Coreano get out of the sedan and walk over to the mound. They kick the dirt off the body. Casually, Che takes a shiny silver surgeon's saw from under his loose jacket and, with the easy skill of a man trained in the medical arts, cuts off the hands of the dark mulatto.

Half-grimacing, half-joking, Raúl says to Che, "I thought you were a doctor, not a butcher!"

Nobody laughs.

Silently they burn the hands of the mulatto a short distance from where they leave his body. Then Raúl gives back to El Coreano the pistol that Fidel had taken from him that morning. The three men shake their heads together. Each knows that if the body is somehow found, and the six bullets are somehow traced to the murder weapon, then it will now be back in the possession of El Coreano.

Fifty-two years later, telling Arturo and me this story in his windowless office on Federal Boulevard in West Denver, Miguel Sanchez smiled as he emphasized what he had learned that night: "I was totally expendable."

Later Arturo said one part of the story did indeed ring true.

"What part?" I asked.

He said, "Raúl is known for telling bad jokes. He's not as charismatic as Fidel and he doesn't deliver his lines as well."

Probably we'll never know how much of El Coreano's story is true. But even assuming parts are exaggerated, we all understood the deeper meaning of the tale: The little brother was always cleaning up the messes left by his big brother.

Chapter Three
Raúl and Rody

El Coreano did not sail on the *Granma* with the rebels he had helped to train. Instead, he told us, he "became invisible." Not so Fidel, Raúl and Che. They crammed their little band of men onto that little yacht and left Mexico on November 25, 1956, sailing into history. By New Year's Eve, twenty-four months later, they had routed Batista and sent him packing from their island.

Fidel became a darling of the media, a romantic hero who had freed his people from the grip of a bloody tyrant.

In his legal defense after his attack on the Moncada Barracks, Fidel proclaimed his purpose of carrying out a nationalist revolution in Cuba. This was a source of concern in Washington, since the American establishment under President Eisenhower was suspicious and hostile not only of communists but also of nationalist governments in the developing world that were advocating neutrality or equidistance from the two main blocs of Cold War power. The fear, according to Arturo, was that nationalists would not only endanger American economic interests abroad but also weaken Western solidarity against the communist bloc.

The honeymoon between Cuba's new revolutionary government and the Eisenhower administration didn't last long. As soon as Castro began his nationalizations and land reforms, his program clashed with American interests. Castro did try to build some accommodations with Washington, without asking for any aid in return, during two visits to the United States in 1959. He even asked for more free trade between the United States and Cuba, ending the system of sugar quotas that limited Cuban exports to its northern neighbor. The United States also tried to find common ground, often through its ambassador, Philip Bonsal, who insisted on better communication rather than rupture with the revolutionary government.

But by January 1, 1961, the divisive forces of the Cold War had played their role. The United States broke off diplomatic relations with Cuba and responded with sanctions every time Cuba nationalized private property. In turn, Cuba's revolutionary government responded to every sanction with a counterattack against American interests.

Fidel's most radical allies at the time were his brother Raúl and Che Guevara. Both they and Fidel were aware of the overthrow of Jacobo Arbenz in Guatemala by a CIA-sponsored conspiracy in 1954. Since early on, even in Sierra Maestra, Cuba's new leadership knew that a potential conflict against an alliance of the U.S. government and those opposed to the Revolution was likely. To prepare for this eventuality, the radical revolutionaries were ready to ask for help from the Soviet Union.

After their victory at the Bay of Pigs, the revolutionary elite became convinced that the White House would not accept its defeat and would try to overthrow the Cuban government by military means. Fidel, Raúl and Che believed an American military invasion of the island was a probable scenario. Their beliefs were strengthened by the Kennedys' substantial increase in financial, military, and technical support designed to assist sabotage, terrorism, and assassination attempts against them.

Their beliefs were further strengthened by the discovery of a CIA plan (code name "Patty") to assassinate Raúl during the July 26, 1961, celebrations in Santiago de Cuba, where he was scheduled to speak. Simultaneously, a group of anti–Castro Cubans would attack the U.S. naval base at Guantánamo, simulating a response by the Cuban military, blinded by anger over the murder of its leader. This would set the context — or pretext — for a direct American military intervention in Cuba.[1]

On April 21, 1961, just two days after Cuba's victory at the Bay of Pigs, Raúl established the "Eastern Army" with the first regular division of the Revolutionary Armed Forces. Without giving up his position as the head of the FAR, Raúl began to develop the biggest and most powerful military structure in the country, covering almost the entire eastern half of the island.

By the end of 1961, the Eastern Army — headquartered in the northeast, where Raul's Second Front had operated during the Revolution — had twelve infantry divisions, three anti-landing battalions, one artillery brigade, and five mountain groups.[2] Cuba's High Command asked the Soviet Union to provide conventional weapons to face, or in the best scenario deter, a U.S. invasion. The Soviet Union leader Nikita Khrushchev answered with a far more dangerous idea. And so it was, in the northeast of Cuba, under Raúl's command, that the Soviets began to install nuclear missiles in 1962.

According to a Central Intelligence Agency report written by James H. Hansen,[3] "Nikita Khrushchev decided to emplace ... missiles in Cuba in the spring of 1962." Khrushchev's general staff called the operation "ANADYR," after a river than runs into the Bering Sea. Hansen's report states:

Secrecy surrounded the first Soviet delegation that went to propose the auda-cious plan to Fidel Castro and other Cuban leaders. The officials arrived in Havana with little fanfare on 29 May, amidst a delegation of agricultural experts.... The group included Col. Gen. Ivanov and several missile construction specialists and other military experts, whose job it was to determine whether the missiles could be deployed in secrecy. Ambassador Aleksandr Alekseev took Cuban Defense Minister Raul Castro aside to explain that "Engineer Petrov" in the group actu-ally was Marshal [Sergei] Biryuzov [commander of the Soviet Union's Strate-gic Rocket Forces], and that he needed to meet with *el lider maximo* without delay. Only three hours later "Engineer Petrov" was shown into Fidel Castro's office. The Cuban leadership unanimously and enthusiastically gave its approval in prin-ciple.[4]

As reported by Jon Lee Anderson in his biography of Che, the Soviet ambassador later said that he'd seen Raúl, for the first time ever, writing things down in a notebook.[5] The following narrative is derived largely from Ander-son's account.[6]

Fidel told the Soviets to come back the next day. He needed to think things over and discuss it with his advisors. When the Soviets returned, several additional players, including Che, were present. The Cubans said they had evaluated the proposal and were willing to proceed with it, mostly because they believed the missiles would deter the United States from invading the island.

Fidel has described how Khrushchev's proposal put him in a difficult position. He did not ask for nuclear weapons but for conventional weapons. But Khrushchev argued that nuclear missiles in Cuba were necessary to create a new strategic balance between the U.S. and communist forces. The defense of Cuba, according to Khrushchev, would be part of the defense of the socialist bloc.

According to Fidel, Cuba could not expect the Soviets to sacrifice while refusing to be part of the common defense of communist interests.[7] So, in the summer of 1961, Cuba and the Soviet Union developed two military cooper-ation agreements. The Soviets began to provide Cuba with critical military equipment and resources. From the Cubans' perspective, the emphasis was on protection against invasion, not mere cooperation with the Soviet hegemon. When discussions with the Soviets turned to the possibility of such an inva-sion, Che exclaimed that anything that could stop the United States was worth a try.

Immediately, the Soviets and Cubans began locating missile sites. To find the right locations, Fidel assigned Raúl the task of accompanying Soviet Marshal Biryuzov, who had originally come to Cuba as "Comrade Petrov." After the tour, and knowing the characteristics of the operation, Raúl reported to Fidel that it would be very difficult to install the missiles without being discovered by American intelligence.

Fidel therefore demanded a more formal agreement — a third one — that required the clarification of certain principles in case of trouble with the Americans once the missiles were discovered. He wanted guarantees against invasion, as well as the return of the U.S. naval base at Guantánamo. He said he would send Raúl — his defense minister and little brother — to Moscow to finalize the agreement.

The Soviet ambassador spent the next week with Raúl, drafting the agreement in Spanish. Raúl and one of the visiting Soviets signed each page. Then Raúl personally carried the draft to Moscow. According to Hansen's account, Khrushchev met with Raúl twice over the following week before the agreement was actually signed.[8] An alternate account[9] says that when Raúl arrived in Moscow with his wife, a Central Committee advisor named Korionov was instructed by Prime Minister Alexei Kosygin to accompany him to pick them up at the airport. The group went directly to a safe house. Once inside, Korionov, Kosygin, and Raúl left the others and retired to the dining room. There was a grand piano in the room. Raúl laid the agreement on it, with all of Fidel's corrections translated into Russian. He and Kosygin signed it. Afterward, Kosygin left, and told Korionov to stay behind.

Raúl and Korionov stayed up all night drinking. They understood the terrible machine they had set in motion. What's more, Raúl had not yet asked Khrushchev the one question Fidel wanted answered before the deal was made: What would happen if the United States found out about the operation before the missiles were in place?

When the question was finally asked later in the week, Khrushchev told Raúl not to worry. If the United States did discover the operation, the Soviet Union would ask the Cuban leadership to invite the Baltic Fleet to the region. Khrushchev said he would send it immediately as a show of support for his Cuban ally. Although Raúl was not totally convinced by the argument, he felt relieved by Khrushchev's approval of the whole package of military support for Cuba.

The island would receive Soviet military support, if it was needed.

Khrushchev figuratively licked his chops. If he could just maintain absolute secrecy until November or December, then he could travel to Cuba for the January anniversary of the Revolution and ink the agreement with Fidel. And if they could reveal it to the world in a sensational fait accompli, then they would gain great bargaining power over the United States.

Raúl left Moscow on July 17. The Soviet ambassador followed three weeks later, carrying the version of the document that Raúl had already signed. Both were confident everything would go smoothly. The missiles were already on their way.

But Fidel did not like the agreement as it was signed. It wasn't political enough. It did not focus enough on Cuban sovereignty. And it did not spell out clearly enough what Khrushchev had already promised — that an attack against the Republic of Cuba would be considered an attack on the Soviet Union. So more changes were made.

And players on the game board also changed. In late August, after the revisions to the agreement were completed, it was time to go back to Moscow. This time Fidel did not send his little brother to do his bidding. Instead, he sent Che Guevara. On August 30, Che met with Khrushchev, who agreed to the amended language. But the Soviet leader did not want to sign the final agreement until he came to Cuba in a few months for a previously scheduled visit.

Che scoffed. He wanted the agreement signed and made public. He wanted to rub the whole thing in the Americans' faces. But Khrushchev refused, insisting on continued secrecy until after the missiles were installed. Che repeated Fidel's concerns about a premature discovery of the missiles by the United States. And Khrushchev repeated his pledge to send in the Baltic Fleet if a problem were to arise.

Che was not convinced, but what could he do? He had to accept the pledge.

Meanwhile, U.S. intelligence had learned to keep tabs on Che's movements, and it was watching his activities in Russia with a wary eye. A Central Intelligence Agency cable speculated there might be more to Che's visit to Moscow than merely economic and trade issues.

By early September, American U-2 spy planes had detected the Soviet military buildup on the island. There would be no more secrecy. Within weeks the entire world (including me, a 12-year-old boy in Omaha) would be watching as Adlai Stevenson challenged Valerian Zorin to deny that Soviet missiles had been installed on Cuba. Or, as Jon Lee Anderson writes, "[T]he deal concluded by Che would bring the world to the brink of nuclear war."[10]

And in that statement lurks a reality Raúl has faced — and accepted — all his life. He might have been the guy who did the serious heavy lifting — cleaning up after Fidel in Mexico, warning him about the impossibility of installing the missiles in secrecy, negotiating the agreement with the Soviets — but it would always be someone else who would get the credit, usually either his charismatic older brother or the romantic radical Che. This tendency to underplay the role of Raúl in the critical events of Cuban history permeates the literature and the media.

In their groundbreaking work, *The Kennedy Tapes: Inside the White House During the Cuban Missile Crisis*, Harvard historians Ernest May and Philip Zelikow carefully compiled transcripts of all of the tapes made by President Kennedy during the meetings he had with his advisors throughout those fateful days in October 1962.[11] The book is 725 pages, and it mentions Raúl's role in the affair only four times: once in the actual transcripts and three times in the commentary. That means throughout the high drama that brought the world to the brink of nuclear war, the Kennedy administration — and later the historians — would virtually ignore the man in charge of Cuba's military.

Brian Latell, a former U.S. National Intelligence Officer for Latin America, continues the trend in his more recent book, *After Fidel: Raul Castro and the Future of Cuba's Revolution.*[12] That subtitle admittedly sounds promising. And on the back cover a reviewer calls it "the first ever Raul Castro biography." But between the covers Latell focuses more on the past and Fidel's life story than on the future or the role Raúl has played or will play in Cuban affairs. Aside from a handful of colorful anecdotes about the relationship between the brothers, the first ten chapters read more like a biography of Fidel than Raúl. And while the final chapters — about 50 pages — do focus more on Raúl, they still look to the past. In addition, this book was written months before the little brother was actually elected president of Cuba and before the reforms he initiated once he formally took office.

Arturo says Latell is "not merely a Cold Warrior, but a Cold Warrior who lets his ideology guide his analysis." In the 1980s Latell wrote a report that described Fidel as "a man on the ropes," and in another controversial report, Latell claimed Mexico was on the verge of falling into communist hands. Many viewed the report as "psycho-fiction," according to Bob Woodward,[13] yet Latell employs the same basic approach in his book. It is very one-sided. There is virtually no mention of the dreadful conditions suffered by Cubans under Batista or of any of the Revolution's notable achievements. Whether he is writing about Fidel or Raúl, the author demonizes rather than analyzes. It is curious how Latell presents Raúl as more market friendly and pragmatic than Fidel, but does not elaborate about potential implications that could lead the United States to adjust its policy toward the island.

A more balanced approach comes in Daniel Erikson's book, *The Cuba Wars: Fidel Castro, the United States, and the Next Revolution*, published in 2008.[14] Erikson is now a senior Cuba advisor at the State Department. When he wrote the book, he was a think tank analyst for the Inter-American Dialogue and a well-respected authority on U.S.-Cuba relations. Still, his book continues to focus far more on Fidel and the past, though he does offer much greater insight on events that were current when he wrote it. Mostly, however, Erikson dissects the tensions between Cuba and the United States during the 1990s and early 2000s. And this is very important material.

The key is the codification of the embargo by the Helms-Burton legislation.[15] Before Helms-Burton, the Cuban embargo was a wall built of differently shaped bricks stacked loosely together. There were statutes and executive orders and administrative regulations and guidelines. Then on February 24, 1996, Cuban jets shot down two small airplanes operated by a right-wing exile group called Brothers to the Rescue. The group had been playing fast and loose with the rules of civil aviation, flying over Cuban waters and distributing leaflets from the air. Several Cuban and American security analysts had expressed concerns about the possibility of a military incident or an accident as a result of these unauthorized flights.

The shooting down of the planes happened at a critical moment when relations between the United States and Cuba had begun to thaw after new migration agreements had been signed by the Clinton administration. There were hopes that some parts of the embargo could be lifted. That may explain why Brothers to the Rescue and other groups were increasing pressure on the Cuban government. After all, 1996 was an election year, Florida was a swing state, and exile leaders expected that any incident with Cuba could give them some leverage to strengthen the embargo — especially with a Republican Congress in which Jesse Helms was chair of the Foreign Relations Committee.

Bill Clinton has said that Fidel later sent him a message, "indirectly of course," recognizing that shooting down the planes had been a mistake. "Apparently he had issued an earlier order to fire on any aircraft that violated Cuban airspace and had failed to withdraw [it] when the Cubans knew the Brothers to the Rescue planes were coming."[16] In any event, the incident definitely stopped all momentum in favor of more engagement between the two nations. Only two weeks after the shooting, Congress passed the Helms-Burton Act, which in effect mortared all those bricks together in a stricter, tighter, more rigid configuration.

No longer could a U.S. president wipe away the embargo with a single sweep of his hand (if one ever really could). Under the Helms-Burton Act, the president would need a jackhammer for the mortar. Though some actions can be taken without congressional approval — engaging in more direct diplomacy or licensing multiple travel categories, for example — the complete dismantling of the embargo has become a more carefully controlled process. Even without Helms-Burton, a new ambassador could not be posted to Cuba without the "Advice and Consent of the Senate." Our system that separates the powers of government, checking and balancing them against each other, requires the president to work with Congress in reversing fifty years of policy.

Arturo says it differently: "The embargo is like a sinking ship and it needs just one big hole — like lifting the travel ban for all Americans — for it to go down." Whatever metaphor is used, there will be a process of deconstruction. And it will likely involve a series of steps and initiatives both unilateral and bilateral that will form an elaborate, sometimes passionate dance between the new administration in Washington and the new administration in Havana. It will be a new dance, too: salsa rhythms, hip-hop beat.

Barack Obama and Raúl Castro are already performing that dance. Congress — driven by changing politics and changing demographics — is starting to learn the music. The days of Helms-Burton are numbered.

Yet throughout 2008, 2009, and even 2010, more people in the United States and all over the world waited for Fidel to die than watched what his little brother Raúl was doing. Even those academics who called for the "decolonization" of the Cuban Missile Crisis — by shifting emphasis away from the U.S. and Soviet hegemons and toward the conduct of the people of Cuba — failed to give Raúl his due in their reframing of history.[17]

When Steven Soderbergh's bio-epic of Che finally hit American theaters, after garnering cheers at the Latin American Film Festival in Havana in December 2008, Raúl's screen time remained surprisingly scant. Here was the man who had visited the Soviet Bloc while he was still a youth, who had introduced Che to Fidel in Mexico City, who had negotiated the agreement for the Soviets to install their missiles on the island, who had stood by his older brother for five decades, remaining in that giant shadow, quietly running the military — and even after he becomes president of Cuba, Che and Fidel still hog the spotlight!

In January 2009, there was a billboard outside Santa Clara that had a line drawing of Raúl in the lower right corner and three giant words emblazoned across it: *"Sí se puede!"— Yes we can!*

I originally thought a description of that billboard would make the perfect ending to this chapter. But I forgot a cardinal rule: getting from Point A to Point B in Cuba is always an adventure. So the billboard became instead the opening of this part of the chapter, and with that gentle mental shift, everything fell into place.

I had come to Santa Clara in the central part of Cuba, a 3-hour drive from Havana, the afternoon before, riding in the backseat of Ernesto's aging white Peugeot. In the cabin there were three new additions: Yael, Ernesto's Argentine wife, a bright and handsome woman; their toddler daughter, a cute fidgety thing; and a Kenwood DVD player a neighbor had helped Ernesto install. The DVD player was loaded with Cuban hip-hop and Reggaeton. It never got played.

I sat in the backseat with Ernesto's wife, who was cradling her drowsy, drooling child. Parenting — the universal language — broke the ice between us. She said the years 2 to 3, the so-called terrible twos, were so difficult. I recalled that when my two daughters were that age, they both experienced an explosion in consciousness. Potty training showed them they could control

Billboard at the entrance to Santa Clara, extolling the city as the vanguard of the Revolution (Arturo Lopez-Levy collection).

their body, clothing, and environment. And speaking, even some early reading, showed they could interact with other people, and get things they wanted, without throwing fits. "It's powerful," I said.

We had both been to Cuba many times before, foreigners in this strange land. I asked her how she'd come to see it, being married to a Cuban. By now we were cruising along the nearly deserted highway. She shifted the infant on her shoulder and said, "I love the people but hate the way they live. Just look. They have DVD players but no food. I play a game with my friends here. It's called 'What's Better? What's Worse?'"

"How does it work?"

"Oh, you know, the schools are better, because they have this new rule that makes the student-to-teacher ratio 20-to-1, and that's good. But the schools are also worse because they don't have enough trained teachers to satisfy the new need, so they've put all these teenagers in the classroom, and they're not teachers, and it's not working out."

"Like the new Chinese buses," I said. "Public transportation is more widespread, and that's better, but the pollution is so much worse."

"Exactly. Or take hospitals. The facilities have gotten better. But they're worse, too, because many good doctors are sent to Venezuela in exchange for oil from Chávez."

Soon dusk was falling, then night, and it got dark on the highway. We stopped talking and I started staring out the window. There were scattered cars and trucks, and pockets of cops, but no neon and no advertising, just a divided highway, in fairly good repair, with sprinkles of light speeding by. The headlight beams of the Peugeot were none too strong and all of us were relieved to arrive in Santa Clara.

Ernesto negotiated the streets where he had grown up, pulling his car in front of a modest two-story apartment in the middle of a block on a side street a short distance from the central plaza. We got out. We had come for the 102nd birthday of "Chicha," Ernesto and Arturo's grandmother, who was really a great aunt but had always functioned as their *abuela*. The festivities were the next day and when that day came, Arturo told me they were going to stay over an extra day. Their grandma was not feeling well and they needed some extra time with her. I wanted to return to Havana that day as planned and Arturo said I could take a bus, hire a taxi, or wait for his friend Rody, who was going later in the day. How much later? Probably noon, Arturo guessed, or maybe one o'clock. I opted for Rody. Then I stood by and watched while a bouquet of 102 red roses kicked off the party. Chicha, shriveled and birdlike, beamed like a star with so much family around her, including Arturo and Ernesto and his wife and daughter as well as all the others who had come: a great niece from San Francisco, the same generation as Arturo; a couple of aunts and uncles; a few cousins; and Rody with his Swiss partner Bruno.

Rody — short for Rodolfo — is simply one of the most striking men I've ever met. He is a boyhood friend of Arturo and Ernesto, but he is as different from them as night is from day. He has flawless ebony skin, close-cropped black hair, smooth cheeks, a sharp nose, slender body, thin lips, and the most beatific smile I've ever seen on a middle-aged man.

The problem wasn't Rody. It was the car he and Bruno had rented at the airport. It started the day with a flat rear tire, so Ernesto went to change it, take the flat for repair, return and reinstall it on the rental. Meanwhile, Arturo borrowed Ernesto's white Peugeot and took me to see Che's mausoleum outside town, where there was a fairly predictable display of memorabilia from the Revolution. One wall was covered with a giant photo by Osvaldo Salas that showed a fully bearded Fidel on the left, in a rakish beret, looking off in the distance, caught mid-sentence; a fully bearded Che on the right, also in a beret, laughing at Fidel's comment; and Raúl in the middle, in a cap with a visor and barely a wisp of moustache on his upper lip, his eyes turned up, glued to his older brother.

After we visited the mausoleum, Arturo couldn't get the white Peugeot to start. There was no juice going from the battery to the ignition. There wasn't even a hopeful little click. And Arturo didn't have Ernesto's cell phone number with him, so he couldn't call him cell phone to cell phone. So Arturo

Rody, Arturo, and a neighbor in Havana (Arturo Lopez-Levy collection).

called his friend Juancho in Havana and had him call Ernesto, and soon
Ernesto was there with the rental, driving up by himself.

I thought: There it is again, the younger brother — cheerfully ready, willing, and able to bail out the older brother. Just like Raúl and Fidel.

Ernesto popped the hood of the Peugeot, took the handle of a large
screwdriver, and banged on the battery terminals. Once, twice, three times
each. That's all it took. The engine turned over and we headed back to
Chicha's. What else could go wrong?

We arrived to find Rody busy putting color in some of the women's hair.
It was like they were having a grand "spa day" in celebration of the birthday.
Rody was part of the family; that much was clear. Arturo had confided to me
that in the old days, when there was still a lot of discrimination against homosexuals, his father had been uncomfortable with his association with Rody.

But that was all in the past. Arturo's family had changed its attitudes
toward homosexuality along with many other Cubans, who tend to be very
tolerant of people with different sexual preferences. That is one of the greatest
changes of the last few decades in a Latin macho society. The new generations
and particularly women — like Arturo's mother, aunts, and cousins — helped

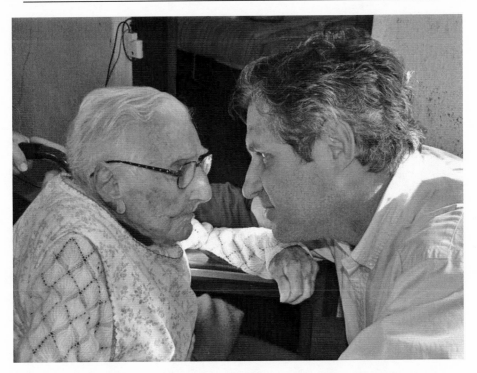

Arturo and his beloved Chicha (Arturo Lopez-Levy collection).

to push this change. As result, older men began to be more tolerant and opened their minds to the injustice of denying respect to homosexuals. Engagement, social contacts, and conversations also helped to dismantle negative stereotypes.

At the political level, Mariela Castro, the daughter of Raúl and Vilma Espin, helped to organize the gay community. Gays are now out of the closet. Rody believes that it would be very positive if the same progress achieved against homophobia could inspire more action against the racism that still colors the system and the nation.

But there was none of that at Chicha's that day, because Rody was family — period. There was only good cheer and a dominoes game for those not getting washed and rinsed. Also plenty of fine Havana Club because this was, after all, Cuba.

Bruno — pinkish white skin, medium build, earrings, short brown hair and a bemused expression — sat with me off to the side, talking about international politics. Mostly Obama and the global financial crisis and the prospects for lifting the embargo. Bruno also expressed interest in my last book, *On the List*, which was in part about the growing global markets for human transplant organs and the need for organ transplant reform in the United States and around the world.

Rody and Bruno lived together in Zurich, where Bruno was a social worker for abused children. He and Rody were plainly in love. After Rody finished with the women's hair, he turned to their nails, doing them quickly; by then lunch was served and finally — now it was late afternoon — we were ready to leave for Havana.

After hugs and kisses good-bye, Rody, Bruno and I set out in the rental whose tire had gone flat. Outside town we passed that giant billboard that grabbed my attention — Cuba's first new president in decades with those 3 words: *"Sí se puede!"*— *Yes we can!*

I sat in the back, Bruno drove, and Rody sat in the front passenger's seat, occasionally resting his hand on Bruno's thigh, above the knee. We laughed about the billboard and talked about my daughters. Then we talked about guy things like stereos and cars. We stopped and bought a kilo of cheese from a peddler on the side of the road.

An hour into our drive, I told Rody that Arturo had said it would be okay for me to ask him about the changes he saw in Cuba from the gay point of view. Rody beamed his beatific smile at me — white even teeth against ebony skin!— and said, *"Claro."*

He explained he had left Cuba nine years before, when the government was still very repressive against homosexuals. I had seen the movies *Strawberry and Chocolate*, much of which was filmed at my favorite *paladar* in Havana, and *Before Night Falls*, which depicted the struggles of the gay Cuban poet Reinaldo Arenas, so I had superficial familiarity with the topic. But it had never been a subject of my research, and I had never talked to someone who had experienced the repression first-hand.

Rody did not want to dwell on the past, however. He wanted to talk about how much better it was for him now when he visited his home country. There were still problems, prejudices, and stereotypes. Some policemen were still hostile to homosexuals walking hand in hand or the celebration of gay parties. But he said he saw big changes, not only in the attitudes of the government but also in those of the people. He delighted in his ability to be openly gay with his partner, in public and in private.

Bruno glanced over his shoulder and nodded.

I was sitting in the middle of the backseat, leaning forward over the transmission, between the two front seats. Rody turned and squeezed my hand in a gesture of such breathtaking affinity that I was taken aback. He emphasized that the huge changes he was describing were making huge differences not only for him and his partner but also for his family and friends. They no longer suffered for his sexual orientation.

I recalled Arturo's remark about his father's discomfort with his relationship with Rody as a youth. And later, when Rody and Bruno dropped me off at Arturo's father's home in Nuevo Vedado, I duly noted the warmth of the hug Rody gave Arturo Sr. Perhaps, I thought, things really have changed.

However, before that big hug took place, we'd had to overcome one more hurdle.

Two hours into the drive, with dusk falling, we stopped at a gas station — which were few and far between — so Rody could stock up on cigarettes and drinks. Water for me, orange soda for Bruno (spiked with a little rum), and a cold Cristal for Rody. I didn't really mind the alcohol consumption, I just wasn't in the mood. But I did wonder why Bruno was not gassing up the car. I assumed he was supposed to return the rental empty, but the gas gauge showed it was already close to that, and we still had an hour to go.

Sure enough, halfway into that last hour, the dashboard indicators said we were about to run out of gas. I took a deep breath. It was just another Cuban adventure. But it was really dark outside and there weren't many other vehicles on the road and there were no signs or billboards. Then Bruno asked, "Do you think we have enough to get there?"

Rody leaned sideways, glanced at the dashboard lights, and shrugged.

I blurted out, "*Sí se puede!*" And we all got a laugh out of that.

But it was no laughing matter. The indicators kept telling us they were serious and nothing was in sight. We began to chant, "*Sí se puede!*" — as if it were our mantra.

Finally, we reached the outskirts of Havana. The car was sputtering. Bruno pulled to the curb and asked someone where the nearest Cupet station was. The guy shrugged, so we crept ahead a little more and pulled over again and asked another guy, who said there was one a mile away. Turn right at the next main street.

Did we have enough fuel to get there or would we have to push?

We coasted into that Cupet station on vapors, laughing, "*Sí se puede!*"

I didn't take many pictures during my January 2009 visit to Cuba. But I took one, with a little SONY digital camera, that for me symbolizes the four big truths. It shows a crusty old Jew with mottled pink skin and a scrawny white beard, wearing a simple white yarmulke and a filthy brown shirt caked with dandruff and buttoned to his neck. He is standing in front of the Star of David on the wooden door of Adath Israel in Old Havana, staring at the camera with weary blue eyes, his face drawn and grizzled.

Arturo says the old man's name is Salomon. Pinned to Salomon's filthy brown shirt is a shiny white campaign button that he must have gotten from

Old Salomon in front of Synagogue Adath Israel in Old Havana, January 2009 (Harlan Abrahams collection).

a tourist. A perfect circle of white. On it, a familiar logo: a blue half-circle over three red stripes converging at the horizon. It reads "OBAMA" in dark blue letters over "BIDEN" in lighter blue.

On both sides of the Straits of Florida, the transfer of power is now complete.

PART II

THE NEW CUBA

Chapter Four

The Economy in the New Cuba

Arturo and I went shopping for produce in Nuevo Vedado. Arturo wanted to take some *fruta bomba* and *guayaba*—papaya and guava—home to his father and stepmother. Knowing that Raúl was allowing the farmers to sell their excess fruits and vegetables for their own account, and in markets not run by the state, we made it a point to target the new farmers markets scattered around the neighborhood.

We came to one a few blocks from Arturo's father's home. Its flimsy stalls were only half full and its garbage-strewn aisles were less full than that. Arturo whispered, "It's the hurricanes. It was very hard on the farmers and their crops this year."

I recalled having run into a Cuban Jewish scientist named Jose Altshuler, a former vice president of the Cuban Academy of Science, just outside the Patronato with Arturo. The scientist had expressed great concern over global warming, the seriously increased hurricane activity it was triggering in the Atlantic, and its impact on the Cuban economy.

Arturo stopped in front of a stall, behind which a scrawny, ill-clad farmer waited to make his sale. Arturo's eyes ran over the farmer's produce. It was not in particularly appetizing condition. I figured Arturo would pass it by. But he didn't. He selected the best *fruta bomba* he could find, reached into his pocket, and drew forth some CUCs.

CUCs—pronounced "kooks"—are Cuban convertible pesos, one of the two currencies allowed at this time on the island. Why two currencies? Economists can give more technical reasons, but it started when the Soviet Union collapsed, taking with it a third of the Cuban economy. No longer could Fidel rely on subsidies from his comrades. He announced a "Special Period of Austerity." Cuba desperately needed hard currency. Opening the island to tourism and remittances from Cubans living overseas in 1993 provided the source. After 1995, the Cuban economy began a recovery marked by inequalities and inefficiencies associated with the dual-currency system.

Meanwhile, despite congressional codification of the embargo in Helms-

Burton, the Clinton administration was lax in its enforcement of the travel ban. Ry Cooder's Buena Vista Social Club exploded on the scene and it became a romantic adventure to travel to the forbidden city of Havana (usually through Mexico or Canada) to taste some of that hot Latin culture colliding with cold communism. Tourist dollars flooded into Cuba and the Cubans welcomed them. It became legal to trade in U.S. currency.

But only those who dealt with the tourist industry and foreign investment, or who had relatives abroad, had access to those precious American dollars. Many Cubans remained trapped in the peso economy. Dollars bought luxury goods while pesos bought ration card essentials. This created two classes of Cubans — and oddities like doctors and engineers driving taxis to get access to tourists, or serving as barmen and waiters.

Still, it worked, after a fashion, until George W. Bush tightened sanctions against foreign banks doing dollar transactions with Cuba. Following the same historical pattern from the beginning of the Revolution, as if nobody had learned anything in forty years, Fidel then denounced the sanctions as another aggression against the Cuban nation and retaliated by taxing these transactions in American dollars. Flirtations with Canadian dollars and euros led in time to the adoption of the convertible peso, the CUC, to fill the role formerly filled by the American dollar. It's a highly dysfunctional system.

Arturo handed his CUCs to the farmer. They were old and wrinkled from being wadded in Arturo's pocket. The farmer looked at them with horror and waved them off. I was surprised and so was Arturo, who launched into a rapid exchange with the farmer. The farmer just shrugged. He didn't take the money, though it was 100 percent legal currency. Arturo put the *fruta bomba* back where he found it and we left the little farmers market.

"What was that about?" I asked.

"My money," he said.

"What was wrong with it?"

"It was too wrinkled," he said. "And the edge was torn."

"That makes no sense," I said. I had seen the tear in one of the CUCs. Trust me, it was no big thing. "These guys are supposed to be entrepreneurs, aren't they?"

Arturo shrugged and we walked on. Perhaps I should have realized that, being a small farmers market in the heart of a neighborhood far from the tourist areas, the place might have hosted farmers who actually preferred pesos over CUCs. We arrived at a second small farmers market, a few blocks — and more crumbling sidewalks — further on.

And sure enough, the exact same scene unfolded, replayed like something from the Bill Murray classic, *Groundhog Day*. Arturo looked over the fruit, selected some, reached into his pocket, and offered his CUCs to the farmer.

The farmer waved them off and harsh words were exchanged. We left the market without any fruit.

After our third failure, we gave up. Arturo stormed off, his blue eyes flashing. He headed straight for an outdoor market run by the state, a few blocks away. When I caught up with him, he was muttering "Wrinkled!" or something obscene in Spanish.

We arrived at the market run by the state.

Arturo explained that this market was not part of the ration system, but managed by the army, selling at lower prices than the private farmers but closer to the market prices. The differences were immediately apparent: The stalls were filled with fresh produce, the aisles were swept clean, and the customers were plentiful. And the greater number of people wasn't for any sort of ideological reasons. Rather, the fruits and vegetables in this market were simply cleaner, fresher, and healthier-looking than those in the private markets.

Arturo, for the fourth time that afternoon, stopped in front of a stall. This one was fully stocked with fresh, ripe produce, arranged in a colorful display. Arturo carefully scanned the produce. He selected a big round *fruta bomba* but left behind the *guayaba*. He reached into his pocket and pulled forth his wrinkled CUCs and handed them to the man tending the stall. The man took them without fanfare, harsh words, or drama.

We left the market shaking our heads, exchanging thoughts telepathically:

HARLAN: If those farmers selling their own crops, who are supposedly trying to be private entrepreneurs, think they can be choosy over how wrinkled their currency is, then how can they ever hope to succeed?

ARTURO: They're not used to having to compete. They're used to having the state run their lives. A lot of things, including the culture, are going to have to change.

HARLAN: But it's a way of thinking that's just not compatible with capitalism.

ARTURO: The way they think won't change overnight. It can't be all at once. The typical advice of the casual Cuba observer is to emphasize the absence of private property and markets. But change is more complex than that. Cuba does need to change. As you say, it's all about the economics, the politics, the rule of law, and culture—all in the right sequence. That is why it is so important to take a gradual and integral approach.

I didn't press the issue. After all, I had met many industrious, ambitious Cubans; I shouldn't judge the private farmers so quickly. Still, I have been haunted ever since by the specter of fledgling capitalists rejecting legal tender.

The next day Arturo and I walked along the Malecón, the famed sea wall that protects Havana from the Straits of Florida. The haunting had begun. I said to him, "You grew up inside the system. For a while you were part of the system. Why do *you* think property rights are more important than the communist government thinks?"

Arturo turned his eyes to the sea. It was cloudless, in the mid–1970s, not too humid by Havana standards. Young lovers walked hand-in-hand over the crumbling sidewalk; an old man and his dog were fishing from the shoals at the bottom of the wall. We had left the Melía Cohiba, where I had been using the wireless in the lobby bar, and were going to the Hotel Nacional, where I meant to buy some Coronas Especiales to take home.

Arturo replied that growing up in a country where private property was almost entirely absent, it became evident to him that the aversion to private property was one of the fundamental flaws of the Cuban Revolution. For years, the economic life in Cuba, and what everyone was taught in schools, was based on the idea that private property was intrinsically wrong and the basis of all exploitation. By contrast, cooperative property was typical of

The famed Malecón of Havana, with the Hotel Nacional to the far right (Harlan Abrahams collection).

socialism, but destined to disappear with the progress to communism. Companies owned by the state were the promoted model, in which exploitation would end.

I wasn't sure I understood everything he was saying.

But Arturo pressed on: "I was born in 1968, the year Fidel Castro launched his 'Revolutionary Offensive,' a process by which most of Cuba's small businesses — stores, bars, and cafeterias — were nationalized by the government. In the countryside, during the 1970s and early 1980s, the government began the process of collectivization by which small private farmers were encouraged to join cooperatives or give up their land and become workers for state companies."

We slowed our pace. I had been on the Malecón countless times — had sweated in the summer heat and marveled at the waves crashing over the wall during hurricanes — but this time would be different. I would be getting a lesson on Cuban economics. Arturo explained that the actions taken by the state against small property owners in 1968 were the expression of Castro's independence of mind, because by that time in the communist world there some were already questioning the most radical economic policies. Within the communist bloc, the radicalism of Cuba had only one parallel: the Cultural Revolution in China. Czechoslovakia, Hungary, and Poland were already beginning to implement economic reforms and liberalization, allowing significant space for small and even medium-sized private businesses. Contrary to what some have written, said Arturo, the Cubans have nobody but themselves to blame for the magnitude of their mess.

I said, "Tell me more."

He said, "While I was growing up, I saw the deterioration of the quality of services in the stores and cafeterias. The quality went down with the replacement of the old workers by new generations who were not trained in the culture of servicing clients. They had no idea that 'the customer is always right.' Back then my great aunt Guiselda was the principal of a primary school. She was strict but loved me so much that my mother later put me in another school to avoid any favoritism. Guiselda's husband Raúl had owned a small produce shop in the plaza during the times of capitalism. He took his values with him into the times of socialism. He managed a shoe store at one of the corners of the main square, next to a newspaper kiosk and bookstore I loved. He was all about servicing his customers. Though shoes were sold through government coupons, he would come out of his office and do his best to satisfy them. He would personally go to the back room and search for the right kind of shoes for the children, women, or men."

Arturo paused to explain that in those days, the culture of serving people, of being nice to the customers, was still present. Workers had developed a

Classic old buildings along the Malecón; imagine the views from those windows! *Bottom:* More buildings and cars on the Malecón (both from the Harlan Abrahams collection).

work ethic for decades and socialism's lack of rigor did not destroy that ethic immediately.

He edged toward the specter that had begun to haunt me: "Around the late 1970s, the disaster was evident. The cafeteria at the corner of my block was badly mismanaged. The hygiene of the place deteriorated and the lines were long. Even with coupons, it was hard to find products to buy. I remember a place we called the *hortaliza*, a piece of land near where I played soccer. When I was little, our diet included fresh tomatoes, lettuces, radishes and other produce we bought at this place. My grandmother — Chicha — loved to go there. The vegetables were taken directly from the land. Sometimes there was a line but it was always short. The owner of the place and his workers made good money by Cuban standards and worked very hard. Then one day the *hortaliza* was closed by the state. Chicha was always protesting the closing of the *hortaliza*. She was a friend of the workers there, who treated their customers with great kindness. She used to say the *hortaliza* did not hurt anybody and the quality of services it gave the community could not be replaced by the state."

I asked, "Did a lot of your family think that way?"

"No, my parents were far less sympathetic. They would say that building a just society requires sacrifice. Small businesses were the seeds of capitalism. My mother would argue with my grandmother about it, and Chicha would predict that the closing of the *hortaliza* would be terrible and the centralized system of agriculture would not be able to sell good-quality vegetables to the people. My mother would argue that perhaps that was true, but produce would be better distributed because the prices of the *hortaliza* were higher and lower-income people could not buy there often. So Chicha would say that while she supported the Revolution, she could not understand the logic of making some people worse off to achieve equality. Suffice it to say, history shows my grandmother won her bet. Every time somebody tells me that property rights don't matter, I remember this story. Those workers, as in many other small and medium-sized businesses, were the managers and the owners, but at the same time, they worked hard because they had the right incentives. I will always miss my fresh vegetables from the *hortaliza*."

Arturo's lesson moved forward in time. He said that in the 1980s, the state experimented with some small forms of private property. The government allowed free farmers markets — *mercados libres campesinos* — where peasants and cooperatives could sell their products. In Havana, Cathedral Square became a place where artisans could sell shoes, dresses, and other products. But in 1984, Fidel began criticizing the peasants and artisans for getting rich off the scarcity of things they acquired from the Revolution. They got their raw materials at subsidized prices, Fidel said, or by patronizing the black markets for goods stolen from the state. He promised to guarantee these goods and services at prices accessible to all and closed the private markets.

Arturo's father said at the time that he wasn't sure the government could honor Fidel's promise and give everyone the products they were selling. "This was one of the first times I heard my father disagree with Fidel," recalls Arturo. "I didn't dare ask him in those terms, but he said that noneconomic incentives played a very important role at the beginning of the Revolution, but in the long run they did not replace economic incentives. This did not square well with Fidel's call for pure and simple moral mobilization."

By that time, Arturo was in high school and many of his classmates were from the countryside. He used to visit some of their homes, and the idea that they were becoming rich was hardly true. They were, in fact, improving their living standard — buying some electrical equipment or old American cars, and building slightly bigger houses — but they were not wealthy by a long shot. Compared to the lives of the leaders of the party, the Revolutionary Armed Forces upper echelons, and the government elites, the lives of the peasants were by no means better.

Another shift forward: "By the end of the 1980s, I was going to the Higher Institute of International Relations in Havana, where I took my first formal classes in economics. It was called 'The Political Economy.' A joke among the students — most of them were members of the Young Communist League — was that our courses on political economy were really about the economy of capitalism. That's because the political economy of socialism was really science fiction. It described a future none of us would ever see."

The specter nagged at me, announcing that none of the sons and daughters of those students would ever see that future, either. Arturo explained that *perestroika* in the Soviet Union opened a debate in Cuba about private property, foreign investment, and the potential for cooperatives. Until then, the Soviet Union was thought to be Cuba's best friend. And, to be sure, Cubans never did hate the Soviets in the way they were despised in Poland, Czechoslovakia and Hungary. But Cubans began to hear a lot about the reforms that were happening within socialism and the reevaluation of the socialist experiments in Czechoslovakia and Hungary during the 1960s. Some of Arturo's professors and classmates began to openly take positions in favor of reform.

Most people were already in favor of economic change without questioning the dominant rule of the Communist Party. One of Arturo's friends, a charismatic young woman named Johanna Tablada,[1] spoke at a students' congress, blaming the bureaucrats who would not tell Fidel that things were not working well. That may have been naïve, but many people, including Arturo, thought that she presented the problem correctly.

In any event, during the extensive discussions about and preparations for the 4th Congress of the Communist Party, many advocated for the restoration of the farmers markets and the possibility of opening small businesses, according to Arturo. By then, I already had learned, there was a large black market growing in Cuba. People coming from Miami would bring products to their relatives, who would sell them to others. Some built thriving businesses selling second-hand clothes, though they were persecuted by the police and the CDR — local watchdogs — for their antisocialist practices.

We paused across from the U.S. Interests Section, the ugly tan and blue glass monolith halfway between the Melía and the Nacional, the scene of the Elián González protests, where a makeshift stage had been erected for the "spontaneous demonstrations." Later, a permanent stage had been built there, so more frequent protests could be aimed more effectively at the Americans. Then, George W. Bush began broadcasting propaganda from the Interests Section to the protesters gathered at the stage. So Fidel installed giant flagpoles between the Interests Section and the stage, so he could fly a mass of flags to block the view when the Americans were broadcasting their propaganda.

In January 2009, no flags were flying.

Arturo continued: "The idea that those advocating for reform were against Castro is false. Most who fell in this category were revolutionaries who believed the country should be changed. They trusted the party to have an honest discussion of the economic, social and political problems. There was already a history of small reforms from the past. This history supported some of the arguments made in favor of reform from within. The party could survive in power, said many, even while allowing small business to prosper."

"Tell me," I said, starting to walk again, "later — when you were studying for your master's [in economics] from Carleton — did you think about these experiences?"

"Of course," said Arturo. "Studying economics in the Carleton program in 1996 was truly great because I learned about capitalism in parallel with the opening of small businesses like the *paladares*— you know, the small family restaurants that are run out of Cuban homes. My little brother Ernesto had a girlfriend named Yamilet. Her family opened a *paladar* named Los Cactus. Ernesto helped in the restaurant and one of our neighbors worked in the kitchen, helping the cook. I used to go there to have lunch with Ernesto and Yamilet. This was a great experience because I could see for myself the problems they faced."

"Like what?" I asked.

Arturo said, "First, there was no fiscal culture. The government created a National Office of Taxes and it was doing nothing more than improvising its policies. The private owners of the *paladares* had no idea of how to manage their accounting and tax situations, but even if they did, the arbitrariness of the tax inspectors was pervasive. Many were looking for bribes or wanted a free lunch. Facing them, or people who would eat and not pay, the owners of the restaurants lacked any protection. There were no appropriate legal mechanisms to solve disputes. There was no rule of law. In the case of Yamilet's restaurant, a conflict arose with the neighbors who lived upstairs — a couple who were both lieutenant colonels in MININT — and this led to a flood of inspections by the police and finally the closing of the restaurant."

Arturo shook his head and said, "Another problem was the stability of the labor. Though workers in the restaurants were making 20 times more than the average salary, the discipline standards were low, and often Yamilet would fire someone because they were not properly working or were stealing from the kitchen. It was a matter of culture. These workers needed to be considered members of the family, because the restaurants were required to be family owned and operated."

"So how did your education — in classes and reality — affect your thinking?"

"I began to endorse serious economic reform beyond the mere toleration of private property. While we studied the fundamentals of market economics, we saw how the planning capacity of the Cuban command economy collapsed. The central planners could never have the necessary information to regulate the economy in the absence of market prices. At the same time, I saw that the problems of reform were not limited to private property and the redefinition of property rights. I became suspicious of market fundamentalism. Perhaps because I was becoming a religious person, I distinguished the realms of science and religion. Some of my classmates adopted market fundamentalism with the same religious fervor I had seen before in the believers in communism. I am convinced they were not in search of rational analysis but were instead seeking an alternative belief system. In contrast, the news from the Soviet Union — where health and life expectancy rates were collapsing along with the communist system — led me and many of my classmates to reject the 'shock therapy' prescribed by the neoliberals. One thing was our understanding that a transition to a more market-oriented economy was badly needed. Another was the challenge of endorsing a new fundamentalist philosophy, replacing blind trust in the socialist government with blind trust in the market."

We neared the small cliff where a small waterfall and a big Cuban flag mark the intersection of La Rampa with the Malecón. Arturo told me that one of his best friends from those days is Juan Carlos Portal, a student of economics and business. Juancho's father Marcos was the minister of energy and basic industry. In the early 1990s, Arturo's mother became the director of the Management School and Scientific Division at the Ministry of Mechanical and Steel Industries. She admired Marcos' efforts to modernize. Following his lead, she tried to create a program that combined Che's strong work ethic with techniques of capitalist management.

We came to the cliff, turned right, and headed up La Rampa.

Arturo said, "Once I invited an Argentinean professor named Juan Carlos Lerda, who was a prominent economist at the U.N. Economic Commission for Latin America, to have dinner at my house with Juancho and some friends. When Dr. Lerda asked me how I looked at the reforms, I said I was seeing some progress, not so much in property rights, but in the creation of better-prepared and more market-oriented managers. Dr. Lerda then took a piece of paper and said a transition requires more than the redefinition of property rights. It must include — he wrote this on the paper — 'markets, regulations, and a whole new economic culture, including a new generation of managers.' Before he left that night we asked him for guidance. He said, 'Do not think in terms of an ideal market or ideal government. The goal is enhancing society's welfare. Markets and governments are just tools to use without bias.' Now this was inspirational. The School of Economics at the University of Havana was undergoing major changes at the time. New master's programs in economics and business administration were being opened with the support of the Spanish and Canadian governments. The curricula were being changed and students began to learn about market-oriented micro- and macro-economics. They began to use a lot of pirated copies of textbooks from U.S. and Spanish universities."

Another right, off La Rampa, and we were just a block from the palm-lined drive of the famed Hotel Nacional. Arturo fondly recalled, "It was interesting to see how the class once called 'Scientific Socialism' became 'Problems of the Contemporary World.' One of my old friends, Carlos Manuel Estefania, was a Marxist philosopher who had one of the best libraries of Western Marxism in Havana. He said when he asked what he should teach on 'Scientific Socialism,' the response was that it was up to him — at his discretion — because nobody knew what it meant any longer."

We paused again, this time in front of a line of taxis — old Soviet Ladas and even older American cars — stretched along the drive. This was the Havana most tourists saw.

Arturo said, "As soon as any news of failure of the transition in Eastern Europe and the Soviet Union happened, the state publicized it through the newspapers and TV. The Cuban system found solace in the fact that the former communist countries were suffering similar or worse problems. Being a policy-oriented person, I thought some of my classmates and professors were not paying enough attention to the problems of privatization and other policies they favored in the context of a society that for decades had pursued equality. It made me see the need for *gradualism* in Cuba." He emphasized the word. "Even if privatization could be achieved without corruption, people could react badly against a sudden disparity in the distribution of income and wealth. This could be bad both economically and politically."

I was getting fidgety. I wanted my Coronas.

Arturo pontificated. He said that it showed great progress in Cuba that almost everyone was accepting the fact that market reforms were necessary, yet would bring with them income and wealth inequalities. Still, he had heard many followers of the Revolution demand that a good public education system and a good health system must be guaranteed no matter how the economic reform goes.

I began inching along the drive toward the entrance to the lobby.

Arturo continued: "After the collapse of communism, markets were presented as a panacea. Any idea of the need for social justice and government intervention was considered bad. Ideological visions, like the 'trickle-down' effect of the markets and the promotion of privatization as the solutions for every problem, were the trend. Many of these recommendations were given to Cuba by supporters of 'shock therapy.' But I am glad Fidel refused to follow this program. It would have destroyed Cuban social fabric and produced a humanitarian and economic catastrophe — as well as a political disaster throughout the Caribbean. What I am *not* glad about is that Fidel let his anti-market ideology block the possibility of opening the country up, and doing market reforms as they happened in Vietnam or China. In Vietnam, for example, the fact that the Communist Party had institutional mechanisms for leadership renovation led to the anticipation of the end of the Soviet Union and the development of a market-oriented alternative. By the middle of the 1990s, Vietnam was growing and the United States was forced to reconsider its embargo."

Then Arturo became more insistent: "I had already questioned the communist aversion to markets by the time I took the Carleton program. And I was learning this one absolute truth: *economics and politics always go hand in hand.*"

I slowed my pace. He said, "I didn't try to silence these market fundamentalists, as some members of the party in the program did, but I disagreed with them. My way of thinking gained support when we began receiving a number of Latin American professors in the program. Coming from underdeveloped countries, they had a less rosy vision of the market and the definition of private property rights as a way to lead the Cuban economy out of its crisis. I realized a new type of economy would mean a redefinition of Cuban politics."

We edged closer to the present. Arturo said, "There were people, at this time, who were at the limits of desperation, having trouble eating properly, and wasting hours every day trying to catch a bus just to go to work for a tiny salary. By August 5, 1994, there were even riots, which surprised many people, but not MININT, which had already been alerted to the explosive social situation. The riots began in Central Havana, where the dollar stores offended a population whose standard of living was deteriorating."

Arturo took a deep breath and continued: "To make my point about the need to preserve the achievements of the Revolution for the social and political stability of the country, I raised the topic of health care in a class taught by Professor Archibald Ritter, the coordinator of the Carleton master's program. We had already covered topics like foreign investment, educational initiatives, and technical training — all key to developing a managerial class wishing to compete. Many people were viewing the Cuban example positively but questioning how sustainable it was outside communism. I said, 'The challenge, from a non-ideological perspective, is not how to dismantle the Cuban achievements in health care and education, but how to make a transition to a market economy that preserves them.' This statement triggered a discussion about whether that was possible. I believe it is not only possible but also necessary."

Arturo was correct: There can be no transition to a market-based economy without recognizing the gains made by the Revolution in health care and education — and without doing all that is possible to keep those gains for the people.

We reached the lobby of the hotel and I bought my Coronas. As soon as we were back on the street, Arturo started up again. He said that when we talk about the reforms of the 1990s, we must distinguish mere adjustment from real reform. There was significant tightening of government spending by relocating workers to more productive work or sending them into agriculture. There was also a desperate effort to obtain hard currency. This caused a reorientation toward tourism and the creation of hotel chains, all under state control. And this was when "apartheid tourism" began. The state prohibited Cubans from staying in hotels that demanded payment in hard currency. That was a bitter pill to swallow, an insult to the equality and nationalism on which the Revolution was based. Facing high inflation, workers and professionals gravitated to the dollar economy, where they could earn more in tips in a day or week than they could make during the month in the peso economy. The increasing role of the dollar was reinforced by the increasing role of remittances when Cuban Americans began to send money home.

We were heading up La Rampa and when we passed Coppelia, I noted the lines were not very long. The global economic crisis was hitting the iconic ice cream store!

Arturo continued his lecture. In 1993, he said, Fidel announced the legalization of dollars and other hard currencies. This was a major development because dollars were identified as the currency of the enemy. Hundreds of people who had been jailed for using and possessing dollars were released. The demand for dollars and hard currency explained the opening to greater foreign investment. Foreign investment had been allowed in Cuba since 1982 but it had been very limited. Some of the joint ventures had been Cuban efforts to break the embargo and import goods and technology from the United States through third countries. Sometimes the corporations were Cuban but registered in Panama to avoid the problems the Cuban government faced because it was not paying its debts to other countries. The need for hard currency led to the decentralization of foreign trade opportunities, which allowed for direct contact between foreign producers and Cuban companies. This was a major departure from the communist model in which the Ministry of Foreign Trade centralized most transactions with foreign economic agents. Eventually the state created new controls and regulations to deal with the chaos. In 1996 a new law liberalized foreign investment even more, allowing up to 100 percent foreign ownership in some cases and including Cubans who were living abroad among those who could invest. This law, however, preserved case-by-case approval of projects by government functionaries and created a long and excessively regulated process that allowed the state to block foreign investment at different stages. This level of discretion was a major source of corruption and traffic in influence, said Arturo.

"What other effects did these changes have on the economy?" I asked.

"The law," he answered, "was a major impulse for investment from Spain, France, the Netherlands, Canada, and even Israel. This was a real ideological change. The Cuban debate evolved from aversion to all foreign capital to more focused efforts to solve the problems of globalization, foreign investment, and multinationalism. Finally, policy debates focused on the conditions under which Cuba could maximize the benefits of foreign investment and minimize its costs."

"How did all this change affect you personally?"

"After 1996, when my resignation from the Young Communist League and the Ministry of Interior was accepted, I wasn't able to get any professional job. So I worked as an independent tour guide. Through the Jewish community, I met several Israeli businessmen, including Rafi Eitan, who was one of the legendary Mossad agents involved in the capture of Adolf Eichmann in Argentina. BM, the Israeli company managed by Eitan, worked with the FAR to recover the citrus plantations around an area crossed by Cuba's central highway near the Bay of Pigs. An orange juice factory was built near the main highway as a sign of new times. I also — how should I say it? — dealt with the problems of several well-intentioned people trying to invest in Cuba but not ready to pay bribes or play the game of endless lunches with the officials. I will not say that most officials were corrupt, but it was clear the system allowed some corrupt ones to block the entrance of good foreign investors. The law kept a lot of discretion and red tape in the hands of Cuban bureaucrats, who were using their power to accumulate capital and influence."

I choked on some of those awful fumes that now filled the air of Havana. Arturo, though asthmatic, was oblivious.

He explained that another change came in the definition of events taking place in Cuba so that people could discuss globalization. For years, the main event regarding these issues was organized by the Trade Union Central. It was called the "Workers Meeting against Globalization and Neoliberalism." During the 1990s, however, the Economists Union, with Fidel's full support, began to organize a separate conference that was titled "Globalization and Development," with less hostility toward all market-based systems and attacking more narrowly what was called "neoliberal globalization."

"You mean market fundamentalism?" I asked.

"Yes, the international version of market fundamentalism — the ideology that says the markets can work everything out, if only the government will leave them alone."

"No regulation, totally free markets — in the extreme."

"Yes. Four Nobel Laureates in economics — Robert Solow from MIT, and three from Columbia — Robert Mundell, Joseph Stiglitz, and Edmund Phelps — came to speak at the event. Later, while I was at Columbia, I talked to Stiglitz, who was my professor, and to Phelps. They had met with Fidel and were impressed by the interest of Cuban economists in learning and developing their own thoughts about how to move the country toward a more market-oriented economy and the Chinese model. One area where reform was urgent was agriculture. In 1993 and 1994, the nutrition of Cubans dropped. This was a self-inflicted wound. While Vietnam reacted to *perestroika* by adopting market reforms with a gradual, sequential strategy that anticipated the end of Soviet subsidies, Cuba did the opposite. Castro began a campaign — 'the rectification of mistakes' — to reaffirm his communist ideology. It was very anti-market, especially when it came to agriculture. The state went after the private farmers markets, emphasizing voluntarism and support for state farms. Even in the 1990s, when the crisis was intense, Castro insisted on communism. He started the Food Plan — *Plan Alimentario* — sending people from the cities to work in the countryside and establishing a rotation system through which people from factories and offices would have to go periodically to work in the fields. It didn't work."

"What was the mood of the country — during the Special Period?"

"By 1993," said Arturo, "people who had been committed revolutionaries were risking their lives to escape. Discontent was growing. Raúl began a tour of the armies. He would lead debates with the military and political leaders in the provinces. He coined the motto of the time: *Los frijoles son mas importantes que los cañones* — 'Beans are more important than cannons.' Once he chastised a leader of the party in Sancti Spiritus who attacked his idea of reopening the farmers markets. The state began to restructure agriculture with new types of cooperatives. For coffee and tobacco, parcels of land were delivered to peasants and they began to receive payment in convertible pesos — what are now called CUCs. Later, after Raúl took control of the government in 2006, the process of delivering more land to private owners speeded up."

"It sounds like Raúl has a long history of being in favor of reform."

"Perhaps, but it is more complex than that. To manage his initiatives, he assigned José Ramón Machado Ventura, a hard-working, austere, and orthodox party bureaucrat from Vueltas, near Santa Clara — and a good friend of my Uncle Guillermo. Machado fought against Batista with Raúl on the Second Front. My father always described him as an austere man with an incredible capacity for work. I never liked his speeches and his obsession with party discipline. However, he has long been a key figure in Cuba's power structure. Now that Raúl has become the president, Machado is second in command."

"Were there other reforms at the time?"

"Yes. One was the 'process of entrepreneurial perfecting.' It began in the companies associated with the FAR, where better systems of accounting and management were implemented. During the 1990s, this reform was expanded to all state companies. The role of the military in the economy — and that meant the role of Raúl — was growing. Leading this growth was General Julio Casas, another veteran of the Second Front and Eastern Army. His right hand in GAESA — the Grupo de Administración Empresarial — was my cousin Luis, the husband of Raúl's daughter. Today GAESA is larger and more powerful than many of the ministries. It owns the largest tourist group in the country, including airlines, hotels, ground transportation, and marinas. To talk about the Cuban economy without mentioning GAESA would disregard a major part, perhaps the most dynamic part, of the Cuban economy. That is why reform must include the interests of these business groups that are linked to the military. *They are already major actors and shapers of reform.*" Arturo emphasized that last sentence for me.

We angled to the right, onto Calle 26, and headed toward his father's home. Arturo said, "While studying with Professor Stiglitz at Columbia, I learned the worst problem with these state-owned conglomerates is not that they are public, but that they lack competition.[2] All of them exhibit the problems of monopolies. They are too big, consumers lack any protection against them, and they breed corruption. Because it is not the bureaucrats' own money that is at stake, no one bears the cost of bad decisions. True, Cuba needs to focus on gradualism, but excessively postponed reforms can cause great harm since some changes that are implemented cannot produce positive results without other accompanying measures. After twenty years of discussing potential changes, Raúl's government should be able to propose a proper sequence of reforms to minimize corruption and maximize competition. It is scandalous how politically well-connected officials and bureaucrats are taking advantage of the new opportunities associated with foreign investment and marketization, and also the rent-seeking opportunities of the old communist structure. Without consumer protection and transparency, the removal of central control through privatization and decentralization can lead to the rule of corrupt former communist mafias, as seen in the former Soviet Union. Major U.S. investments regulated by the Foreign Corrupt Practices Act would be good for Cuba. U.S. laws against corruption are much stricter than in other capitalist countries."

The long walk wasn't getting to me, but the fumes from the Chinese buses were.

Arturo finally wrapped up his lecture: "The major reform of the 1990s was the authorization of more than 300 categories of self-employment, from ox trainer to shoe maker. The treatment of these activities varied in different parts of the country, however. It depended a lot on the attitude of the local party leaders. Reforms are still needed in this area. During the 1990s and early 2000s, the state was very erratic in over-taxing, over-regulating and often asphyxiating these small businesses. But Fidel Castro's retirement has opened possibilities for major reform. By now most Cubans recognize that the incentives of property ownership are very effective."

And with that, our conversation ended, exactly where it had begun.

"Gradualism," in this context, is another word for the process of incremental, decentralized, and ground-up economic reform in Cuba. It emphasizes the need for a proper sequence and timing of the changes. The transition from a command economy to a market-oriented economy is a major economic and political challenge. Capitalism has proven more successful than communism, but there are still different types of market-oriented economies. In the developing world, there are many countries in which capitalism has not been successful at the task of creating prosperity and growth. Cubans must decide for themselves what type of market economy best fits their needs and how to implement it with the minimal cost for their economy and society.

Gradualism in Cuba also means a transition that includes a definition of private property rights *and* an emphasis on creating institutions — legal, social, and political — that are necessary to provide a positive environment for contracts in a mixed economy. In Cuba, these institutions and the political atmosphere, which are well established in the capitalist developed world, cannot be taken for granted. The experience of transition in the former Soviet Union shows how — without adequate institutions — the policies of rapid privatization and liberalization can become fertile ground for corruption, rent seeking, civil wars, and the growth of political mafias. In contrast, Vietnam and China have demonstrated the value of an incremental approach in the presence of great uncertainties.

The most important political challenge to Cuba's transition will be the creation of a development state in which the government intervenes in the economy to complement the market but not to replace it. This task is not easy because a powerful state with strong discretion in economic matters can potentially lead to a predatory government. That is why gradualism must prepare the Cuban population to live in a market-oriented economy, developing anti-corruption institutions and a cadre of talented managers, workers and accountants able to succeed in a globalized world. Cuba needs not only a new private sector but also a new state, with new politics and new laws.

In the current Cuban context, gradualism specifically means continuing with reforms like more freedom for the farmers, the taxi drivers, and other self-employed entrepreneurs as seeds for the development of small and medium-size private companies. A gradual strategy also means creating a serious tax authority as part of comprehensive tax reform for the *paladares* and other private businesses; expanding the categories of allowable private and self-employment; and permitting private businesses to hire labor — reforms that came to pass in a rather spectacular fashion during 2010 and 2011.

Not that major companies from other countries aren't also a factor. Many have already come to the island. Cuba is happy to do business with Spain, Canada, Venezuela, and the BRIC nations — Brazil, Russia, India and China. And it would love to do more business with the United States. It's all part of that elaborate dance: salsa rhythms, hip-hop beat.

Finally, gradualism in Cuba also means gradualism in U.S. policy toward Cuba. Still, savvy dancers on both sides of the Straits are growing impatient when it comes to the development of the oil that has been discovered off Cuba's northern coast.[3] Allowing American oil companies to participate in this development makes great sense. It's far cheaper to bring a drilling rig from the Gulf of Mexico than from China. And American regulations are much stricter because the United States has a great interest in preventing oil spills in the Gulf. So why not create a new exemption from the embargo — adding to the existing one for agricultural products[4] — for energy development companies?

But, to banish the specter that's been haunting me — that capitalist farmer who wouldn't accept legal tender — it will take a reformation and reeducation of the population. And that's already happening. It comes with more TVs and DVDs and computers and Internet and tourism. Tourism is, indeed, the second big industry that Cuba wants to develop with American companies as soon as it can.

When Arturo and I spoke with Carlos Alzugaray during our January trip to Cuba, he talked specifically about the opening of economic opportunities on the island. He said the government's gestures most likely will be in the nature of economics rather than politics: capitalism and markets, not democracy and human rights. He noted that this approach is consistent with the Chinese model. He told us that Spain and Canada were "the most popular capitalist countries in Cuba." There was lots of trade with those countries.

"Canada sends over 600,000 tourists to Cuba each year," said Dr. Alzugaray. "After the United States drops its travel ban, it could send 2.5 million more! Some estimate a total of 5 million tourists coming to Cuba from everywhere in the world. Imagine. It would be a really big dynamic. It could unleash everyone."

Whatever the pace of reform, this decentralized, ground-up market economy is likely to be a demand-driven market economy. No more supply-side economics. Extreme market fundamentalism is on the retreat. Credit the crash of 2008 and the recession of 2009. Tomorrow's market economy, in Cuba and the United States alike, is more likely to be a matter of trickle *up* than trickle *down*.

To be sure, the rise and fall of command economies demonstrates the limits of central planning and the importance of market prices in conveying decentralized information to economic agents. But the history of capitalism and advances in economic theory both show that externalities like market failures are more pervasive than what the neoliberals recognized. Particularly in the context of nations in transition or under development, governments might well enhance the welfare and development possibilities of markets.

Whatever the exact sequence of openings and reforms — steps in the dance — there will be a need to visit the intersection between capitalism and the rule of law. As the Peruvian economist Hernando De Soto explained in his classic *The Mystery of Capital*, there must be certain basic types of laws in place to support a capitalist system.[5]

These basic laws include property laws, such as land, personal property, investments, and intellectual property; contract laws to enforce the transactions that drive capitalist buying and selling; antitrust laws to keep capitalist companies from running amok and becoming monopolies; bankruptcy laws to allow for the orderly exit of losers from the markets (which by definition create losers as well as winners); and finally regulatory laws for industries that do not adhere to capitalist principles.

Note in particular the need for regulatory laws. In a "flattened" world of complex interconnections and instantaneous response, we need regulatory laws to harmonize the chaotic elements of the system, domestically and internationally. The recession of 2009 proved in a decisive manner just how incredibly connected the world markets are.

And with the inevitable but gradual return in the West to a more heavily regulated economic environment — due to necessity and not ideology — an interesting phenomenon should occur. There should be a commingling and convergence of styles of market-based capitalist economics. In full retreat from the extreme "market fundamentalism" of the old Conservative Right, the West should be expected to adopt more economic regulations, and these will include more and more social regulations because the two are inseparable. This process of re-regulation has already begun. Some will involve financial reform at the national level, through legislation and regulatory agencies like the SEC and the Federal Reserve. Some will involve reform at the transnational level, through existing institutions like the International Monetary Fund and the World Bank. Not so long ago debates over the stimulus and bailouts dominated the public space.

It's somewhat ironic that in 2008, the same market fundamentalists who decried socialization could so easily accept nationalization — at least temporarily. In any event, more government involvement in the economy in both the short term and the longer strategic term is not just inevitable. It's upon us. At the same time, more countries on the opposite side of the political and economic spectrum have retreated or are retreating from the more radical economic policies of the Old (communist) Left. The defenders of unconstrained statism in economic matters are also in retreat. In the long run, Brazil — a country in which successive governments have idealized neither the market nor the state — will likely play a greater economic role in the Americas than Venezuela, as Carlos Alzugaray predicted during our interview. And as more and more New Left countries become more market friendly — and more "pragmatically progressive" — they will tend to look more like the most heavily regulated countries of the West.

Obama will meet Unger in the middle.

This commingling and convergence of market economies will spawn a new era of globalization. And Cuba will have a role to play in it. Beyond oil and tourism, even beyond the traditional staples of tobacco, rum, sugar and nickel, Cuba has particularly important contributions to make in the realms of health-care delivery and biotechnology. It is little known that the island boasts an extremely advanced biotech sector that includes genetics and the development of unique vaccines.[6] Cuban scientists were among the first to develop vaccines for hard-cell lung and brain cancers, and they have also developed vaccines for various strains of hepatitis and meningitis. Yet only sporadically has the United States granted licenses to American companies to help develop these innovative life-saving drugs; in fact, many cannot be imported into the United States because of the embargo.[7] Still, despite the global recession, Cuba is plunging ahead with its biotech programs.[8]

To be sure, the island is not leaving its old economy behind, but it is developing a new economy both domestically and internationally with its Brazilian, Russian, Indian, Chinese, and Venezuelan trading partners. The embargo has sidelined many American competitors. Indeed, the Russians — the Russians!— have already beaten the United States to the punch in securing deals to develop Cuban oil fields.[9]

Yet everyone knows the future remains dependent on that dance between Havana and Washington. And the majority in the United States — including 74 percent of the Cuban American community — knows the embargo has been a terrible failure.[10] It plainly hasn't worked, and it cannot work because it violates two of the critical conditions that typically must be satisfied for economic sanctions to achieve their objectives.

Studies done over the past decades have confirmed that for economic sanctions to work properly, they must be both multilateral and targeted at specific conduct rather than vague ideas.[11] The U.S. embargo of Cuba is not multilateral. It is, in fact, spectacularly unilateral, since no other countries in the world honor it, and it is widely condemned. Also, it is not targeted at specific conduct. Getting Iran or North Korea to drop their development of nuclear weapons would be specific conduct. Regime change is not.

But of course regime change is exactly what the embargo is really all about. Witness the provisions in Helms-Burton that require both Castro brothers to be out of office before the sanctions can be lifted.

The damage the embargo causes to U.S. foreign policy is increasingly evident. Sanctions could perhaps be deemed rational if they were the best of all policy choices. But they are not. Indeed, from a foreign policy perspective, the gains of a policy of engagement toward Cuba in terms of public diplomacy, relations with U.S allies, the possibility of influencing Cuban elites and the population, promotion of American economic and strategic interests, and human rights are significantly positive, while the embargo balance is overwhelmingly negative for American national interests.

Still, legislators can change legislation, and even Republican legislators are calling for change in U.S. policy toward Cuba. In January 2009, Republican Senator Richard Lugar of Indiana sent his staff to Cuba, and in late February they issued a report to the Committee on Foreign Relations, titled

"Changing Cuba Policy — In the United States National Interest."[12] The report is remarkably nonpartisan and realistic. It recognizes that leadership has changed in both Havana and Washington, and that the embargo has not been effective. It includes a particularly useful appendix listing those actions that could be taken by the president to ease the embargo without congressional authorization and those actions that must be taken by Congress in order to lift the embargo completely.

The guts of the report are its findings and recommendations. The findings are entirely consistent with the gospel I have been preaching: First, "The Cuban regime is institutionalized." That's right. It remains strong despite the "deep problems" that plague everyday life on the island. A popular uprising is highly unlikely. Second, "Positive developments are occurring in Cuba but they should not be mistaken for structural reform." Third, "Popular dissatisfaction with Cuba's economic situation is the regime's vulnerability."

Now Arturo disagrees, but only to a certain extent. While he agrees the regime is strong and a popular uprising is highly unlikely, he believes the Cuban government is already in the final phase of a transition from charismatic leadership to institutionalized leadership. This makes a policy of engagement more pertinent because there are more possibilities to influence and shape the process by ending the unifying factor that American hostility represents to the different Cuban nationalist factions. In any event, Arturo and I both do believe the seeds of structural reform have already been planted.

Go back to item 3. The literature constantly links the development of democracy with the development of a nation's economy. As stated by political science professors Ronald Inglehart and Christian Welzel in *Foreign Affairs*:

> During early industrialization, authoritarian states are just as likely to attain high rates of growth as are democracies. But beyond a certain level of economic development, democracy becomes increasingly likely to emerge and survive.... The strong correlation between development and democracy reflects the fact that economic development is conducive to democracy.... Washington should do what it can to encourage development. If it wants to bring democratic change to Cuba, for example, isolating it is counterproductive. The United States should lift the embargo, promote economic development, and foster social engagement with, and other connections to, the world."[13]

And now for the fourth and final finding in the Lugar Report: "The regime appears to be open to some bilateral dialogue and cooperation." The priorities of Cuba and the United States remain wildly different but the desire for change is widespread and deep.

The recommendations are also straightforward.[14] They envision a "steady series of gradual measures ... sequencing this process of engagement." Early in his presidency, Barack Obama took the first step by lifting all limits on family travel and remittances to the island. The Lugar Report next recommends "bilateral talks on drug interdiction and migration" and allowing "investments in alternative energy," because Cuba wants to upgrade its energy infrastructure and the United States can help. Next, removal of the Bush-era limits on agricultural and medical trade. Finally, creation of a "bipartisan commission and a multilateral framework" for resolving America's differences with Cuba.

The Lugar Report pulls no punches. It concludes that "increased dialogue through appropriate channels, coupled with looser trade terms, would lay the groundwork for more substantial discussions between the USG [the U.S. government] and GOC [the government of Cuba].... [T]he USG should begin treating Cuba as it does other nations with whom it has fundamental disagreements but where engagement advances broader interests.... If reform in U.S.-Cuba policy were to occur in the direction of sequenced engagement, the impact on the region would be swift and to the benefit of the security and prosperity of the United States."[15]

Not surprisingly, the economic arguments have blurred into political arguments.

Chapter Five
Politics in the New Cuba

Carlos Alzugaray asks the big question: Can the single-party system survive? As economic reform leads to political reform, can Cuba walk the walk China now walks?

Not if Yoani Sánchez has her way. Age 36, thin as a whip, with long black hair, thick dark brows, a long straight nose, and a pointed chin, Sánchez lives in Havana with her teenage son and her husband, an independent journalist. She holds a degree in philology, the intersection of linguistics and literature. She is an expert in information technology. And she writes *Generación Y*, named by *TIME* as one of the 25 best blogs of 2009.[1]

Translated into 15 languages, featured frequently on the *Huffington Post*, and read by millions throughout the world, *Generación Y* takes its name from the fad among Cubans during the 1970s of giving their kids names that began with or contained a Y. These kids, she says, "marked by schools in the countryside, Russian cartoons, illegal emigration and frustration," are the Yanisleidis, Yoandris, Yusimís, and Yunieskys.[2]

Sánchez invites everyone on the island, but these Cubans "especially," to post their own entries on her website, DesdeCuba.com. But it isn't easy for her or them or those who want to read the blogs.

To post her entries, Sánchez often dresses like a tourist and sneaks into hotels that have Internet access for foreigners. She uses a flash drive, writes her entries quickly, and sends them — at $6 an hour — as emails to friends who live abroad and post them for her. Her site is hosted on a server located in Germany. It's cumbersome and expensive. And Sánchez risks being arrested for using the Internet connection without proper permission.

Though Raúl has opened limited access to the Net, it's not a favorite of the state. Much of the Web is filtered or blocked. Ordinary Cubans can send and receive emails, but the lines are long at the youth clubs, post offices, and few Internet cafes with access. Government control is very strict, even worse than in China. To get around these restrictions, many buy black market dial-up accounts or use the passwords from authorized accounts that hackers steal or otherwise acquire. Whatever technique is used, more and more Cubans are accessing the Internet, trying to "flatten" their worlds.

In this environment, Sánchez often cannot read what she writes because it is blocked by the government. That is not surprising. The criticisms that appear on *Generación Y* are sharp and direct. They call for an immediate overturn of the Cuban political system and barely toe the line of legality. In 2008 *TIME* listed Sánchez among the 100 most influential people in the world; *Foreign Policy* named her one of the 10 most influential Latin American intellectuals; and Spain bestowed on her the prestigious Ortega y Gasset Prize, its highest award in journalism. When Sánchez applied for a visa to go to Madrid to accept the prize, her application was denied.[3]

By early 2009 *Generación Y* was getting 14 million hits a month, mostly from outside Cuba. Sánchez had become a darling of the media, a symbol of resistance in the digital age. And that was the problem. She became a symbol to the outside world more than to her fellow Cubans. Arturo believes her influence is greatly exaggerated and her posts increasingly put her in the camp of the opposition — in contrast to the reformers. Outside Havana, he says, in places like Santa Clara, few people know who Sánchez is. He offers three specific criticisms: (1) there is greater reform going on within the system than a focus on the opposition blogosphere would suggest; (2) the promotion of human rights should be as nonpartisan as possible — facing challenges to their freedom of expression in Miami, some Cubans wonder why there is not a shared prize for a Cuban defending the right to free speech in Cuba such as Sánchez and another Cuban defending freedom of expression in Miami; and (3) the closer Sánchez gets to the pro-embargo lobby, as she did when she received an award from the Cuban Liberty Council, the further she places herself from most Cubans in Cuba.

Nevertheless, in 2009 Sánchez was placed on the jury for the International Documentary Film Festival in Prague. She again applied for a visa, this time to go to the Czech Republic to sit on the jury. Here is part of the blog entry she wrote on March 20:

> When you read this post I will be sitting in the waiting room of the Plaza Municipality Office of Immigration and Emigration. Among military uniforms, my passport waiting for a permit to travel that has been denied me on two occasions. During the last year, the obedient soldiers dedicated to limiting our freedom of movement have not permitted me to accept international invitations. In their databases next to my name there must be a mark condemning me to island confinement. The possessive logic of this Daddy-State sees it as normal that I, as a punishment for writing a blog, like a box on the ears for having believed myself to be a free person, will not receive the "white card." ...
> I confess that I do not want them to allow me to travel as if it were a gift, rather I fantasize that — this very day — while I am waiting for the third "no," someone

will come out and announce that this regulation that is such a violation was just repealed. I have a feeling that I will leave Cuba when everyone can do it freely, but in the meantime, I will continue besieging them with my demands, my posts and my questions.[4]

And this is what she wrote the very next day when her application was promptly denied:

This time they've been more direct: "You are not authorized to travel," the woman told me quietly, almost nicely, dressed in her olive-green.... I have never been charged in court yet I am condemned not to leave this Island. This restriction has not been dictated by a judge, nor could I have appealed it to a jury, rather it comes from the great prosecutor ... the Cuban State. That [same] severe magistrate determined that the old woman sitting next to me in the office at 17th and K would not receive the "white card" because her son "deserted" from a medical mission. The boy who waited in the corner couldn't travel either, because his athlete father plays now under another flag. The list of the punished is so long and the reasons so varied, that we could establish a huge group of forced islander "stay-at-homes." It's too bad that the vast majority are silent, in the hopes that one day they'll be allowed to leave, as one who receives compensation for good behavior.[5]

The first entry appears under a photo that shows a Cuban passport in a meat grinder and the second under a photo of a bird sitting on a wire fence. Both are powerful images. And Sánchez is irrepressible.

Just a few days after she was denied a visa to go to Prague, she wrote about the wonderful time she had spent the night before at the Wifredo Lam Center, a showcase for contemporary art housed in a fine old building on Calle San Ignacio. A performance artist named Tania Bruguera had staged a podium and microphones before a large red curtain as part of an interactive installation in the center's open courtyard. This is a fairly large space where perhaps two hundred people could gather. Anyone who wanted to speak could simply step up to the podium and say whatever he or she wanted. The only condition was that the speech had to be kept to a minute or less.

Sánchez had been told about the set-up by friends ahead of time. She seized the moment and delivered an impassioned one-minute speech about freedom of expression, the Internet, blogs, and censorship. When she blogged about it the next day, she wrote, "In front of the lenses of national television and protected by the foreign guests at the Havana Biennial, I was followed by shouts of 'Freedom,' 'Democracy,' and even open challenges to the Cuban authorities. I remember one boy of twenty who confessed that he had never felt more free."[6]

Compare two prior efforts to inject change into Cuban politics: the Varela Project and the Ladies in White. The Varela Project[7] was launched in 1998 by Oswaldo Payá of the Christian Liberation Movement. It was named for Felix Varela, a famous Cuban Catholic priest who advocated independence from Spain during the first half of the nineteenth century. Because of his ideas, Varela went into exile in the States, where he preached among Italian and Irish immigrants as the general vicar of New York.

The Varela Project circulated a proposed law — in the United States we would call it an "initiative" — calling for a referendum on democratic reforms in Cuba, including freedom of speech, freedom of association, freedom of the press, freedom to start private businesses, freedom to travel, and free elections. The proponents relied specifically on Article 88 of the Cuban Constitution, which allows citizens to directly propose laws for discussion by the National Assembly if 10,000 people who are registered to vote sign the petition and include their national identification numbers and addresses.

Having gathered over 11,020 signatures, the Varela Project presented its proposed law to the Cuban National Assembly in 2002, a day before the arrival of President Carter in Havana. President Carter even mentioned the initiative in his speech at the University of Havana on May 14, with Fidel Castro and most of the communist elite seated in the front row. The initiative was not, however, welcomed by all.

The opposition to Payá among radical exiles was seen when he visited Miami after receiving the Sakharov Prize from the European Parliament. Frequent dismissals of his leadership came through the "hot air" of Spanish radio programs repeating the phrase "ni pa' ya, ni pa' aca," a word game using Payá's name to indicate a move to nowhere.

For its part, the Cuban National Assembly immediately gave the initiative to the Constitution and Legal Affairs Committee. Meanwhile, the Communist Party arranged for a number of trade unions, student groups, and other organizations to respond with their own counterinitiative to make permanent the socialist nature of the Cuban state.

The government-sponsored plebiscite was held in June 2002 and the counterinitiative won decisively, according to the government. The outside media reported that many Cubans felt pressured to vote for the counterinitiative and the U.S. State Department claimed widespread harassment, arrests, and short detentions of Varela activists.

In March 2003, the state arrested 75 dissidents and activists, among them 21 activists who were associated with the Varela Project. In less than a week they were tried, convicted, and jailed for a variety of offenses related to their political activities. Some of them were accused by the Cuban government of accepting foreign political support from the U.S. government — which is illegal in both Cuba and the United States. Some of the activists, like economist Oscar Espinosa Chepe, denied these charges.

All over the world, people from right to left condemned the crackdown. Arturo notes that, at the time, three other men were convicted of hijacking a boat with guns and knives "to escape to freedom." Their cases, he says, are distinguishable because the state always has a legitimate interest in preserving the public order. It is hypocritical to call such desperate men engaged in common criminal activity "dissidents." Often these distinctions are not so carefully made. Yet Arturo believes that the fact that such serious issues were resolved in just four days shows the trials were neither fair nor impartial, as demanded by basic principles of human rights and the Cuban Constitution.

Soon after the arrests, the Ladies in White — wives and relatives of the dissidents — started gathering at a Catholic church in Miramar, on the modern west side of Havana, to protest.[8] They came to Sunday mass in white dresses, wearing buttons with photos of their relatives and the numbers of years of their sentences. After attending Sunday mass, they would silently march along Fifth Avenue, one of the most frequented thoroughfares of Havana. In 2005 the European Parliament awarded the group the Sakharov Prize for Freedom of Thought.

Over the years the Ladies in White garnered a fair amount of media attention outside Cuba. On the island itself, their protests drew occasional state-sponsored counter-demonstrations, though many people said they respected the women's peaceful ways, humanitarian cause, and good manners. The protests did not, however, result in widespread political change in Cuba and many among the population tended to view their significance, and level of support, as minimal.[9]

So neither the Varela Project nor the Ladies in White prompted deep reform.

However, I believe that the full impact of the Cuban bloggers — to say nothing of the newer social networking sites — has yet to be determined. Dissident movements and daring individuals are not without their impact, to be sure. But seldom are they enough, without widespread popular support, to effect change on their own.

The safer bet is this: Whatever political changes come to Cuba, they will be elements of a *process and not an event*. They will spread first among the population. Like the economic reforms discussed in the last chapter, and exactly as predicted by Dr. Alzugaray, political changes in Cuba will start from the ground up. They will be grassroots and populist in nature. And they will be driven by political demand.

Arturo cautions against too much optimism. He admonishes against giving the opposition too much clout, and insists the existing regime remains strong, a conclusion echoed in the Lugar Report. He notes that the dissidents in Cuba actually constitute a fairly small, dispersed, and divided segment of the population. And he argues that political reforms from within the single-party system are likely to be more significant in the long run than loosely

An empty balcony at the Gran Teatro de la Habana, facing the Parque Central, draped with a banner celebrating the 50th anniversary of the Cuban Revolution, January 2009 (Harlan Abrahams collection).

organized opposition movements that lack any real plan for addressing the central concerns of the Cuban people, such as building more houses, keeping the health care system functioning, and reducing crime.

Some disagree with this assessment. As Carl Gershman of the National Endowment for Democracy and Orlando Gutierrez of the Cuban Democratic Directorate wrote in early 2009 in the *Journal of Democracy*,[10] Cuba's internal or civic opposition is more widespread in terms of the sheer number of its groups — and also more varied in its organizational structures and activities — than the democratic movements in the Eastern Bloc in the late 1980s. The Eastern European movements included mostly dissident intellectuals, whereas the Cuban movements are more diverse and include many segments of society. The authors point to Cuba's dissident intellectuals and independent journalists, its Catholic and Protestant activists, its students and farmers, professionals and unionists, writers and artists and young rock-and-rollers. And yes, they point in particular to Cuba's Internet bloggers. They admit these groups are diverse but argue that they are unified in purpose.

Arturo counters that there is a major gap between (1) the human rights agenda of a segment of the dissidents, many intellectuals, the religious communities, and those reformers who are promoting change within the system; and (2) the agenda animating the actions of the USAID programs, the exiles, and those dissidents connected to the exiles. A survey by Freedom House in four Cuban provinces identified the right to own private property, the right to travel, and welfare issues like food, housing and transportation as the central concerns of the Cuban population.[11] In Washington, among the right-wing exiles and those dissidents working in their orbit, the central issues are compensation for properties nationalized in the 1960s, elections in six months or a year, and freedom to create independent trade unions.

Ironically, I agree with both Arturo and those with whom he disagrees. I believe the key to resolving their differences lies in the ability of today's tools of communication — the Internet and cell phones and social media —*to accelerate and magnify* the forces of change already at work at the grassroots level.

As Arturo says, "The Internet will change people's hearts and minds not because they read the blogs of the dissidents and those in the opposition — although this would be an expansion of the opinions they can read. Rather, the Internet will change people's hearts and minds because they will start reading about things that are happening in China, Vietnam, Paris, and Spain. People will be able to look at a Canadian website abroad and learn how they can apply for a fellowship. A professor in one of the more than thirty universities developed after the Revolution will be able to send a paper to a conference without the party or his boss telling him that he has been assigned to present a paper in Canada instead. A writer will be able to send his book to a publisher abroad without any interference from the Writers' Union. People will be able to buy and sell things regardless of what the government says."

And clearly Arturo is right when he argues that the process of reform from within should not be taken lightly. A year into his presidency, Raúl replaced several top officials who were close to his brother. The next day Fidel wrote a blog — a blog! — on the government website Cuba Debate, approving of the action and condemning the seductive "Honey of Power."[12] Gone was Foreign Minister Felipe Pérez Roque, the youngest at 43, who had served as Fidel's personal secretary and was often mentioned as a possible future president; gone as well was Carlos Lage, who was replaced as cabinet secretary by Homero Acosta Alvarez, a lawyer from the Armed Forces with a master's degree in public law from a Spanish university; and gone were several other prominent long-time figures. Also, at the same time, several ministries were consolidated to achieve what Raúl called a "more compact and functional structure."

At the time, Arturo joked, "It's a massacre!" Some said the "reformers" were taking a blow. In hindsight, Arturo and I agree that the move was less earth-shattering and more consistent with Raúl's natural desire to create a unified leadership with loyalists from both the party apparatus and the Armed Forces. It was also consistent with Raúl's enduring administrative savvy.

What is clear is that politics both inside and outside the party, among the elite and the broader population, are already changing. And politics between the United States and Cuba are also changing. Recall that in February 2009, Senator Richard Lugar issued his report, "Changing Cuba Policy — In the United States National Interest," and the next month he and several other senators introduced legislation to drop the travel ban for all Americans.

In April, Raúl and Fidel met with members of the Congressional Black Caucus,[13] and President Obama, on the eve of the Summit of the Americas in Trinidad and Tobago, fulfilled his campaign promise to lift all restrictions on family travel and remittances by Cuban Americans to the island.[14] At the same time, in an equally important but less heralded move, the Obama administration also began the process of issuing licenses to allow telecommunications companies to provide cell phone, satellite television, and computer services to the island, and to allow family members to pay for relatives in Cuba to get those services.[15] The effect of such measures was to show how the embargo and the American policies of official hostility were blocking a rational approach toward Cuba.

It was only the beginning, however. The moves by Washington did not address the problems associated with the unfair inclusion of Cuba on the list of terrorist countries. Because Cuba is on such a list — though no terrorist action has been connected to Cuba in the last 25 years — American citizens can sue the Cuban government and raid Cuban funds or property in the United States. In fact, and astoundingly, courts in the United States have retroactively adjudicated compensation from these funds for incidents that happened before the list was even created.[16] All this contrasts sharply with cases concerning Iran, the sponsor of terrorism par excellence, in which the American government has argued that its courts have no jurisdiction in lawsuits against the Tehran government for the taking of the hostages in 1979, because this event occurred before the inclusion of Iran on the list.[17]

In any event, there was — quite ironically — agitation in the United States to drop all limitations on travel to and telecommunications with Cuba at exactly the same time that there was agitation in Cuba to ease the government's limitations on travel off the island and telecommunications by ordinary Cubans.

In other words, the new leadership in Washington started its dance with the new leadership in Havana on both economic and political grounds. And what style did the new American president display? Certainly it was less ideological than that of his predecessors. Justin Ruben, executive director of MoveOn.org, told the *New York Times* in early 2009, "Here's a label if you want one — pragmatic populist progressive."[18]

It's a good label. By design or by coincidence, it combines two words — "pragmatic" and "progressive" — that are not infrequently associated with Obama's former law professor, Roberto Mangabeira Unger, who served for two important years as the Brazilian minister of long-term strategic planning. Note, too, the word that connects the two — "populist," which gives the label a nice ground-up connotation.

As Unger has written in *Democracy Realized*, for change to be truly successful — for "political practice" to become "transformative" — it must "unite action from the bottom up with action from the top down."[19] That means that whatever direction change comes from, it must connect the people to their state.

And connections are what the 21st century is all about.

What will politics between Cuba and America look like after the embargo? Whatever party controls Congress and the White House, the likely scenario finds the countries actively engaged, with Cuba clinging to its one-party system while the United States pushes for democratic reforms through a new balance of carrots-and-sticks diplomacy. The decades of refusing to engage — and letting the Cuban exiles dictate the U.S. agenda — are over. Perhaps despite those decades, democratic change will come to Cuba.

What will that change look like?

Two myths must be debunked. The first is the idea that the United States has a monopoly on democracy. Ours is not the only form, or even the dominant form, of democracy in the world. Indeed, American-style democracy is not a pure democracy, but a republican — or representative — form of democracy. And who, after all, would deny that England's older parliamentary system constitutes a democracy? In other words, the Cubans have plenty of other models of democracy to inspire them.

The second myth, equally pernicious, is the idea that democracy is expressed primarily through elections, however contrived. Americans have forced their dogma — "elections equal democracy, so elections must come first" — on parts of the world to the detriment of building democratic institutions that must operate in real time between the periodic treks to the voting booth. The results have been the election of Hamas in Palestine, Hezbollah in Lebanon, and dysfunctional administrations in Iraq and Central America.

Hopefully the United States has learned that the building of democratic institutions must at least accompany the holding of elections, or, more properly, precede them. Multiparty elections are indeed essential to a modern democracy, but holding elections without properly building democratic institutions can have tragic and destabilizing consequences.

Separating the powers of government among branches that check and balance each other; creating an independent judiciary to adjudicate criminal cases and private disputes; implementing a rule of law that supersedes the cult of the single-party system; expanding freedom of expression and association; allowing the creation and operation of a loyal opposition; and honoring the basic human, economic, cultural, social, civil, and political rights of its people: these are all critical steps in crafting a functioning modern democracy. And they will most likely proceed in Cuba, a nation with a strong constitutional tradition, in a gradual, decentralized, and incremental manner.

Indeed, Arturo and I do agree on this: Political change will come to Cuba in a manner that mirrors the gradualism that will likely characterize its economic reforms. We returned to the island exactly 100 days into Obama's presidency to see, once more, what was happening there.

We arrived in Havana late that night. Our taxi dropped me at my *casa particular* on Calle 6 near Calle 23, before it becomes La Rampa. Gisela, my landlady, greeted me, entered my passport number in her register, and left me with the keys to my room and the front door. I quickly unpacked and collapsed on the thin mattress.

Arturo picked me up early the next afternoon and we headed to Old Havana for the last day of the Décima Bienal de la Habana — the art festival that was drawing crowds from around the world. Along the way, we started a dialogue about Cuban politics that lasted throughout our trip.

"Okay," said Arturo, "here is how I see it. Some of the changes that have been proposed involve political reform inside the one-party system. Many are intended to improve the system by making it more democratic and sustainable. I believe, however, that a more open one-party system, with greater responsiveness to the people's problems and greater freedoms like the right to travel or have access to the Internet, will make the system more viable in the short run only. In the long run, the plurality of interests and ideas in Cuba will lead to the creation of more political parties. That doesn't mean the Communist Party will disappear — just that other parties will develop."

After walking two-thirds of the way along the Malecón, I suggested that we should cut through El Centro to slice off the curve. Arturo shrugged and led the way.

He continued: "For a while, change inside the system will appeal more to the revolutionaries than a multiparty system. There are many who reject the rigidity of the current system. They criticize its refusal to reflect a variety

A backstreet in El Centro, complete with ancient American cars (Harlan Abrahams collection).

of points of view. But at the same time they are very critical of multiparty systems. There are several reasons for this criticism: First, the Cuban Republican experience from 1902 to 1959. While Cuba achieved significant progress between 1940 and 1952, there was also significant violence, exclusion, and corruption in what Cubans call La República. Racism was everywhere. Only 10 years after independence — conceived as a social revolution with significant participation by the black masses — there was a massacre of those who tried to create a party for the advancement of people of color. Second, Cuba's sovereignty, a premise for democracy, was severely limited by U.S. intervention. Before 1934, the United States intervened under the Platt Amendment. After this formal authorization to intervene was derogated, there was a reduction of the level of intervention, but still, as one U.S. ambassador in Havana later said, 'The U.S. ambassador was the second most important man in Cuba and sometimes the first.' This dependence was not the main cause of Cuba's problems, but it did artificially limit the way Cubans think about solutions to their problems."

"What else?" I asked, never ceasing to be amazed that Arturo really talks like this.

The Hotel Sevilla, one of Havana's oldest hotels, just off the Prado, near the Malecón (Harlan Abrahams collection).

"Third," he said, "there are high levels of indoctrination by the government propaganda machinery against the idea of representative democracy. These efforts are based on legitimate criticisms of the flaws in the systems in the United States and Latin America, but they generally distort and exaggerate their versions of the realities of other countries in comparison with an ideal presentation of the one-party system."

We emerged from El Centro at the Prado near the old Hotel Sevilla. I noticed it had been freshly painted. Arturo gestured at a gathering of people, talking in tight little knots of twos and threes, under the shade of the trees that lined the colorful promenade.

"Those people," he said, lowering his voice, "are swapping houses. The state won't let them buy or sell their houses but they can exchange them with others. Here is where they hold their market." Then he raised his voice and was back in lecture mode:

"Fourth, there is the nationalist appeal to Cuban cultural and political resistance. Many believe the country needs a political system that manages differences within restricted limits as a way of avoiding divisions among

Cubans that would eventually weaken the nationalist capacity to resist foreign pressures."

We crossed the Prado, walked a block, and landed in front of a giant modern building with giant cockroaches climbing up its side! They appeared to be metal but on closer examination proved to be carved from wood. And each one had a human head! They were part of an elaborate Bienal installation. It was time to pay attention to the art.

We went inside the Museo Nacional de Bellas Artes, directly across the street from the Museo de la Revolución, and took a spin around the familiar galleries.

Emerging from the art museum, we could see, across the street, the old *Granma* — the actual yacht — displayed inside the Museo de la Revolución. Arturo returned to his analysis: "Many of the changes that are proposed are related to specific areas of work while others are more general. In 1990, when the call to the Fourth Congress of the party opened debates, people of different positions, including me and some of my friends from the Higher Institute of International Relations, people who are now in the Ministry of Foreign Affairs, advocated a change in the party name."

Giant wooden cockroaches — with human heads!— climb the walls of the Art Museum (Harlan Abrahams collection).

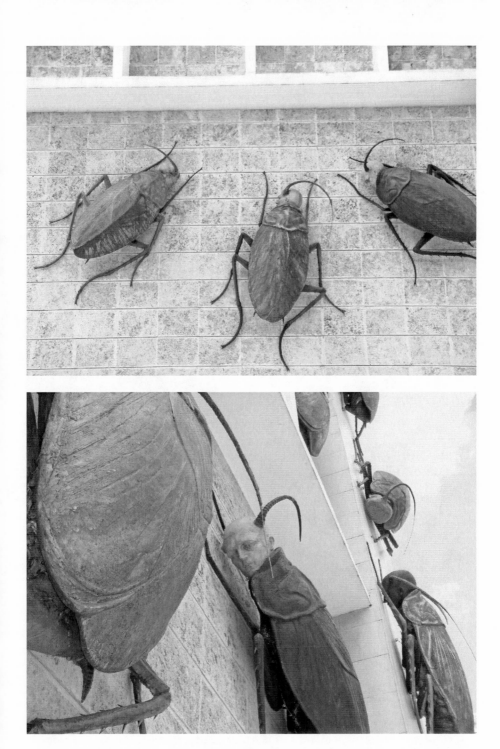

Top and bottom: Giant wooden cockroaches — with human heads! — climb the walls of the Art Museum (Harlan Abrahams collection).

Large sign for the Décima Bienal Habana, placed just outside the Art Museum (Harlan Abrahams collection).

"What did you want to call it?"

"We wanted a more open ideological setting — democratization inside the party — and within Young Communist League elections. So the name we proposed was the Cuban Revolutionary Party, as José Martí had called his own party. The idea was that people who were nationalists but not communists could have a place within the party, with equal standing regardless of their religious views, their preferences for a market economy, or their rejection of communist views about culture. Some further questioned the doctrine of 'democratic centralism,' which forced party members to defend the party line once it was adopted even if one disagreed with it."

"What happened?"

"Well," said Arturo, "the Fourth Congress answered this discontent by elevating José Martí's thoughts to the official ideology of the party, which from then on declared itself 'Martiano' first and Marxist-Leninist second. During these years, there was a large renewal in the membership of the Central Committee and the party recruited thousands of young people. This was different from before, when almost nobody under thirty was a member of the

Communist Party. At the time, young leaders from the Student Federation and the Young Communist League were promoted to leadership positions inside the party in the provinces and Politburo. These included Roberto Robaina, Carlos Lage, Felipe Pérez Roque, and Juan Carlos Robinson Agramonte, who were later removed, but also people like Miguel Díaz Canel, María del Carmen Concepción, and Misael Enamorado, who stayed in the second tier of the party and government, or were in charge of provincial party sections or governments. These people are now very important in the functioning of the country."

We wandered along Calle Obispo, deeper into La Habana Vieja, stepping into a cluttered bookstore where Arturo quietly showed me this or that subversive element in this or that new text. "See," he said, waving his hand, trying to emphasize his point, "there is a loosening of censorship on the island."

"Give me your best example," I challenged. "Hit me with your best shot."

He held up the biography of a former foreign minister named Raul Roa, who had not agreed with Soviet-style socialism and defended representative democracy before Castro's triumph against Stalinism. "Not long ago," said Arturo, "this book would not have been on the shelves, or some parts of it would not have been published, as happened with some of Che's criticism of the Soviet Union. This is not the sort of change that gets noticed by the tourists, or the journalists, or the people who come here for a week and leave with the certainty that they are now experts about Cuba. These changes are slow, gradual, and incremental."

He segued back to his lecture: "Of course, we must distinguish between people who were speedily 'helicoptered' by Fidel and people who were promoted through normal party mechanisms. Those promoted by Fidel would go to work for him directly and immediately become visible and powerful. At the same time, they would not develop their own networks of support within the system. Those promoted through the mechanisms of the party would grow more steadily. They would be put in charge of specific problems, their connections were diffuse, and they were monitored for longer by the internal control agencies. I believe Raúl prefers this type of functionary, who has been socialized inside the party and has a more institutional view. A main feature of his rule is less charisma but better management. His cadres are less improvised and better trained. In this way, there is more opportunity for building trust and alliances among the factions inside the system — from different areas and generations — like the party, the FAR, and the massive economic organizations that are controlled by the FAR."

We arrived at the Wifredo Lam Center for Contemporary Art — the very place where Yoani Sánchez had taken the microphone only a month before.

A group of mostly older Cuban musicians — some well known — were tuning their instruments in the large courtyard. Folding chairs were set up for the audience. We sat in the back and waited for the small concert that would signal the end of the Bienal.

Arturo told me that one reform proposed for the party and state institutions was the development of term limits for the leaders in the provinces and also the establishment of a compulsory retirement age of 70 for all of the members of the Politburo or the Central Committee. Recently, a popular singer named Pablo Milanes, known for his love songs and his commitment to the Revolution, had said in an interview in Spain that he didn't trust the capacity of any ruler over 70. This idea was especially relevant in Cuba, and it had already been adopted in some form by other communist countries like China and Vietnam. However, Arturo explained, one obstacle to the adoption of term limits in Cuba was the campaign by Hugo Chávez against it. A friend from the Higher Institute of International Relations, working in the Cuban Ministry of Foreign Affairs, had told Arturo that in this sense, Chávez's influence on the island was particularly negative because instead of promoting an institutional approach to socialism, Chávez was more like Fidel in promoting charismatic rule like a Latin American *caudillo*.

A few more people wandered in, sat down, and waited for the music to begin. Arturo said, "Another reform that has been proposed is a better separation between party and state functions. Many advocate less heavy-handed political intrusion in the direct management of the daily problems of housing, transportation, and food. Even old party members say it loses credibility when it tries to micromanage things. They say the party should focus on strategic plans and monitor the government, and let those with initiative run the daily affairs of the country so long as they don't deviate from established policies. Since the 1990s, reformers have sought an expanded role for the National Assembly as a legislative power, controlling, inspecting, and monitoring the way the government does business. They say the National Assembly should have longer sessions, with a more professionalized staff and more direct reflection of what people think. They reject the unanimity of sessions, where discussions consist of reaffirming political loyalty, not arguing about different positions and disagreeing over how to proceed. They propose a more technical participation in committee sessions with greater transparency. They say experts should testify publicly and openly about problems in the economy and society. And they want to continue basic election reform. Before 1992, members of the National Assembly were nominated and elected by provincial assemblies. And before the Fourth Party Congress, people advocated for direct election of deputies. This was approved in part, but with important limits. Today, unlike nominations to the municipal assemblies, where two or more candidates must stand for each position, in elections for the National Assembly there is only one candidate for each position. The voter has three choices: he can leave the ballot blank to express his dissatisfaction with the system, as the political opposition suggests; he can vote for some members on the list but choose not to vote for others, showing his dissatisfaction with some of those nominated; or he can cast the 'united vote' for all of the candidates. Since 1992 the major trend, contrary to government wishes, has been toward the second — voting for some but not for others. After living in America, I've also come to value more the idea of a bicameral congress in which the upper chamber is partially elected every two years. If there is a transition to a multiparty democracy in Cuba, then I hope it will include a separation of legislative chambers. This will allow more direct representation in the lower chamber, but also provide the current elite with the confidence to democratize, since control of the upper chamber could serve as a break against any sudden upheaval in the political mood."

Arturo abruptly stopped talking. He noticed a familiar face at the bar, raised his chin in that vaguely aristocratic manner of his, and soon we were sitting at a small bistro table, drinking cold Bucaneros with a stout, dark-haired man who had a square, friendly face and big floppy ears.

The man was Jose Camilo López Valls, the director of foreign relations for the Bienal and the Wifredo Lam Center. When he excused himself for a moment to talk to one of his staff, I asked Arturo, "How do you know him?"

"We were in Cuban Intelligence together," Arturo answered casually.

I noted that he said "Cuban Intelligence," not "MININT," but did not remark on it.

He added, "We resigned at the same time." Then he returned to his previous thoughts as we waited for Camilo to return: "The list of candidates for National Assembly elections is made by a commission of organizations controlled by the party and the trade unions. Defenders of the system say the party does not intervene but this is very hard to believe. In fact, the party gives clear directions about how they should run the show. Therefore, one of the most important reforms being proposed is that more than one candidate must run for each seat in the National Assembly. Candidates should compete against each other and explain their positions to the people. This idea is presented by some as appealing to the complexity of society in Cuba. It is important, they say, to give space to the expression of differences inside the electoral system. Another proposed reform is to nominate judges to the provincial courts and the People's Supreme Tribunal for longer terms or even for life. They say that the judges could then exert more independence from the political authorities. Others have proposed a reform that would imitate China's creation of an anticorruption agency in charge of monitoring the expected increase in corruption during the transition to a more market-oriented economy."

Camilo returned to our table. He and Arturo began to reminisce about the old days in rapid-fire Cuban Spanish. I quickly finished my Bucanero, thanked Camilo, and excused myself, leaving the next installment of my political immersion for the next day.

The next day was May Day and I awoke at 6:00 to the sound of loud-speakers on the corners blaring patriotic music. Arturo arrived early to pick me up. He made it clear he would be taking me to the parade only to show me what it was like. We marched with several hundred thousand people down Zapata and through the Plaza of the Revolution, past the giant white statue of José Martí and the wide reviewing stand, just to get a brief glimpse of Raúl. Ironically, we mistook him for a short general in uniform when in fact he was wearing a simple white *guayabera* and a straw peasant hat.

The giant white statue of José Martí in the Plaza of the Revolution (Arturo Lopez-Levy collection).

I noticed one middle-aged couple in particular, marching with their arms around each other's shoulders. She was plump and wore a bright red T-shirt that proclaimed, "The Blockade Is Genocide." He was thin and wore a bright blue T-shirt that advertised, "Capital One." It was the perfect yin and yang.

Arturo returned to his thoughts on politics as if nothing had stopped him the afternoon before: "Two areas of increasing political debate involve the racial divide and the necessity of confronting legacies of exclusion and discrimination against people from the eastern provinces, homosexuals, women, and blacks. In the case of race, there are discussions about affirmative action programs for tourism jobs, the mass media, and other sectors of the economy. In the case of homosexuals, CENESEX — the Centro Nacional de Educación Sexual, a group under the leadership of Mariela Castro — has advocated for greater tolerance and participation in different parts of Cuban life. There is even a proposal for allowing homosexual marriage. But I believe the most important political reforms that have been proposed are the elimination of controls on travel abroad and easier access to the Internet." Now we were getting to the guts of the matter, for the party elite, many of them from the older generation, were clinging to their ideology while the younger generation was demanding more reforms. And the reforms most often demanded were more private property rights, more freedom to travel, and more Internet access.

Arturo said, "There is an emerging convergence of people who live within the system — workers, artists, intellectuals, and students — advocating for reform. A year ago, a video was made of a meeting between students from the Computer Science University and Ricardo Alarcón, the president of the National Assembly. Several students asked him about official policies like the lack of information and critique in the Cuban press, the mechanisms of elections, and of course travel and the Internet. One of the most circulated and popular parts of the video occurred when a student questioned Alarcón about the right to travel. Alarcón said the state opposed this so-called right because if everybody could travel, then the skies of the planet would be filled with airplanes. People laughed and made fun of this view. Recently Soledad Cruz, one of the best-known propagandists for the government, wrote a piece on the website *Kaos en la Red* supporting freedom to travel for all Cubans."

The crowd was thinning out. Arturo said he wanted to wait for some friends. Before he sent me on my way, however, he finished with these thoughts: "Last month, Silvio Rodriguez, a popular revolutionary singer, was prevented by the United States from traveling to New York City for a concert in honor of Pete Seeger, who popularized the well-known Cuban song 'Guantanamera.' Silvio protested the denial of his visa, but his protest was questioned by Adrian Lopez Leyva, a Cuban Christian Democrat living in Miami, with whom I exchanged friendly emails before he died trying to return to Cuba. Adrian agreed the United States had acted improperly by not granting Silvio a visa for a cultural event based on his nationality and politics, but he reminded Silvio that Cuba was doing the same to its citizens. In response, Silvio declared his opposition to the Cuban travel ban 'as a mistake of our migration policy hurting the Revolution.' So the issue is getting aired more and more in public. People crave travel and communication without regard for politics. And the forces of politics will eventually give way."

"That's optimistic," I said, "coming from you."

He said, "I am concerned about bigger, more structural issues. One problem that could stand in the way of reform is the lack of discussion about how to check and balance the power of the higher authorities within the party and the relation between the different branches of the system. There are formal checks and balances among the branches in the Cuban Constitution, but there is virtually no check on the power of the Communist Party or civilian oversight over the FAR. Checking the party is hard in a culture characterized by lack of transparency and minimal, if any, scrutiny from the media. I think we need to enhance the 'republican components' of every modern democracy in order to have effective checks and balances against abuse. This is where the reforms could go astray."

I left Arturo to meet his friends, walked to the Meliá to check my emails, and rejoined him at 4:00 to visit Adrián Pellegrini del Riego, a rising Cuban artist. We drove to Adrián's fine art deco home on the outskirts of Havana with Arturo's friend Camilo and Camilo's wife, a pregnant gynecologist who listened a lot and spoke only rarely.

Adrián was a dark, trim, balding 29-year-old painter whose work leaned far more toward the abstract than the expressionist style. His larger canvases could fetch $8,000 outside Cuba and his intricate pen-and-ink drawings evoked images of *Alien* and *Blade Runner*. His home was filled with gadgets from iPods to laptops and telescopes, including an old Soviet missile warhead in his kitchen. And his life and demeanor proved the importance of the youth and their Internet and travel. Our visit with him couldn't have been more different from our visit with Pedro García Espinosa during our previous trip in January.

We drank vodka — except for Camilo's wife, who drank tea — while Adrián told us about himself. He pointed to the gold Star of David hanging from his neck and explained that his people were Sephardic Jews, originally *marranos*, who migrated to Cuba via Portugal, Holland, and France. He and Arturo had not been acquainted during Arturo's involvement with the Cuban Jewish community. He wore a white linen shirt without a collar and had the faint shadow of a moustache and beard on his lip and chin. He had been painting since he was 3 or 4, and grew interested in his Jewish heritage when he became attracted to the signs and symbols of the Kabbalah.

"I'm not political in my actual life," said Adrián, "but I am in the transcendent future sense. I don't believe in borders, for example. And I think we should do more with less. I've learned a lot from living in France for a year and from traveling through Europe, Latin America, and even the United States. I was there twice in 2004. It's a really free country all right, but I do not feel a lack of freedom here. I have friends in high places and we simply do not discuss politics — we talk about women and art and cigars."

According to Adrián, Obama was for America the right guy in the right

Alien meets **Blade Runner** in the art of rising Cuban artist Adrián Pellegrini (courtesy Adrián Pellegrini del Riego).

place at the right time. The United States faced a crisis in credibility after Bush, and Obama responded. Still, Adrián insisted, in the United States there is the "sensation of freedom because there are so many choices available, but the real freedom is not in economics — it's in your head."

At 5:38 on May 1, 2009, the skies over Havana opened with a hard, driving rain.

We interrupted our conversation to go out on Adrián's balcony. There we reached out and gathered drops from the first rain of May in our hands. We rubbed them on our faces for good luck, according to Cuban custom.

I thought, *Adrián doesn't fully realize just how lucky he is.* He had talents and gifts galore, to be sure, but he had used the tools of his youth to magnify them and market them in an extremely tough environment. Adrián projected a hopeful vision for Cuba's future. I would learn much more about him when he visited me in Denver in October 2010.

On October 10, 1868, Carlos Manuel de Céspedes rose early. A lawyer by training and planter by profession, he rang the bell that summoned his slaves for their day's work. As soon as they gathered around him, he granted them all their freedom. The same day he declared independence from Spain and launched the Ten Years' War. He became Cuba's first president in April 1869 and is called the Father of the Country. His picture appears on the currency and streets in Havana are named for him.

It's 140 years later — late Saturday morning, the day after May Day — and Arturo and I are sitting with the great-grandson of the Father of the Country. Monsignor Carlos Manuel de Céspedes is the general vicar of Havana's archdioceses. That makes him an influential man in the most influential of the institutional religions on the island. He's also an exceedingly kind, gentle, intelligent, articulate, and savvy man — a teacher and a leader who has met with popes and presidents — and plainly shows a warm affinity for Arturo, his former student.

His air-conditioned office in the rectory, attached to the San Agustín parish church in Almendares, has high ceilings and walls filled with maps of Cuba, paintings and pictures of his family and forebears, mementos and photos with those popes and presidents, and bookshelves crammed with the worn volumes read by a learned man in his 70s. His desk is cluttered and so is the workspace around his computer, to the left of his desk as he would face it, though he sits today in an overstuffed chair with a white lace doily behind his head.

The photos show Father Carlos Manuel as a vibrant, pudgy, balding man in black glasses and clerical garb. Before us, he seems shrunken, though he still fills out the belly of his dark blue, long-sleeved *guayabera* (custom-made, I assume, because it sports a white priest's collar). His mind is as sharp as ever but his face and scalp are spotted with scabs from the skin cancer that has spread to his lymph nodes — and is killing him.

After introductions and niceties, I say to Father Carlos Manuel, "It is my understanding that the Church is very involved in efforts to democratize Cuba."

Arturo with Monsignor Carlos Manuel de Céspedes in his rectory (Arturo Lopez-Levy collection).

Immediately he corrects me: "Liberalize is a better word than democratize. This is not because democracy is bad — I like it — but we don't need to pre-judge the current government ahead of a dialogue. Encouraging dialogue is important to the Church. Dialogue not limited to religion. Dialogue that encourages recognition of the plurality of Cuban society, of its different parts here and in other places around the world where many Cubans now live."

"Are there specific goals you want to reach?"

"We would like to see more free speech and free press. The Church is involved in many publications. We write what we want" — Arturo interjects that he is writing an article for just such a publication at this time — "and the government might or might not like it but it doesn't say anything about it, either. We try to be respectful of everyone's position in the name of dialogue. We are not an opposition party. We fight to have all patriotic voices heard."

Arturo says, "Father Carlos Manuel is very well known for coining the phrase 'House Cuba,' which means when you're having your lunch on Sunday..."

"Every Cuban should be welcome at the family table," says our host. He talks about plurality within the one-party system and says it's hard but possible. He mentions that Raúl has said that the single-party system can survive only if it allows more diversity of opinions — though some people on the island say Fidel quickly told his little brother to stop talking like that. As for Obama, Father Carlos Manuel looks forward to having better relations between United States and Cuba. Then he waves toward the photos of him meeting with presidents Ronald Reagan and George H.W. Bush. Changes under Raúl have been real, he says, but they mostly have involved land reform and generally have been more economic than political in nature.

He laughs and says, "There are people whom we would like to remain retired."

Though, he admits, the changes that have involved religion began under Fidel.

Arturo interjects that these changes were the result more of the success of the religious communities' strategy of adaptation to the situation after the Revolution, though to Fidel this opening undoubtedly showed a great political mind.

"Today we can celebrate mass in prisons," says Father Carlos Manuel.

"So you do have a political agenda?" I ask.

"Not really. We would like to see more education and more opportunities for the Church to be involved in education — not a private school system, mind you, but some sort of an accommodation, a presence."

I marvel at the monsignor's excellent English.

He continues, "The Church is not counter-revolutionary. We do want to see the country move forward and not back. This is a great moment of great opportunities." Then he gestures at the computer on his side desk and says, "I have a computer, you see, but no Internet. I can send and receive emails, but I cannot browse the Web. So of course I want more Internet access — for information, not for some improper political purpose. The real question becomes, who should be able to pick and choose what I get to see? I think the Internet is so important for the education of our people, and that means it's all about our young people."

I'm thinking: Here is one of the oldest, wisest men I have met in Cuba, tying together two of the themes that have not only emerged but also risen to the top as keys to the future. Then he hits on the third: "I have traveled to so many places. To Spain, Italy, the Vatican, the United States — sometimes three or four times a year — to Latin America, and France. I like Spain because I adore the language, and I lived in Italy for four years. Then there's Austria, Philadelphia, New York, Boston, Washington."

"Where would you like to go where you haven't gone before?" I ask.

He looks sad. The cancer has slowed him down. He says, "I want to visit Israel."

That leads to a discussion of what normalization might look like between Cuba and the United States after the embargo is lifted. He agrees with Arturo and me that dismantling the embargo is a process, not an event. He believes Cuba and the United States will be very close, like Cuba is with Spain and Mexico. He doesn't, I notice, mention Venezuela.

Arturo later tells me that he doesn't believe Father Carlos Manuel sympathizes with Chávez's political views, though he is a great admirer of José Martí and his dreams of a community of Hispanic American nations.

Finally, Father Carlos Manuel says, "With the Church, as I said, it is more about social action than politics. Now in specific cases like hurricanes, the state is letting us get more involved. There is a lot of aid coordinated by the Church. We provide lunches for the poor at our parishes. We have cultural centers where we teach computer skills and conduct classes in languages, marketing and history."

He's talking about demand-driven, ground-up, grassroots liberalization and about the new Holy Trinity: the youth, the Internet, and travel.

We wrap up our interview. Father Carlos Manuel shakes my hand warmly and I step aside as he and Arturo exchange many hugs. After Arturo tears himself away from his old teacher — and after the monsignor fades into the dark hallways of the rectory — Arturo lowers his voice and whispers to me, "Every time I leave Cuba, I am afraid he won't be here when I come back. He is such an open-minded person and a great teacher."

We left Father Carlos Manuel and went to the nearby Hotel Kohly to look for a cousin of Arturo's who worked there. His cousin wasn't on duty. Arturo said, "My aunt and uncle live over there, across the street, and I'd like to see if they are home." So he called his father to ask if it was okay for him to call his aunt. Why did he do that?

Because Arturo's uncle was General Guillermo — the Rooster — father-in-law to Raúl's daughter Deborah, a man who was strict about his rules. And the rules of the FAR said that officers must not meet with Americans outside protocol and without orders. That meant me, and Arturo as well, since he had become a U.S. citizen.

But Arturo's father said it was okay to call, and soon we were at the door of a home down the block that seemed self-consciously modest in the upscale neighborhood. And soon, after many exclamations, hugs and kisses, we were seated in the living room with Aunt Cristina, her middle-aged daughter, and her 21-year-old granddaughter, called "Little Cristina," a lovely tall and lanky young woman who spoke excellent English.

The living room had plenty of gadgets — a TV and a stereo — but they were not as new or nifty as those we saw the afternoon before at Adrián Pelligrini's house. But the Cuban coffee we were served was hot and the reception was warm. Clearly the three women adored Arturo. He spoke with his aunt and first cousin in his clipped, rapid-fire Spanish, so Little Cristina and I talked in English. She, like Adrián, took an immediate liking to the wide range of blues I had on my iPod: B.B. King, Buddy Guy, Junior Wells, Pinetop Perkins, Susan Tedeschi, Little Milton, and Eric Clapton.

Little Cristina said her boyfriend had given her a program that might allow her to lift the songs off my iPod. We went to the computer in her bedroom, which was girly and messy in the way my daughter Rachel's room was girly and messy at 21. Her computer and iPhone were newer than my iPod, but her boyfriend's magic program failed to lift those blues off that old hard drive.

When she learned my daughters were dancers — and one was appearing in *Phantom of the Opera* in Las Vegas — Little Cristina sighed. Pointing to her long legs, she said, "I've always loved to dance but my body isn't right for it." Then she laughed and added, "I guess that's why I'm taking business and engineering at the university."

She missed her father, a physician who had moved to Florida and had not been able to visit her very often due to the restrictions on travel on both sides of the Straits. "Is it okay that we talk about that here?" I asked, gesturing with my head toward the matriarch of the family in the next room.

"Sure," she said, "they don't understand."

I didn't ask, though perhaps I should have: "You mean they don't understand the English language or they don't understand the language of iPods and travel restrictions?"

Soon we finished our coffee and, after many hugs and kisses, said our good-byes.

Half a block later, Arturo lowered his voice and hissed, "You know, the whole time back there?"

I wasn't sure what he was getting at. "What about it?" I asked.

"My Uncle Guillermo was there, all the time, downstairs in his room."

"And he wouldn't come up and just say hello?" I must have sounded surprised.

"Of course not," answered Arturo.

I processed; I wondered, "Is he angry or stubborn?"

"Neither one," answered Arturo.

"Would it have made any difference," I pressed, "if I hadn't been there?"

"Of course not," said Arturo, sounding a little impatient with me. "I told you, Harlan, there is a rule. And my uncle always follows the rules."

Arturo with his cousin "Little Cristina," granddaughter of Uncle Guillermo, one of the most powerful generals in the FAR (Arturo Lopez-Levy collection).

A photo of Raúl faces a photo of Obama on the back cover of the first issue in 2009 of the Catholic lay publication *Espacio Laical.* Between them, the tagline reads, "*El futuro de las relaciones entre Cuba y Estados Unidos está en las manos de los presidentes Raúl Castro y Barack Obama.*" Inside there is a lengthy interview with our friend Carlos Alzugaray and an article about Cuba's relationship with Brazil.

On a hot Monday evening I met Arturo at the small park on the corner of Bernaza and Teniente Rey in Old Havana to dine with the director, editor, and two staff writers of *Espacio Laical.* All four of them were trim and fit, and all four wore nice button-down shirts and trousers. Three wore glasses.

El futuro de las relaciones entre Cuba y Estados Unidos está en las manos de los presidentes Raúl Castro y Barack Obama

Raúl faces Obama on the back cover of the Catholic lay publication *Espacio Laical* (courtesy *Espacio Laical*).

José Ramón Pérez Expósito, the director, was the eldest: salt-and-pepper hair, clean shaven, bright brown eyes, and an authoritative manner. In the middle was the editor in chief, Roberto Veiga González, a lawyer with sharp, penetrating eyes, somewhere in his forties. Then came two staff writers, roughly a decade younger, one of them a history professor.

In a spic-and-span little conference room behind the church that faced the park, we talked and ate a typical Cuban dinner of chicken, rice, and potatoes. The folks at *Espacio Laical* meant to thank Arturo for his recent contributions as a member of the board of the publication, including the article he was writing for them at the time. Initially we talked in generalities: The magazine, they said, is social, not theological. They want to widen the dialogue but always with respect and civility. Yes, it has political content in the broadest sense, but it is not partisan.

We talked about plurality in one-party systems versus plurality in multiple-party systems, the role of the youth in Cuba, and the pace of change in Cuba. Then we edged toward deeper matters. Because the political culture on the island has been "shaped by the Revolution," they said, there will continue to be a heavy emphasis on sovereignty and social justice in the future, no matter who comes into power. More Internet access and more travel opportunities — in fact, anything, like tourism and foreign investment, that "normalizes the country" — will certainly hasten the process of change.

"But we need oxygen!" said the director.

The editor insisted there should be "no preconditions" on normalization with the United States because that would violate Cuba's sovereignty. The nation's internal affairs should be left to its people and their government. This is a central issue in Cuban culture. "Cubans," insisted the editor, "must be the ones who demand change."

I agreed with him. For advocates of change on both sides of the Straits of Florida, the idea — mandated by the Helms-Burton legislation — that Cuba cannot be deemed to be free and democratic until both Castro brothers are out of power is patently offensive. It is an idea that is widely viewed throughout the world as violating Cuba's sovereignty.

The director added, "But change is difficult because the people in power on both sides of the Straits of Florida have kept the people in the trenches. We need to break out of our stagnation."

Everyone agreed the "shock of normalization" would break the elite and the people out of their "siege mentality." Opening relations with the United States and having a genuinely open dialogue about change inside Cuba would be the best way to promote human rights.

I especially appreciated the editor's emphasis on Cuba's sovereignty. I felt we were talking lawyer to lawyer, for sovereignty is the critical link between politics and the rule of law. Professor Maryann Cusimano Love of Catholic University explains:

> Sovereignty is the form of political organization that has dominated the international system since the Treaty of Westphalia in 1648. Sovereign states have exclusive and final jurisdiction over territory, as well as the resources and populations that lie within such territory. A system based on sovereignty is one that acknowledges only one political authority over a particular territory and looks to that authority as the final arbiter to solve problems that occur within its borders. Sovereign states have four characteristics, three of which are negotiable: territory, population, a government with control over the territory and population, and international recognition. [O]nly international recognition is non-negotiable. If a political entity has territory, population and a government but lacks international recognition, then it is not ... a sovereign state.[20]

In other words, in the 17th century people in Western Europe stopped fighting over religion and started fighting over politics. If you had a population, a territory, a government to rule, and broad international recognition, then you had sovereignty and other nation-states would not interfere with your internal affairs. Of course, the idea of "broad recognition" is inherently flexible, so sovereignty has always been somewhat less absolutist than its connotation would suggest.

More recently sovereignty has become even more flexible. As I have written elsewhere, "During the Twentieth Century, organizations composed of nation-states took on powers and functions formerly reserved to 'sovereign' states. The imposition of economic sanctions by trans-sovereign organizations like the U.N. grew to new heights. Justice went international. The war crimes trials at Nuremberg set enduring precedents.... Over time the relative nature of sovereignty became accepted. The number of quasi-states, failed states, 'statelets,' pseudo-nations, and conquered nations proliferated."[21]

Today the "non-intervention principle" that lies at the heart of sovereignty remains strong despite the challenges posed by economic globalization, the international desire to promote universal human rights, and especially the prohibitions against genocide, war crimes, and crimes against humanity. Those prohibitions remain the clearest examples of the non-absolutist nature of sovereignty in the 21st century.

Finally, Arturo and I pushed back from the table to say our thanks and good-byes. I kept mine brief, shaking hands with each of our hosts in turn. Then I waited patiently outside for Arturo while hugs were exchanged and long sentences spoken in Spanish.

Once we talk about sovereignty, we have to talk about politics between Cuba and the rest of the world. Most countries understand that Cubans value their sovereignty — their nationalist identity — even more than they value their communist identity. That is why Havana has more diplomatic missions, embassies, and international conferences than almost anywhere else. The United States and Israel may not have diplomatic relations with Cuba, but everyone else does. And Israel is a major investor in several Cuban industries.

Cuba will continue to have vibrant relations with the nations of Latin America, especially Venezuela and Brazil. It will continue to be a leader among the so-called non-aligned nations, including countries in the Middle East that are not friendly with the United States. It will continue to expand its relations with China, Russia, India, and the European Union. The only question is this: When will the United States accept the failure of its isolationist strategy and come to the party?

We heard the government was cracking down on the use of wireless Internet connections in the major hotels by Cubans—especially bloggers like Yoani Sánchez. Already I had noted every time I went to the Meliá to buy wireless access—at 12 CUCs for two hours!—they took down my passport number. We left Cuba for a conference in Canada on May 6 and four days later, Yoani Sánchez reported this on *Generación Y*[22]:

> Yesterday, May 9, I went to the Meliá Cohiba hotel to check if the Internet access limitations for Cubans continue. Several friends had told me that the measure had been rescinded ... but I wanted to check for myself. So Reinaldo and I went and made this little video. The "tourist" who appears to be reading the newspaper *Granma* is me. [There follows both the video and a transcript.]
>
> REINALDO: Good afternoon, Miss. I'd like to buy an hour of Internet.
> MUJER: May I see your passport please.
> R: No, what I have is an identity card.
> M: No, I can't sell you an hour of Internet, because the connection here is only for foreigners...
> R: Since when is this?
> M: Since one month.
> R: I came last week and connected.
> M: And who sold you the ticket?
> R: I don't know the name... It was eight days ago.
> M: There's a resolution that says it's only for foreigners. Look here...
> R: But is this only in this hotel? Is this being done in all the hotels? Because I frequently connect in the National.... Is this a resolution ... of the Meliá?
> M: No, it's a resolution from MINTUR [the tourism ministry]....
> R: Look, I don't have an argument with you ... you are a person who is just doing your job.
> M: Yes, you can go to Reception and lodge any complaints you like.
> R: Because you know this violates my constitutional rights. Because it's written in the constitution of our Republic that discrimination based on national origin is prohibited. And I feel discriminated against because my national ori-

gin is Cuban. It's as if they said here: "This Internet is for the whole world except Mexicans." It's the same ... I'm being discriminated against for my national origin. There's not a single law or internal regulation that can supersede the constitutional rights of citizens. Aren't I right?

So, exactly as economics blurs into politics, politics blurs into the rule of law.

Chapter Six
The Rule of Law in the New Cuba

I approached Passport Control in Varadero amid the raucous laughter of 100 Canadian college students freed from dreary winters of study. Now that was the first strike against me. I was a U.S. citizen traveling on a charter flight from Toronto to the premier beach resort on the northern coast of the island, rather than a more typical entry at José Martí International Airport outside Havana.

The officer behind the glass in the booth ran my passport through his scanner.

I smiled casually and said, *"Buenas noches."*

He looked me up and down and nodded curtly. Canadian college students zipped past me in droves to my left and right. The officer asked, "Is this your first time in Cuba?"

"No," I said. "I'm sure your computer shows you that I have been here before."

"Where are you staying, here in Cuba?"

"At a *casa particular*" — a private home licensed by the state to rent rooms and provide limited services to foreign visitors — *"en La Habana."*

And that was a swing and a miss for a big strike two. I was not staying at a resort in Varadero or even a tourist hotel in Havana. I was staying in a private home and that is not the typical place for an American tourist. The officer behind the glass gestured with his chin and immediately another uniformed officer appeared at my side. He spoke better, though still broken, English, and asked, "And could you tell us, please, what is the address of this *casa particular* where you are staying?"

"It's on Calle 6 between Calle 23 and Calle 21 in Vedado."

"Yes," replied Number Two, "but what is the address?"

"I don't recall," I said, "but I have a card with the address on it in my suitcase."

"Ah," said Number Two, "I see."

From behind the glass, Number One said, "You know, my computer says you come here a lot. Yet you have filled out a tourist visa. Coming here as a mere tourist is not allowed under the laws of your country, isn't that right?"

"Yes," I said, slowing my speech and thought, sensing for the first time that something might be amiss.

"Unless you have a *permiso*, isn't that right?" asked Number Two.

"Yes," I said, "that's right."

"And do you have a *permiso*?" asked Number One.

"Yes, I do."

"May I see it?"

I had no choice. I took my "specific license" from the U.S. Treasury Department from my pocket, unfolded it carefully, and handed it through the glass. I didn't realize it yet, but that was another swing and a miss for a gargantuan strike three. At the time, Number One merely studied the license and made some more entries on his computer. Nothing earth shattering.

Number Two smiled patiently and said, "And have you, by chance, remembered the address of the *casa particular en La Habana?*"

"No," I said, "but I told you, it's in my suitcase."

"And so," said Number Two — and here he nodded at Number One behind the glass in the booth — "I will see you on the other side." He smiled and left.

Number One made one final entry on his computer, stamped my entry visa, handed me back my passport, my license and the visa, and buzzed me into the baggage claim area. I noted Number Two was already waiting for me, leaning casually against the far wall. The instant he saw me collect my suitcase, he was at my side.

"Excuse me," he said politely, "but I must get that address now." He smiled.

I opened my suitcase, reached inside, and retrieved the spiral notebook that held the business card from my *casa particular*. I gave him the address and he wrote it down on a little pad he kept in his pocket. He nodded at me and said, "You may go now."

And for a moment, I thought that was all there was to it. I would pass through Customs and meet Arturo on the other side. But no. The young woman in uniform who was checking entry forms at the Customs gate on the far side of the baggage claim area took one look at the stamp Number One had put on my visa and motioned me aside. Immediately a new guy — Number Three — was quietly and politely leading me and my suitcase and my small computer bag to a cramped windowless room that had a table for me to put my luggage on, and precious little in the way of air circulation.

Number Three was even trimmer and tighter and tougher than Number One and Number Two. His olive MININT uniform was carefully creased.

His English was clear, crisp, and articulate: "I'm sorry to have to detain you, but I am sure you understand..."

"Of course."

"Would you please put your suitcase and bag on the table and open them?"

"Of course." I complied while he pulled on latex gloves.

Then Number Three carefully examined, layer by layer, my clothes and my shoes, my toiletries and prescription bottles, and especially my computer and cell phone cables. He took a glance at the book I had brought to read — *The Adventures of Sherlock Holmes, Volume I*— and got a quick laugh at that. He muttered, "You are a very organized man," while he pulled off his latex gloves and fished a small notebook from his shirt pocket. "Please," he said, "you can put it all back together the way you want it now. I am sorry to have to keep you here, but I have to ask you some questions."

"Of course," I said, trying to stay cool despite the closeness of the quarters.

Number Three began by going over all the things I had written on my visa application and then moved to my passport and license. Then he dropped the very thermonuclear bomb I had hoped to avoid: "Please," he said, writing carefully in his little notebook, "explain for me how it is that you are entering Cuba as a tourist but your Treasury Department has given you license to enter for some reason other than tourism."

I began sweating. It was getting hot in there. The air was getting stuffy. And no matter how cool you think you are, no matter how many people you have interrogated as a lawyer, you might well sweat like I did if you don't have the perfect answer to the $64,000 question: What are you *really* doing here?

Arturo had told me not to talk about writing a book about Raúl because that would certainly send them up the walls. So I had to answer truthfully but not completely. And I am a terrible liar, so I stammered something about being a lawyer and a former law professor and a consultant on trade with Cuba and a writer of narrative nonfiction.

Number Three was writing feverishly. But he wasn't fooled by any of it, for he was probing for the very thing Arturo had warned me about: my failure to have a proper "research visa" issued by the Cuban government if I was trying to enter the country to do professional research. I did not have that piece of paper. I had foregone that formality, despite Arturo's admonitions, because I could not afford to waste the several months it usually takes an individual to get a "research visa" and because I was not interviewing government officials subject to limitations on talking to me without such a visa.

So Number Three was entirely right in asking me the big question.

I tried giving him a more coherent version of my bullshit. But he didn't buy it. He grew frustrated and excused himself, leaving me alone. As I waited in that stuffy little room, I sweated, and as I sweated, I thought about the path that had brought to me to this place. I knew it began long before I started traveling to the island, long before I ever thought about writing novels and narrative nonfiction. It began in the autumn of 1974.

Back then Langdell Hall housed the world's largest law library and the offices of the oldest professors at Harvard Law School. The office of Paul Abraham Freund was on the first floor. He was a modest, kindly man: overweight, with thick glasses and unruly tufts of white hair sprouting from the sides of a shiny bald head. In 1932–1933, he had served as the law clerk for Supreme Court Justice Louis Brandeis, and he later called his clerkship "the most important year in my life." He joined the law school faculty in 1939, taught and wrote for nearly four decades, and knew his stuff. He could quote from cases with excruciating detail and analyze issues with Olympian perspective. He had once been short-listed for the Supreme Court, but President Kennedy picked Whizzer White instead.

Freund's office was cluttered with stacks of books and piles of scholarly papers, dog-eared and marked with notes and highlights. An old electric typewriter sat on a metal stand. I sat on a wooden chair, waiting to hear what Freund — my faculty advisor — had to say about my LL.M. thesis. It was early in the process, so I had given him only an outline and draft of the first thirty pages. He couldn't hate it too badly.

Then again, he could. I had been particularly harsh on a case whose lead opinion was attributed to Justice Brandeis, though I knew it was actually his law clerk, the young Paul Freund, who had drafted it.

Freund frowned at me sitting like a schoolboy ready to be scolded. He arched his eyebrow and said, "Are you still planning to go back to that firm in Beverly Hills?"

He meant the securities law boutique that had recruited me two years before.

"Yes?" I said tentatively, wondering what he was driving at.

"But you don't really want to, do you?"

How could he have read my mind so easily? I was shocked.

"That's right," I said, "how did you know?"

"I've read your draft," said Freund. "You want to be a law professor, don't you?"

"That's right," I said again. Was it that plain from my writing?

"Well," said Freund, waving me up and out of his office, "then get back to work. Don't bother looking for jobs. There are people who call people when they need someone to teach con law. I'll get back to you."

The following fall I was teaching constitutional law at the new law school at Southern Illinois University. I've also taught con law at the University of Puget Sound, where I earned tenure, the University of South Carolina, and the University of Denver. And I have a guilty pleasure I must confess: Justice William O. Douglas is my hero.

Wild Bill Douglas — the Great Dissenter, rugged outdoorsman, judicial iconoclast, vocal defender of fundamental freedoms, and champion of the environment — the guy who argued that "trees should have standing" to sue to protect themselves — replaced Justice Brandeis on the Supreme Court in 1939.

In 1958 Justice Douglas wrote in *Kent v. Dulles*, one of my all-time favorite cases for teaching purposes:

> The right to travel is a part of the "liberty" of which the citizen cannot be deprived without due process of law under the Fifth Amendment.... Freedom of movement across frontiers in either direction, and inside frontiers as well, was part of our heritage. Travel abroad, like travel within the country, may be necessary for a livelihood. It may be as close to the heart of the individual as the choice of what he eats, or wears, or reads. Freedom of movement is basic in our scheme of values.... Freedom of movement also has large social values.... Foreign correspondents and lecturers on public affairs need first-hand information. Scientists and scholars gain greatly from consultations with colleagues in other countries. Students equip themselves for more fruitful careers in the United States by instruction in foreign universities. Then there are reasons close to the core of personal life — marriage, reuniting families, spending hours with old friends.... In many different ways, direct contact with other countries contributes to sounder decisions at home.[1]

Note how unequivocally Justice Douglas wrote his opinion. That is the hallmark of a *rule*. It is definite, clear, and unequivocal. Six years later, in 1964, he emphasized the rigidity of his rule, concurring in *Aptheker v. Secretary of State*:

> Those with the right of free movement may use it at times for mischievous purposes. But that is true of many liberties we enjoy. We nevertheless place our faith in them, and against restraint, knowing that the risk of abusing liberty so as to give rise to punishable conduct is part of the price we pay for this free society.
> Freedom of movement is kin to the right of assembly and to the right of association. These rights cannot be abridged....
> War may be the occasion for serious curtailment of liberty. Absent war, I see no way to keep a citizen from traveling within or without the country, unless there is power to detain him.... And no authority to detain exists except under extreme conditions, e.g., unless he has been convicted of a crime or unless there is probable cause for issuing a warrant of arrest by standards of the Fourth Amendment. This freedom of movement is the very essence of our free society, setting us apart.[2]

But can you tell? Something very important had happened in the six years between the *Kent* and *Aptheker* cases. The unequivocal views of Justice Douglas — which had carried a narrow majority of 5–4 in the earlier case —

garnered only his vote in the later case. His rule — absent war, there is no way to keep a citizen from traveling abroad — proved too rigid for the rest of the Court.

Justice Goldberg delivered the majority opinion in *Aptheker*, using a different methodology. He wrote a "means-to-ends" or "*strict scrutiny*" opinion:

> Although previous cases have not involved the constitutionality of statutory restrictions upon the right to travel abroad, there are well-established principles by which to test whether the restrictions here imposed are consistent with the liberty guaranteed by the Fifth Amendment. It is a familiar and basic principle ... that "a governmental purpose to control or prevent activities constitutionally subject to state regulation may not be achieved by means which sweep too broadly and thereby invade the area of protected freedoms." ...
>
> "[E]ven though the governmental purpose be legitimate and substantial, that purpose cannot be pursued by means that broadly stifle fundamental personal liberties when the end can be more narrowly achieved. The breadth of legislative abridgement must be viewed in the light of less drastic means for achieving the same basic purpose."[3]

The Court's shift in methodology is subtle but important. Once the walls of the rule have been breached, it's possible to make exceptions. Justice Douglas entertained only one exception — war. By contrast, under the means-to-ends approach of *Aptheker*, however difficult it may be to write laws that pass the test of "strict scrutiny," it can be and has been done. If the governmental purpose is compelling enough, and the means chosen to achieve it are among the least drastic available, and they are also well tailored for achieving the compelling purpose, then the restriction will pass muster.

Only one year passed before it was shown how weakened the original rule had become. In *Zemel v. Rusk*, the secretary of state had refused to validate a citizen's passport for travel to Cuba. The Supreme Court upheld the refusal. This time it was Chief Justice Earl Warren who delivered the majority opinion of the Supreme Court:

> The right to travel within the United States is of course also constitutionally protected.... But that does not mean that areas ravaged by flood, fire or pestilence cannot be quarantined when it can be demonstrated that unlimited travel to the area would directly and materially interfere with the safety and welfare of the area or the Nation as a whole. So it is with international travel. That the restriction which is challenged in this case is supported by the weightiest considerations of national security is perhaps best pointed up by recalling that the Cuban missile crisis of October 1962 preceded the filing of appellant's complaint by less than two months.[4]

Both Justice Douglas and Justice Goldberg dissented. They saw exactly what the chief justice was doing. He was *balancing* the interests of the individual against the interests of the state, and in so doing, he was "balancing away" the fundamental right of travel by forcing it to yield to so-called weightier concerns.

Of course, in 1965 the Cold War was raging. The awful specter of nuclear doom, barely averted in the missile crisis, hung over the Supreme Court — heavy, frightful, and real. Still, two decades later, after things had settled down, in *Regan v. Wald* a conservative majority of the Court, led by Justice Rehnquist, saw the opening left by *Zemel* to further eviscerate the right to travel abroad:

> We see no reason to differentiate between the travel restrictions imposed by the President in the present case and the passport restrictions imposed by the Secretary of State in *Zemel*. Both have the practical effect of preventing travel to Cuba by most American citizens, and both are justified by weighty concerns of foreign policy.
>
> Respondents apparently feel that only a Cuban missile crisis in the offing will make area restrictions on international travel constitutional. They argue that there is no "emergency" at the present time and that the relations between Cuba and the United States are subject to "only the 'normal' tensions inherent in contemporary international affairs."... The holding in *Zemel*, however, was not tied to the Court's independent foreign policy analysis. Matters relating "to the conduct of foreign relations ... are so exclusively trusted to the political branches of government as to be largely immune from judicial inquiry or interference."... Our holding in *Zemel* was merely an example of this classical deference to the political branches in matters of foreign policy.[5]

Follow the pattern. In 1958 the right to travel abroad was stated in the rule crafted by Justice Douglas in unequivocal terms. In the 1960s it was restated in a means-to-ends analysis that was difficult, but possible, for the government to get around. Next the right was balanced away until finally the gig was up. The Rehnquist court found it easy prey. Poof! No more fundamental right!

And so it sat in 2009 while I waited for Number Three to return to that stuffy little room at the airport outside Varadero. I knew that younger generations of con law jocks belittle the legacy of Wild Bill Douglas. But to me, he was still a hero. Many of the classic right-to-travel cases dealt specifically with the restrictions placed by the American government on travel to Cuba by non–Cuban American citizens. So I faced the legacy of my hero every time I boarded a plane to the island and every time I disembarked on Cuban soil. I had never had any trouble getting *into* the country before. Why this time?

Number Three returned with two more MININT officers, Numbers Four and Five. We crowded together in the stuffy little room while all three looked me up and down.

Number Five spoke to Number Three in rapid-fire Spanish and Number Three nodded crisply. Numbers Four and Five left the room. Number Three asked once more, "Why did your Treasury Department give you a license if you are just a tourist?"

In hindsight, I should have said all along, "Because I am a professional writer and I am here to cover the last day of the Bienal de la Habana." That likely would have ended it there, but the police in a police state know they can rattle your cage just by putting you in a cage and interrogating you for 50 minutes while the last bus to Havana leaves and you are stuck feeding them crap and hoping they let you go or put you on the plane back to Toronto — anything but more questions in this stupid shitty little room!

"...so you see, officer, I have several legitimate reasons for being here this time," I found myself saying, "but none of them, I had believed, required anything other than a typical tourist visa. I have, after all, been here before, on an academic mission, and as a journalist to cover the Film Festival, and I have always entered on a tourist visa..."

This time Number Three made a single-word entry in his notebook, closed it, smiled at me, and said, "I am sure you understand why we have to ask these questions. We hope we have not inconvenienced you. You may go now." And he motioned with his head in an unmistakable gesture that said, "Get out while you can."

I gathered my suitcase and computer bag and left the terminal, heaving a sigh of relief. Arturo was waiting for me in the near-empty parking lot and he was plainly not happy. "They stopped me and questioned me too," he snarled, "because I was from Denver and you were from Denver and so they figured that we had to be traveling together."

"And what did you tell them?"

"The truth. That I was entering to see my family and you were coming to soak up the current situation because we write articles together about Cuba and Latin America."

We hailed a taxi and negotiated the price for our trip to Havana. Once inside Arturo made his feelings clear: "I told you that you should have gotten a research visa."

I didn't want to revisit the issue. I had just spent an hour with five Cuban security agents and had gotten the point. But Arturo wouldn't let it go: "They probably already had a file on you because you come here so often. But if they didn't before, they do now. And so you will be followed. If you were staying at a hotel, your room would be bugged. If you left your computer in your room, someone would come and copy your hard drive. I've tried to warn you about these things. The government here really believes that the government of the most powerful nation on the earth is at war with them and they act consistently in accordance with that belief. Now perhaps you will take me seriously."

Adding insult to injury, a few days later Carolyn emailed me an article that I read in the lobby bar at the Meliá Cohiba after paying 12 CUCs for wireless access. It was about a former Cuban intelligence agent, now a defector, named Delfín Fernandez.

"My job was to bug their hotel rooms," stated Fernandez, referring to the long parade of Hollywood celebrities whose rooms he claimed to have bugged during their visits to the island. "With both cameras and listening devices. Most people have no idea they are being watched while they are in Cuba. But their personal activities are filmed under orders from Castro himself... [And] not just the rooms, we'd also follow the visitors around. Sometimes we covered them 24 hours a day. They had no idea we were tailing them."[6]

At least for once I had been warned.

The first time Arturo called for me early, to take me to the May Day parade, Gisela, the landlady at my *casa particular*, laughed cheerfully and said, "I am not such a good revolutionary." The second time he called for me early, this time without an excuse, she laughed cheerfully and promptly served him the same breakfast she was serving me: a single fried egg, a single slice of fried cured meat, some sliced fruit, dark coffee, orange juice, and a single bun, hard on the outside and fluffy soft on the inside.

Arturo started shoveling it down as soon as Gisela served it. He returned to our continuing dialogue as if nothing had interrupted us: "Most of the good work that has been done on transitions to market economies and representative democracies discusses the importance of the rule of law, Harlan, but I do not understand it as well as you. There are scholars of the Chinese and Taiwanese experience who have even talked about an intermediate phase of the rule by law. What does the rule of law mean to you?"

I sipped my strong Cuban coffee and said, "There is no single definition. Most people think it means that a nation's political and legal system must be run according to laws and not according to the whims of its leaders. 'We're a country of laws, not men,' you know. And today that usually means you've got to have a constitution, usually a written constitution. And that constitution will typically define and separate the powers of government among branches that check and balance each other. It will typically create an independent judiciary to try criminal cases and private disputes. It will typically allow the creation and operation of multiple political parties. And it will honor, in varying degrees, the human, civil, and political rights of its people."

"But there is no single magic formula," ventured Arturo.

"That's right. It varies from country to country and from society to society."

I told Arturo about Lon Fuller, a great scholar of jurisprudence, and an icon at Harvard Law School, whose debates with H.L.A. Hart defined the dilemmas of modern legal philosophy. Fuller's masterwork, *The Morality of Law*, was written in 1964. It remains the bedrock of the subject. In it Fuller wrote that you must have eight elements to have the rule of law: First, laws must exist and be obeyed by everyone, including government officials. Second, laws must be published so people can have notice of them. Third, laws must be prospective in nature so that the effect of the law may only take place after the law has been passed. Fourth, laws should be written with reasonable clarity to avoid unfair enforcement. Fifth, laws must avoid contradictions. Sixth, laws must not command the impossible. Seventh, laws must stay relatively constant through time to allow for the stability of rules, but they must also allow for timely revision when the underlying social and political circumstances have changed. And finally, eighth, official action should be consistent with the declared rule.[7]

Whenever I recall Fuller's list, I add what I believe is a critical *ninth* requirement: The establishment of a strong independent judiciary to adjudicate disputes among citizens and between citizens and their government.

"So it's not just the written word," said Arturo, "but also the practice of adhering to the written word."

"Exactly," I said, wiping some egg from my plate with a wad of soft fluffy bun. "As you know, I believe that constitutional law — which makes the rule of law specific to any particular country — provides the third great force, or dimension, when it comes to explaining world events. You can't just have the economic and the political forces or dimensions. And you can't just study the interactions between those two great forces. To fully understand the limits on economics and politics that are placed on a government by its people, and to understand the mechanisms by which economic and political interest groups make their votes and decisions effective, you've got to include the rule of law, that critical third dimension, both domestically and internationally."

And that took us to a discussion of human rights.

For Arturo and I agree: Cuba is not a national security threat to the United States. And the United States should not violate Cuba's sovereignty by trying to dictate a form of government not chosen by its people. But, as part of the international community, and within the margins of international law, the United States does have a legitimate gripe against Cuba when it comes to human rights. Many freedoms that Americans take for granted and value highly — freedoms of speech, press, and assembly — are severely limited in Cuba as of 2011.

Unfortunately, a legitimate concern for human rights has not driven U.S. policy toward Cuba for many decades. Rather, that policy has been driven, until quite recently, by the strident oligarchic fantasies of the right-wing exile community: *Just you wait. When the Castro brothers die, we'll move back to the island and take back the country they took from us!* This is what Ann Louise Bardach presents as the struggle between two kinds of "royal families" — the Castros and the Diaz-Balarts. But, you ask, what about the Cuban people? *Well, they should just say thank you.*

Indeed, consider these basics: Sovereign states are primarily responsible for human rights inside their boundaries. The Universal Declaration of Human Rights, adopted by the U.N. General Assembly in 1948, provides a list of substantive rights of individuals and imposes the responsibility upon nation-states to implement those rights. Human rights treaties or covenants are norms of international law by which states have codified the bundles of interdependent and indivisible rights they owe to their peoples.

"It is very important," insisted Arturo, "that we always view human rights as consisting of bundles, not a menu from which a state may freely pick and choose."

In terms of specificity, he was referring to the Universal Declaration and the six basic international instruments: the International Covenant on Civil and Political Rights; the International Covenant on Economic, Social and Cultural Rights; the Convention for the Elimination of Racial Discrimination; the Convention against Torture; the Convention for the Elimination of Discrimination against Women; and the Convention on the Rights of the Child. These instruments have widespread support in the international community.

Indeed, Cuba has signed all of them, though it has not actually ratified all of them. By contrast, the United States has signed all but the last one. And there is the rub. In theory, human rights are interdependent and indivisible, and that means economic, social, and cultural rights are as important as civil and political rights. But in reality, each nation does in fact emphasize some rights over others, according to the ideological preferences of those in power. The United States has historically protected the civil, political, and capitalist property rights of its people more than it has protected their economic, cultural, and social rights. Cuba, by contrast, is seen by many as protecting the economic, social, and cultural rights of its people more than their civil, political, and property rights.

"And there are," I added, equally insistent, "countless variations." I could feel the tension between theory and reality in our train of thought. We took our coffees outside, to the two white metal rocking chairs on the front porch of Gisela's *casa*, a cool, shady place lined with pots of tall green palms and lots of white and green tile work.

"Even among Western democracies," I continued. "For example, England's rules concerning free speech and free press allow various forms of

The front porch of Gisela's *casa particular*, with its two white metal rocking chairs (Harlan Abrahams collection).

'prior restraints,' while generally the rules in the United States do not. And all of these different variations are allowed to exist under international law. It's only when violations of human rights become really gross — like in cases of genocide, child soldiering, and crimes against humanity — that international law allows the outright intervention that is implied in a regime change policy."

"You are always seeking that linkage among the economic, the political —"

"And the legal," I said. "That's right. Yes, I am. In fact —"

Arturo interrupted my interruption. "And that's why it is so important to have an independent judiciary. Even though we freely admit the U.S. Supreme Court makes many mistakes..."

"Yes, it does. Take *Bush v. Gore*— or the travel cases — or any number of cases each year. I think some are wrongly decided. But that does not negate the rule of law. Rather, it's about crafting principles, or methodologies of decision-making, like rules, strict scrutiny, and balancing. And it's about using those methodologies in transparent, reasoned ways to resolve real-world cases, not by choosing one value or rule or protected right over another for all purposes, but by accommodating the competing principles and values and interests protected by the Constitution. It's that dynamic — that *application* of methods to real-world problems — that attracts me to law as the third dimension."

"What examples do you use when you are teaching this stuff?"

"I usually point to the four Ps," I said. "Pervasive prejudicial pretrial publicity. In the famous Sam Sheppard case, the case that inspired *The Fugitive* on TV, and the many cases that have followed it, the Supreme Court has allowed limited, case-specific incursions on the rights of free speech and free press by upholding very narrowly drawn 'gag orders' that seek to protect the competing interests and values that demand fair trials for criminal defendants. These are very case-specific accommodations, mind you, not rigid choices that govern all cases for all times."

"I like this idea, the accommodation of competing principles," said Arturo, finishing his coffee. "But you have to admit," he argued, "that our independent judiciary [in the United States] makes a lot of bad decisions when it comes to Cuba."

"You're focusing," I said, "on the few, the obvious, the notable cases — not the great mass of less controversial cases that are correctly decided. Besides, who are we to say what is or is not correctly decided? That's why we need an independent judiciary."

I paused in mid-thought, realizing my response was not entirely responsive. Then, searching more carefully for my words, I said, "It's true, I suppose, that whenever Cuba gets thrown into the mix, the analysis and the results get skewed. Usually in the wrong direction. You know Stan Murphy — that trial lawyer from Alabama who does a lot of Cuba cases — the guy who is speaking at the conference in Canada? He says Cuba has a 'corrosive influence' on American law and discusses four types of cases to prove his point. He starts with the right-to-travel cases, of course, but then he also discusses a series of academic freedom cases, a bunch of child custody cases, like the Elián González case, and most recently, the *Vamos a Cuba* case."

I could see that I had inadvertently pushed a hot button for Arturo. He started winding up, getting agitated, puffing like a viper. He put down his empty coffee cup. Steam was building inside his brain. A flood of words was getting ready to burst forth. He was going to hit me with a tirade about the fact that American courts often treat Iran — a genuine terrorist threat — better than they treat Cuba.

So I held out my hands to block the flood I had triggered with the sound of those three simple words: *Vamos a Cuba*. This was the title of a small children's book — part of a series about visiting other countries — that was removed from the shelves of all public school libraries by the Miami–Dade County School Board in 2006, prompting a lawsuit by the ALCU and proving once again Cuba's "corrosive influence" on American law. The case went to the U.S. Court of Appeals, which did not invoke the rule that applied to "viewpoint discrimination" under the First Amendment: *Absent obscenity or other forms of unprotected speech, a book cannot be removed from the shelves of a public school library simply because the school board does not like it.*

Instead, the court of appeals allowed the "insidious influence" of Cuba — to use another of Stan Murphy's phrases — to color its analysis. It disregarded the usual rule and held that the school board could indeed ban *Vamos a Cuba* because the book inaccurately portrayed life on the island as normal and acceptable. The court went to unusual lengths to point out trivial misstatements in the book. And in November 2009, the U.S. Supreme Court declined to review the case, handing a major victory to the censors.[8]

Never in recent years has there been such a blatant display of hypocrisy when it comes to "the marketplace of ideas." Ironically, the same right-wing conservatives who attack judicial activism have no trouble embracing the act of judicial censorship evident in the case of the innocent little book about Cuba.

I said to Arturo, "I know, I know, the case is a travesty. It's just like Stan says: Our constitutional rights 'become fluid' whenever Cuba is involved."

Then, a little abruptly, we got up and brought Gisela our empty coffee cups.

The winds blew, the skies opened, and the downpour began. Our hostess closed the shutters on the only window that brought fresh air into the room. She didn't start the electric fan in the corner either, so it started getting stuffy fast. I thought of the tight little room at the airport in Varadero where the officers of MININT had grilled me.

Arturo and I were visiting a pair of professors — a father and his daughter — in their tiny apartment in Vedado. Everywhere we looked there were books, books, and more books. Rounding out the parlor were a few old paintings on the walls, a few sticks of worn wicker furniture, a Dell laptop computer and an ancient Acer desktop computer. The father had thick white hair, a thin physique, and deeply tanned skin. The daughter looked like him — small, trim, deeply tanned, high cheekbones — but with long black hair.

The air inside the room was growing stuffier by the minute and the rain showed no sign of letting up. The father complained that the hurricanes had given the government an "alibi" to roll back market reforms: "It's about politics, not economics," he insisted.

The daughter, who had attended Moscow State University and written a very well-received book about José Martí, agreed: "Everything here is about the politics." She did not think it was likely the Communist Party would open itself to more plurality, at least not in the near future. "These people," she said, "are professional revolutionaries. They lead. And the people, the masses, simply follow."

Our conversation ranged from the influence of the American academy on the debates going on in the country to the importance of class versus race in seeking diversity within the party, to nationalism versus socialism — a particular specialty of the daughter. After a time I realized she was talking about a total absence in the present of any real "marketplace of ideas." It simply did not exist at the core of Cuban life.

Arturo disagreed. He thought that reducing the exchange of ideas to a "market" was a terrible analogy. From a human rights perspective, an educated population and the free expression of its ideas are inalienable rights regardless of any market considerations. "Cuba," he said, "has been a vibrant society with intellectuals and academics interacting and producing great research and analysis. Some ideas are censored by the authorities, but there are discussions and positions about Cuban economics, history, legality, and politics expressed openly at Cuban universities and in official institutions and journals. Beyond these official venues there is an extensive network of groups that are tolerated, like the Observatorio Crítico, the Democratic and Participative Socialism Group, the Cofradía de la Negritud, and Cátedra Haydée Santamaría, where debates about national and international issues often take place. Cubans work hard to connect themselves with publications and information from other countries. In most cases they manage to avoid censorship. In short, Cubans have been discussing their own problems for decades."

I turned back to the daughter and said, "The people here are so well educated. Isn't it hard for them to accept?"

She responded, "The big problem here is that people do not even know what their rights are." She described a survey the government started to see how much the people knew about their rights under the Cuban Constitution. It quickly revealed that they knew virtually nothing about their rights. The survey was stopped.

As she spoke I thought of what I had learned of the Cuban Constitution.[9] The problem with the rule of law in Cuba is not that it lacks a written constitution. In fact, Cuba's Constitution is much more detailed — and wordy — than the U.S. Constitution, and the two have many features in common. Both constitutions separate the powers of government into legislative, judicial and executive branches, which check and balance each other to varying degrees. Both declare equality among the people and establish rights of free speech, free press, freedom of religion, free assembly, and procedures and limits on the state's ability to convict a person of a crime. Indeed, like the U.S. Constitution, the Cuban Constitution embraces popular sovereignty, the idea that "sovereignty lies in the people, from whom originates all the power of the state."[10]

The differences between the U.S. Constitution and the Cuban Constitution are, however, the key to understanding the differences between their peoples and the political, economic, and legal systems they have crafted for themselves. The U.S. Constitution leaves the interpretation of many of its critical features to an independent judiciary, which must grapple constantly with its open-ended language. By contrast, and in an abundance of detail, the Cuban Constitution is filled with qualifiers and limits. For example, free press and free speech must be "in keeping with the objectives of a socialist state."[11]

Make no mistake — state socialism as a political, economic, and legal system is embedded throughout the Cuban Constitution: "Cuba is an independent and sovereign socialist state of workers."[12] Detailed provisions cover the people's rights to health care and education. Private property is eliminated, with limited exceptions. One is allowed to inherit a house but cannot sell it. Foreign investment is allowed but tightly controlled by the state. The idea of "socialist state property" dominates.

By contrast, the U.S. Constitution nowhere mentions "capitalism," though it goes to considerable lengths to protect private property. And even more importantly, in Cuba "the Communist Party of Cuba, a follower of Martí's ideas and Marxism-Leninism, and the organized vanguard of the Cuban nation, is the highest leading force of society and of the state, which organizes and guides the common effort toward the goals of the construction of socialism and the progress toward a communist society."[13]

No, the problem with the rule of law in Cuba is not that is lacks a written constitution or basic freedoms that are recognized in that constitution or three branches of government that check and balance each other — or even provisions for holding elections by the sovereign people. The problem is the weaving of the Communist Party into the very fabric of the Cuban Constitution, for in reality the party dominates and directs the implementation of each and every provision of that long and wordy document.

It's hard, after all, to have truly free elections when a single political party or a group of organizations under its control nominates a single candidate to run for the National Assembly and Council of State. It's hard to exercise the freedoms of speech and press when they must be exercised in a manner that's in keeping with the socialist nature of the state, and the state is not shy about limiting communication to enforce the proviso. And it's hard to do much reform outside the party structure when the leaders of the party can call a state of emergency to basically put an end to such foolishness.

Arturo observed, "It has now been over ten years since the last Congress of the Communist Party was held. It's hard to have a debate within the party when the party refuses to hold a congress."

The daughter replied, "They know that's the best way to avoid change. Soon after he came into office, Raúl called a meeting of the Central Committee and said to them, 'We need to hold a congress,' but there has been no real movement in that direction. And, of course, no election of delegates means there can be no debate." She sighed. "There is simply no project for the future!"

There were nods all around. The storm was beginning to let up. The winds were dying down. She opened the shutters of the stuffy room and air freshly bathed by the rain rushed in. We all took a long deep breath. She continued: "There is no clear idea of socialism in the 21st century. They're still selling Cuba as a place of the 1950s, not a place of the future. And there is no clear platform to discuss reform."

Relieved though I was by the cooling of the room, I felt a vague distress over the generally pessimistic views I had been hearing for the past two hours. I respected a need for balance, but sought relief in a single question, pointing at the laptop and desktop computers in the parlor: "Will the Internet take the debate to the people?"

I was thinking of Yoani Sánchez and her influential blog. I was unaware that, roughly at this time, the state was clamping down on Cuban usage of the Internet. Soon Sánchez would be making her secret video of the confrontation at the Melía Cohiba in which Reinaldo, her husband, protests the new restrictions as violating his constitutional right to freedom from discrimination based on his nationality. So I could not take solace in the fact that some Cubans do indeed know their constitutional rights.

The father, who had remained relatively quiet during the conversation, spoke up: "No! Not yet." He made clear that he would like to see more change, but was (emphatically) not hopeful of seeing it soon. He insisted, "There is still much stagnation. And there are not yet a lot of reforms."

The daughter explained, "The party does not have the political will to change at this time. There is simply no political culture where people are trained to give and take their differing views. There is no reward for dissent and so there is not a lot of dissent. We need a debate where dissent is natural."

I paused over that last sentence. Dissent was at the core of reform. And I suddenly appreciated, with a depth I had not fully felt since the last time I taught U.S. constitutional law, the genius of the system to which I had pledged my allegiance. The American system, in its totality, has a capacity for self-correction that is not evident in the Cuban system. Americans exercise their rights to choose among multiple candidates in hotly contested, frequent elections and Americans openly debate their economic, political, and legal differences 24–7 on TV and the Internet.

As of the summer of 2009, Cubans simply did not seem to have the same institutional drive to self-correct, and their way of life reflected it. The economy could be resting in hell and dissident journalists could be resting in jail, but among the people — the masses — there was no deeply felt, widespread demand for immediate, sweeping political change. I often think about my debate with the artist Pedro García Espinosa, Arturo's former neighbor. At one point I had laughed and said, "This debate that we are having today, it is all about your views and my views. The 'thesis' and the 'anti-thesis.' If you are such a good Marxist, then why isn't there more synthesis?"

It's true. The debate was totally polarized. There was no effort at compromise, no common point of view, *no accommodation of competing interests.* And certainly no synthesis of ideas and values. It was just like the talking heads on cable TV.

I left Arturo with the two professors of history and walked back to my *casa* under the shelter of the travel umbrella that Carolyn had forced me to bring. I felt saddened by the less optimistic tone of the afternoon, all the talk of stagnation and the slowing down of reforms. It was a counterpoint I had to hear, but dispiriting just the same.

Still, I couldn't help but grab at the positive. The younger professor, the daughter, was clearly less pessimistic than her father. And the computers they had stuffed into their little parlor evidenced their obvious desire to connect with the world. That was two out of three of the new Holy Trinity: the youth, the Internet, and travel.

Later that night, waiting for Arturo at his father's apartment off Calle 26, I chatted with Arturo Sr. He had made me feel comfortable in his home after many visits. I was younger than him but older than his son and he knew I did a lot of work with his son.

At our feet sprawled his big Siberian Husky with its crystal blue eyes and smooth, sleek coat. I leaned over and scratched him behind his ear. He wagged his tail.

Arturo Sr. said, "Tokker remembers you."

Half-heartedly I asked Arturo Sr. some questions about the business trips he took each year to China. Half-heartedly we talked about the state of Fidel's health and we wondered whether the older brother was still telling the younger brother what to do. Then I asked him, a bit out of the blue, "Out of all the reforms that people are talking about here in Cuba, which one would be the most important to you?"

Arturo Sr. — still thin and sharp, but with a head full of grey, experienced hair — comes from the School of Kindly Gentle Fellows, much like Father Carlos Manuel and Professor Paul Freund. He smiled a smile at me that only a parent can smile, and said, "You know, it is very hard to travel for Cubans. It is hard for us to get the visas. And it is very expensive. Like the Internet, so expensive. But I would like to be able to visit my sons in the United States." He meant Arturo and another two sons who live in San Jose.

"Why," I asked, "do you think it is so hard for Cubans to travel abroad?"

I expected something about the government, the laws, or the politics of the issue.

Arturo Sr. just shrugged and said, "It's a problem of the mind."

When you fly from Toronto to Chicago, you clear U.S. Customs before you board your plane. Arturo and I both declared on our entry forms that we had been to Cuba. There was no need to lie, for we both had the benefit of a license. The initial screening officer predictably sent us to a secondary screening area — a large, brightly lit, separately enclosed space behind a thick glass door — where we would be asked some predictable questions. Probably our bags would be searched as well.

Arturo approached the second screening officer. The officer, named Gomez, according to his name tag, was new to the job and had not faced an American openly returning from Cuba before. He started asking questions and Arturo gave him answers; soon the language was slipping in and out of Spanish and two Latin macho temperatures were rising. Arturo was saying, "If you would just let me see a computer terminal, I would be able to look it up and show you."

Officer Gomez was trying to act as courteous as his counterparts in Cuba had acted toward me two weeks before. But he was having a hard time of it.

I sat in a simple metal and plastic chair off to the side and watched as he said, "Look, amigo, there's no need to get huffy about this. I'm just trying to help you get through. But you've got to help me, too. Tell me again why it's all okay. Tell me in your own words."

In fact, Arturo was also having a hard time of it. He was traveling pursuant to a "general license," which, unlike my "specific license," did not require a piece of paper with the seal of the Treasury Department. He was trying to explain to Officer Gomez but Officer Gomez wasn't getting it. Finally, I raised my hand like a schoolboy and said, "Excuse me, officer, but I think I could help clear this up if you'd let me speak."

Officer Gomez clearly didn't know whether to smack me or thank me. "Who are you?" he asked.

Before I could answer, Arturo said, "He is a lawyer and —"

Officer Gomez said, "Then why don't you tell your client here —"

And I said, "He is not my client, sir. I am not representing him as a lawyer. But we are working together and —"

"Do *you* have a license to go to Cuba?"

"Yes, sir, here it is." I handed him my piece of paper. I added, "I've also made a copy for you for your files. Here it is."

Officer Gomez took the copy and started reading, comparing it to the original. Arturo and I glanced at each other. Between the two of us, one of us must surely have felt a little like that bird on the wire atop that Yoani Sánchez blog. Then Officer Gomez handed my original back to me and asked, "Why doesn't he have one of these?"

I explained, "As of this date, things are changing when it comes to the regulations concerning travel by Americans to Cuba. I am traveling under a 'specific license,' which means I applied to the Treasury Department for permission to travel there — in my case, to do research on a book I am writing about the island — and the Treasury Department gave me the license. Arturo is traveling under what is called a 'general license,' which means the Treasury Department does not require him to get a piece of paper beforehand. It just requires him to be able to demonstrate why he qualifies for the license. In his case, it is because he is an American citizen who has close family — a father, great-grandmother, aunts and uncles — on the island and he went there to visit them. He is also a Ph.D. candidate who is allowed to go to Cuba for the purpose of conducting research there."

Officer Gomez looked askance at me. "Why didn't he say so before?"

"I think he was trying to," I said. "But as you can see, it is very complex."

"Does he have anything that shows he has close family on the island?"

I looked at Arturo, who by now had spread a banquet of documents on the table to demonstrate his bona fides. Arturo selected some pieces of correspondence that showed his father's return address in Havana. Then he selected a previous license he had gotten from the Treasury Department for a trip he had taken back in the days when a specific license was required — just a few weeks before.

"Why does he have this one?" asked Officer Gomez. "And why doesn't he have to have one now?"

I said, "The president has just announced the removal of all restrictions on travel by Cuban Americans to see close family on the island. The regulations are currently in the process of being changed. In March the Treasury Department issued a 'guidance' or notice that said very clearly that you could rely on the presidential order pending the revision of the regulations."

Officer Gomez called his supervisor. Temperatures dropped.

The supervisor arrived, heard what was going on, and called someone else, who immediately appeared in the secondary screening area to show Officer Gomez how to process the OFAC forms that would show his satisfaction that we had been to Cuba pursuant to a legal license.

This room is a whole lot nicer than its Cuban counterpart, I thought. *But we are now up to four different government agents. One more and they'll match what the Cubans threw at me. It's like* Alice in Wonderland.

The fourth U.S. Customs officer looked at my passport, then my license, then inside my bags. He sent me on my way, to wait for Arturo on the other side of Security.

Twenty minutes later, Arturo came out of Security. "Luckily we got here in plenty of time," he said, none the worse for wear. "We still have an hour before our flight leaves for Chicago."

I was a little surprised that he was not more rattled than he seemed. I, after all, admit to having been rattled somewhat by my experience of being detained and interrogated upon entering Cuba. Arturo, I knew, had once before experienced difficulty entering the United States after a trip to the island. Why was he being so cool about the whole thing?

I asked him and here's what he said: "Harlan, you forget what I used to do. When I came to the United States, I told Walter Scheuer — my Jewish friend in New York who sponsored my studies at Columbia — everything about it. He told me to always tell the truth to officials and comply with all the rules, because America is a country of laws. If there are still problems, he said to me, we will hire a lawyer, and we can afford it."

Then Arturo winked at me, an unusual show of humor for him. I could not help but notice that the more we worked together, the more he acknowledged his past.

We walked down the concourse together, chatting amiably, having once again run the gauntlet of economics, politics, and law.

PART III

THE FUTURE OF CUBA

Chapter Seven

Silly Fantasies

We shall begin this chapter with a quiz. What is fact and what is fiction?

[a] At the end of the last century, a mysterious old man wandered around Cuba, preaching political reform. According to many on the island, he may or may not have been the legendary Che Guevara, who may or may not have survived his assassination in the jungles of Bolivia.

[b] During World War II, the novelist Ernest Hemingway, based outside Havana, worked with the FBI to keep tabs on Nazi activity in and around Cuban waters. He even chased German submarines in his fishing boat *The Pilar*.

[c] In the late 1990s, a retired Cuban spy who was once a hero of the Revolution smuggled his family's ancient Spanish treasure off the island. He intended to sell it and invest the proceeds in multinational biotech companies.

[d] Also in the late 1990s, a detective from Moscow traveled to Havana to investigate the murder of a former Soviet agent and uncovered a scheme to assassinate Fidel Castro.

[e] In June 2009, a 72-year-old State Department veteran and his wife — identified in their indictments as "Agent 202" and "Agent 123" — were arrested in Washington, D.C., and charged with spying for Cuba over a thirty-year period.

And the answers:

[a] Pure fiction, and also the plot of a novel titled *I, Che Guevara*, published in 2000 under the name "John Blackthorn," the pseudonym of former U.S. Senator Gary Hart of Colorado, who had been traveling back and forth to Cuba for years on secret backdoor missions for the U.S. government.[1]

[b] Genuine fact, though a highly fictionalized version can be found in the novel titled *The Crook Factory* by Dan Simmons. The government doc-

uments that detail Hemingway's wartime activities on behalf of U.S. Intelligence were released to the public in the 1980s and can be found on the Internet.[2]

[c] More fiction, the plot of a novel I wrote called "Cardozo's Treasure," which has never been published but has been optioned for a movie to be shot on location in Havana. When several Cuban officials reviewed the screenplay, they declared, "There cannot be a contemporary crime drama set in Cuba, because we have no crime." Accordingly, with a few strokes of the screenwriter's pen, my retired Cuban spy in the late 1990s became a clean cop in a dirty department in 1957 — when there was plenty of crime in Cuba.

[d] Also fiction, the plot of *Havana Bay* by novelist Martin Cruz Smith.[3]

[e] And this one is 100 percent true, according to the Justice Department press release that described the arrests,[4] the guilty pleas that were entered some months later, and the federal court that sentenced the State Department veteran to life in prison, and his wife to six years in prison, in the summer of 2010.[5]

Here's what the tapes, allegations, pleas, and findings reveal about Agents 202 and 123: Walter Kendall Myers was 72 in the spring of 2009. A great-grandson of Alexander Graham Bell, he earned his doctorate from the Johns Hopkins School of Advanced International Studies and began working for the State Department in 1977. Initially, he served as an instructor at the Foreign Service Institute. He traveled to Cuba in late 1978 at the invitation of an official who worked at the Cuban Mission to the United Nations in New York. During this trip, Cuban intelligence assessed Myers' potential as an agent.

Six months later, while he and his wife Gwendolyn were living a counterculture lifestyle in South Dakota — growing their own pot in their basement — the official from the Cuban Mission visited them. He recruited them to spy for the Cuban government. After they agreed, Cuban intelligence ordered Myers to return to Washington and seek a job with the State Department or CIA. He went back to the State Department in 1980.

From 1988 to 1999, Myers worked for both the Foreign Service Institute and the Bureau of Intelligence and Research (the INR). He began working full-time for the INR about a decade ago. From July 2001 until his retirement in October 2007, Myers served as a senior analyst specializing in European affairs. He had daily access to classified information and received his top-secret security clearance in 1985.

Throughout these years Myers and his wife kept a short-wave radio in their apartment, which they used to receive encrypted messages from Cuban intelligence. They decoded these messages with a decryption program provided by their handlers. The FBI routinely collects high-frequency messages broadcast by Cuban intelligence to its assets and began to identify messages that were broadcast to the couple's handler. It probed deeper and found emails sent to the couple in 2008 and 2009 by a known Cuban agent.

On April 15, 2009, an undercover FBI source, posing as another Cuban agent, approached Myers outside the Johns Hopkins School of Advanced International Studies, where he had been an adjunct since the 1980s. The source congratulated Myers on his recent birthday and gave him a cigar. He told Myers that he'd been sent by his handlers. Myers agreed to meet again later that day at a hotel and offered to bring Gwendolyn with him. At that later meeting the couple told the source about their activities on behalf of Cuban intelligence. "We have been very cautious ... careful with our moves and, uh, trying to be alert to any surveillance," Myers said to the FBI source.

During this and later meetings, the couple described how they were recruited and how they operated. Walter was known as "Agent 202" and Gwendolyn was known as "Agent 123." They had met personally with Cuban spies in Mexico, Argentina, Brazil, Ecuador, Jamaica, New York, and Trinidad and Tobago. They often passed information "hand to hand" because that way was the most secure. Gwendolyn's favorite technique was exchanging shopping carts in a grocery store because it was "easy enough to do." Walter claimed he typically memorized or took notes about the information he took from the State Department. "I was always pretty careful," he said. "I usually didn't take documents out," though he did on occasion.

An analysis of the hard drive on Myers' work computer showed that from August 2006 until his retirement, he viewed over 200 sensitive or classified documents about Cuba while serving as a senior analyst for Europe. Many were marked "top secret."

On May 4, 2009, Walter and Gwendolyn Myers were arrested and charged with acting as spies for Cuba. "The clandestine activity alleged in the charging documents, which spanned nearly three decades, is incredibly serious and should serve as a warning to any others in the U.S. government who would betray America's trust by serving as illegal agents of a foreign government," declared David Kris, assistant attorney general.

The Cuban Intelligence Service is considered among the best in the world. It has many agents operating in the United States. Cuban spies are notoriously hard to detect because Cuban intelligence specializes in recruiting "true believers" who generally don't leave money trails. Myers was one of them. He and Gwendolyn were planning to sail to Cuba and live there on their boat. They considered Cuba their home. That appears to be fact.

But often it's hard to tell the fact from the fiction — the true from the false — when it comes to Cuba. Fantasies abound. Romantic illusions of a "socialist paradise" distort the views of the left. The right recoils from the "brutal dictator" only 90 miles from U.S. shores. I say, "It's all true." Cuba is a land of deep contradictions and competing truths. And the truths are usually more interesting than the fantasies.

Fantasy #1: The Exiles Go Home and Reclaim Their Properties

On April 4, 2009, Arturo sat on a panel during a conference on Cuba at the University of Miami. Before he boarded his plane in Denver, he winked at me and said, "I am going into the lion's den." Some of his friends and family had advised him against speaking at the conference. It could be a minefield.

Arturo and I had talked about it. He had been approached by Alex Correa, one of the leaders of Roots of Hope, the young Cuban American group that sponsored the panel. Correa, who had read some of Arturo's articles in exile publications, had offered Arturo an opportunity to talk. "I must go," Arturo had told me. "Whatever reasons our parents had to fight their battles, we need to move on. It's time to think about Cuba and Cuba's relations with the United States from new perspectives."

The day before his panel presentation, Arturo explored the audience. His friend Dan Erikson, author of *The Cuba Wars: Fidel Castro, the United States, and the Next Revolution*, who was then working for the Inter-American Dialogue, discussed the advantages of easing U.S. travel restrictions as a way to help Cuba transition to a market economy and a more open Cuba. And Jaime Suchlicki, a University of Miami professor, spoke passionately: "The Jews waited two thousand years to return to their motherland, while we, Cubans, have only waited for fifty years. Let's be patient." Arturo's friend Sheryl Gold opened her eyes in dismay when half the audience applauded Dr. Suchlicki. But Arturo was optimistic; there was another half who behaved rationally. It was for that second half that Arturo had prepared his presentation.

The next day, things got off to a good start. Arturo wore his nice dark suit, a white shirt, and a tie, even though the other panelists dressed casually. The man to his right sported silver hair that was closely cropped and wore a polo shirt. The man to his left was bald and wore an open-collared shirt under a blazer. To his right sat the fourth panelist in shirtsleeves.

Arturo once told me, "I always wear a coat and tie for my speaking engagements. Let the others look casual. This way I show respect to whomever I am talking to."

The panel sat behind a long table draped with the logo of the group sponsoring the conference in both English and Spanish: Roots of Hope — *Raices de Esperanza*. It was supposed to be about Cuban American reconciliation and the morning's discussion was supposed to be about academic exchanges as part of the process.

When his turn came, Arturo charmed the audience with a story about his early days in America. It was only eight months after he had moved to New York City and enrolled at Columbia for his second master's degree. He was living across the street from Grant's Tomb and became acquainted with some folks from the Civil War Round Table who were visiting the tomb. They invited him to go on a bus tour with them to the battlefield at Gettysburg. He went along.

Nearing the battlefield, the bus stopped and everyone on it, except Arturo, changed their clothes. "They were all reenactors!" he exclaimed, delivering his punchline perfectly, amiably, affably — and earning friendly laughter from the audience.

Then he told how he visited the museum on the battlefield and found himself marveling at the photographs from the celebration that had honored the 10th anniversary of the Battle of Gettysburg. "These were people who had fought for the Confederacy and people who had fought for the Union, and they were talking to each other," said Arturo.

The ability of the North and South to reconcile after such a bloody conflict not only amazed him but also caused him to wonder why it should be so hard for Cubans and Americans to reconcile.

It was a skillful lead-in to his presentation about academic exchanges and international reconciliation. Still, when he moved from the battlefield of Gettysburg to the battlefield of Miami, the mood in the audience split. Many remained positive toward him. To some, however, he could talk all about reconciliation being a process and not an event — it didn't matter. And he could talk all about academic exchanges between Cuban and American institutions acting as "bridges, walls and spoilers" — it still didn't matter.

Half of the audience, give or take, turned cold. These people had little interest in hearing about reconciliation or academic exchanges if the message was not about putting the Castro brothers out of power. They had a different agenda. So when the question-and-answer session began, some sparks did fly. Arturo held his ground.

The atmosphere grew heated — you can see it plainly on the YouTube video.[6] That video later drew eleven comments. Several were hostile. One asked, "What is a university doing hiring a former member of the 'Ministry of the Interior' who is still defending a totalitarian dictatorship as a success in the papers?"

Arturo bristles at the allegation: "Even among young people there are still many who are not interested in a real dialogue. Despite growing up under the U.S. Constitution and the First Amendment, they've been as indoctrinated as the young hardliners in Cuba. It is a clash of ideologies and passions without any sense of pragmatism or the need to address urgent issues. Look at any of my articles. You will find people arguing against many things I never wrote, accusing me — McCarthy style — of being a communist, or an agent for Castro, or even assuming that I am a homosexual because I am not married. When they don't have any real arguments to defend the travel ban, they resort to character assassination. For example, my school in Cuba was called 'los camilitos,' meaning 'little Camilos,' in honor of Camilo Cienfuegos, a major hero of the Revolution. But some of my critics don't even know who he was, or the real name of the school, so they talk about 'los carmelitos' as if it were some sort of Catholic Order of St. Carmel. Originally I didn't understand, but now I do. Cuban Americans are a community traumatized by a real revolution, as the Americans, the Russians, or the French were. Revolutions can represent progress but they also can cause many injustices. There are politicians who exploit these traumas to distract and keep the support of the community. And let's not forget the influence of American politics."

The point is that many in the Cuban exile community in Florida have no genuine desire to reconcile. They have a very different fantasy. They fantasize about returning to their family homes in Cuba, reclaiming their properties, and presiding over the quick conversion of the nasty communist state into a lively, prosperous capitalist country — under their rule.

These fantasies — the single most persistent myth when it comes to Cuba — have fueled a battle against not only the Castro brothers but also the people on the island. Remember, the embargo is not made of "smart sanctions," targeting only the elite. The embargo targets the whole country. And this feud, due to the importance of Florida to national politics, has driven U.S. foreign policy for over 50 years. As Arturo has said on many occasions, "The dream of a big conga line with all the exiles dancing in the streets of Havana has been the most paralyzing fantasy in the history of American foreign policy."

But for many reasons, this dream will never come true. It has no business guiding American foreign policy any longer. From a military point of view, there was a revolution — a civil war — in Cuba during the 1950s and 1960s, and Fidel won it. The Cuban Armed Forces of the future will emerge from the Cuban Armed Forces of today. The opposition forces have no military capability and control no part of Cuba's national territory.

In fact, the agreements that ended the missile crisis also ended the ability of the United States to force regime change on Cuba through outright military intervention. No more Bay of Pigs. And recall what was stated unequivocally in the Lugar Report that was issued in February 2009 and discussed in Chapter Four:

The Cuban regime is institutionalized.

The Cuban government remains riddled with deep problems including resource constraints, inefficiency, and corruption, but it continues to function nonetheless. It exercises control over its territory, manages government functions such as taxation, policing, and delivery of social services, and engages in effective international diplomacy.

Though the Cuban Revolution first emerged as a popular movement, the process of institutionalization that began in the 1970s has strengthened and formalized the political structure to the extent that the island's institutions occupy an important role in the governance of Cuba. This process has been accelerated by Fidel Castro's retirement in 2008 and the accompanying departure from his charismatic but erratic leadership style. Under Raúl Castro, decision-making relies on more regularized and predictable channels such as the Cuban Communist Party, the National Assembly, and government ministries.

While a popular uprising against the government cannot be completely ruled out, staff concluded that a sudden collapse of the [Government of Cuba] is unlikely given the institutionalized nature of the regime and the absence of an external war or other catalyst. Moreover, the internal opposition does not appear sufficiently well developed to precipitate a negotiated transition, while external opposition efforts have been proven peripheral. It is thus more likely that the post–Castro era will be led by factions of the current regime.

Consequently, the basic premise of U.S. policy — that a liberal democracy will arise in the post–Castro era without political continuity from the current system — is unlikely. This is not to say that a democratic transition is impossible or inevitable, but rather that Cuba's future leadership will not be tabula rasa. By limiting engagement with Cuba's second-tier leaders, the [U.S. government] foregoes the opportunity of establishing ties that might positively influence the advancement of U.S. interests in the near future.[7]

In other words, Americans should stop waiting for Fidel to die.

The United States should forge ahead with changing its foreign policy toward Cuba. Neither Fidel's death, nor the end of his little brother's presidency, however near or far off in the future it may prove to be, will dictate the future.

Someday monetary reparations, calculated in accordance with international law, might well be paid to Cuban American exiles, as part of an overall settlement incidental to normalization of relations. But nobody is giving the Bacardi family or the Diaz-Balart family or any other family back their plantations and mansions, which, by the way, have long since been subdivided into apartments, distributed among the people, or given as rewards to the elite. In any case, they are crumbling and in sad disrepair. They no longer exist as they did in the dream.

And the dream itself is fading. Cuban American pro-embargo politicians no longer represent the views of their constituency on the Cuban issue.[8] The most strident right-wing Cuban American exiles tend to be older. Many have been dead for years. Others are aging and dying off. Younger Cuban Americans tend to be less ideological and more flexible. They show little interest in joining the "big conga line." They have different aspirations.

Simple demographic changes are killing the dream. In 2007 the Cuban Research Institute at Florida International University released a poll that showed how much these demographic changes were impacting the views of Cuban Americans. Its executive summary states in part:

> Cuban American residents of Miami–Dade County are generally concerned about the need for change on the island but they are far from monolithic in their support for different policies regarding US/Cuba relations. There are major differences of opinion on many issues.
>
> • In spite of the recent occurrences on the island, the Cuban American community is guarded in its expectation of *major political change* occurring in the near future....
>
> • Approximately 65 percent of respondents signal that they would *support a dialogue* with the Cuban government, up from 55.6 percent in the 2004 Cuba poll. The percentage of survey respondents supporting such a dialogue has risen from approximately 40% in the 1991 poll to the current year's mark which is the highest in the history of the poll.
>
> • Although only 23.6% feel that the *embargo has worked well*, 57.5 percent of the Cuban-American population expressed *support for its continuation*. The percentage of the respondents supporting the embargo declined from 66 percent in the 2004 poll. In fact, this is the lowest percentage of the population ever expressing support for the embargo.
>
> • Respondents have specific requirements triggering the *lifting of the U.S. embargo*. Approximately 29 percent of respondents would like to *put an end to the embargo immediately* without any preconditions. Another 8 percent would end the embargo *upon the death of Fidel*. About 11 percent would wait until *both Fidel and Raul* were gone. Approximately 6 percent would wait until the economic system changes on the island (without any changes to the political system) occurred ... while 10 percent would wait until *democratic changes* occurred (without economic changes). Finally, about 35% would wait until both the economic system and political system had changed....
>
> • 55.2 percent would support allowing *unrestricted travel to Cuba*....
>
> • Approximately 57.2 percent would support *establishing diplomatic relations* with the island....
>
> • Approximately 15.6 percent would be very likely and 13.1% somewhat likely to *return to live on the island* if the country's government changed to a democratic form.[9]

The FIU poll showed major changes in the attitudes of Cuban Americans. But more recent polls — taken since President Obama lifted restrictions on travel for family visits and limits on remittances — show an even more dramatic acceleration of the trend. In April 2009, Bendixen & Associates of Miami released the results of a broad survey with these major findings:

- A substantial majority of Cuban and Cuban American adults in the United States — 64 percent — support the changes in Cuba policy announced ... by President Barack Obama that lift all restrictions for Cubans in the United States on travel and remittances to Cuba. Fifty percent of Cubans said that they "strongly support" the policy changes while only 20 percent said that they "strongly oppose" them.
- Approximately 240,000 Cuban adults would like to travel to Cuba....
- Two-thirds of Cuban and Cuban American adults — 67 percent — support the lifting of travel restrictions for all Americans so they can also travel to Cuba....
- The Cuban American community splits on the issue of the commercial embargo against Cuba. Forty-two percent believe that it should be continued while 43 percent believe that it should be terminated....
- President Barack Obama receives surprisingly high ratings from Cuban Americans — a group that has very strong ties to the Republican Party. Two-thirds of all Cuban adults (67%) give him a favorable rating while only 20 percent give him an unfavorable rating.[10]

Reuters reported that "Fernand Amandi, an executive vice president of Bendixen, said Obama's approval rating was the highest Cuban Americans had bestowed on any president since the Republican Ronald Reagan in the mid–1980s and the highest ever for a Democrat."[11] And the *New York Times* said the survey reflected "a stunning change of heart now shared by a wide majority of Cuban-Americans."[12]

The dream of the "big conga line" is dying with the times. Even older, more conservative Cuban Americans are letting go. Amid the economic gloom of 2009–2010, one industry alone enjoyed a booming business: the handful of specialized travel agents, mostly based in Miami, who book flights from the United States to Cuba for family visits. Their business simply exploded.[13]

Fantasy #2: Cuba Becomes the Fifty-First State in the United States

Here's a fantasy that's even more extreme and less likely than fantasy #1. Writing in *Esquire* magazine in 2007, Thomas P.M. Barnett envisioned this version:

- Fidel Castro croaks and brother Raul ends up running things for a bit, experimenting with markets and letting in a trickle of foreign investment from "trusted" sources.
- Raul is soon replaced by some "national unity" committee that reflects the growing splits within the next generation of leaders over how far market reforms should proceed. Meanwhile, the money seeping in from Miami's Cubans grows to a flood and travel restrictions are radically reduced in response to popular demand.
- Within five years, Cuba holds its first roughly free presidential election, and one

or more candidates, with substantial outside financial backing, stumps openly for American statehood.

• Once that match gets lit, watch Florida hold every subsequent American presidential candidate hostage to the Cuba-statehood plank.[14]

This scenario is not plausible. Mr. Barnett should have his tongue in his cheek. A U.S.-centric view of the world that assumes everyone wants to be just like us — indeed, be one of us — finds little resonance in today's Cuba. Recall our interview with the staff of *Espacio Laical* and the editor's insistence that his nation's internal affairs should be left to its people and their government: "Cubans must be the ones who demand change."

The ideals of nationalism, self-determination, and sovereignty remain extremely strong on the island — stronger, in all likelihood, than communism. Cubans have a deep sense of anti-colonialism and oppose any idea of a foreign protectorate handling their affairs. Their Constitution explicitly states the following:

> The Republic of Cuba espouses the principles of anti-imperialism and
> [a] ratifies its aspirations to a valid, true and dignified peace for all states, big or small, weak or powerful, based on respect for the independence and sovereignty of the peoples and the right to self-determination;
> [b] establishes its international relations based on the principles of equality of rights, self-determination of the peoples, territorial integrity ... and the other principles proclaimed in the United Nations Charter and in other international treaties which Cuba is a party to....
> [d] advocates the unity of all Third World countries in the face of the neocolonialist and imperialist policy which seeks to limit and subordinate the sovereignty of our peoples, and worsen the economic conditions of exploitation and oppression of the underdeveloped nations;
> [e] condemns imperialism, the promoter and supporter of all fascist, colonialist, neocolonialist and racist manifestations, as the main force of aggression and of war, and the worst enemy of the peoples;
> [f] repudiates direct or indirect intervention in the internal and external affairs of any state and, therefore, also repudiates armed aggression, economic blockade, as well as any other kind of economic or political coercion, physical violence against people residing in other countries, or any other type of interference with or aggression against the integrity of states and the political, economic and cultural elements of nations.[15]

Cuba is not about to become the fifty-first state. The idea is pure fantasy.

Arturo sees it this way: "One problem with the dream of a return of the right-wing exiles to power in Havana is that it ignores changes in demography on both sides of the Straits of Florida. The traditional exile was white and urban — and likely from Havana. Today's Cuban population is predominantly black and mulatto. These groups are now demanding the attention they never got in Cuban history. During the last four decades, but especially since the 1990s, there has been more discussion about race in Cuba. It is unthinkable to talk about historical claims and reparations in the case of Cuba and focus exclusively on the injustices committed by the Revolution. Why would the injustices of nationalizations in the 1960s be more important than the legacy of slavery or racial discrimination?

"I am always surprised when I tell people about the gap in visions between the right-wing exiles in Miami and the Cubans on the island, including most of the dissidents. Many say those in Miami do not really want to return to their homes on the island and nobody would actually try to recover their little apartments in Old Havana or Vedado. But — as if this were reasonable — they also say the big companies and the big mansions should be open to claims by their former owners who want them back. According to this odd view, basically everybody who took sides against the Revolution and lost a house or property, or suffered a human rights violation, or simply took up arms against Castro and lost, must be entitled to compensation.

"This is nonsense. The first priority of the Cuban state is to improve the living conditions on the island and reduce the possibilities of violent conflict among Cubans. The idea of taxing the Cuban people of today, or using loans from other countries, just to pay compensation to the exiles in Florida is politically and ethically ridiculous. Putting these property claims at the top of the U.S. agenda can only create conflict and hostility. To compensate and distribute wealth — to have a welfare state — Cuba must have wealth.

"The main task facing Cuba today is economic development and there is no reason or important national interest that should stop Washington from helping. Transitions to more open political systems, either through liberalization or through democratization, tend to be more secure and stable when there is economic growth.

"If, after several years of pro-market economic growth, the Communist Party faces a crisis and there is a split among the leaders and a defection of the broad middle class, then major change could occur more quickly. But in that case, a move to representative democracy would happen as a result of the leadership's decision that it should change by getting into some kind of power-sharing arrangement with others. This might well be the best path: increasing democratic contestation and using the existing Cuban Constitution as a basis for expanding popular participation and accountability within the system.

"Based on my conversations with a significant number of intellectuals — college professors, community leaders, and those connected to religious communities — I believe the left-leaning political culture extends beyond the mere members of the party or the active supporters of the regime. These people are very critical of the government's policies from social democratic, Christian democratic, or even more Western liberal perspectives, but they do not belong to the opposition — not out of cowardice but because they do not believe that change will come from that direction.

"Many of these people share the ideas I have about preserving the health care and education systems developed by the Revolution, the need for gradualism, and the wisdom of a sequence of change in which economic reforms and liberalization come first, leaving electoral contests to come later. The idea that the intelligentsia and the people connected to the market-oriented sectors of the Cuban economy are all in favor of a 'big bang' right now is wrong. Many have refused to join the opposition simply because they don't agree with its proposals. It has nothing to do with lacking courage to join with the dissidents and bloggers, as some critics have claimed. These people simply think differently.

"I do agree that a restoration of relations between Cuba and the United States would be a significant turning point in Cuban history. One myth that is dangerous to this goal, however, is the notion that younger generations of Cubans would be better partners for a dialogue with the U.S. than the 'old guard' who made the Revolution or those of my parents' generation who followed them. The simple reality is that Raúl and Fidel are still the leaders in Cuba, with both legal and popular authority. Accordingly, 'since the time for change is now,' the United States should try to solve as many problems as possible with the existing leadership, rather than waiting for another generation. The more agreement Washington and Havana reach now, the less controversial these issues will be later, since nobody could claim to be tougher with the United States than the Castro brothers.

"Something unfortunate that feeds all of these myths and fantasies is a basic lack of understanding about the cultural differences between Cubans and Americans. In the United States the phrase 'you are history' means you don't count anymore — or you are about to die. In Cuba it means something very different. It means 'you are a legend.'"

Fantasy #3: Cuba Remains the Last Socialist Stronghold; Nothing Changes

One night I wanted to take Arturo's father, his stepmother Vilna, and his cousin — a cardiologist visiting from Santa Clara — to dinner at La Guarida in El Centro. It's my favorite *paladar*, and the place where much of the movie *Strawberry and Chocolate* was filmed. But when Arturo called Enrique, the owner, to make reservations, we learned we couldn't get in until 11 o'clock. So we opted for a Chinese restaurant in Barrio Chino.

We drove in two cars because Arturo refused to ride with Tokker and his father refused to leave his beloved Siberian behind. "He loves his car rides so very much," sighed Arturo Sr. as the big dog jumped into the little backseat, wagging his tail.

I rode with Arturo and his cousin in her car. As she negotiated the narrow, winding, rutted, pock-marked back streets of Barrio Chino, Arturo crooned in her ear, "No woman, no drive" — to the tune of Bob Marley's "No Woman, No Cry." We pulled in front of a restaurant on a side street no tourist could ever find, piled out, and entered a large and lively space filled with locals chowing down on chow mein. The portions looked huge and the smells of greasy stir-fry wafted past our noses.

We ordered drinks and appetizers and Vilna, an architect, began talking to me about a problem she was facing in the renovation of an apartment owned by a relative. She drew the present plan of the kitchen on a napkin, then drew the proposal she was working on, then showed me the problem: a support pillar blocked access to the new cabinetry she wanted to install. Presumptuously, I suggested integrating the pillar into the design by building shelves around it for cookbooks and knickknacks. We drew a few more squiggles on the napkins before Vilna said, with some frustration, "I wish we could have more CAD" — computer-assisted drawing — "but we don't have the programs for it."

That led to a discussion about the use of computers on the island and all the ways computers make our lives easier. I told the cardiologist from Santa Clara about an elderly anesthesiologist who had once complained to me that her Internet connection was filtered to the point that she could not access legitimate medical websites from other countries. "That was a number of years ago," I said. "Is this still a problem for you?"

She answered that it wasn't a problem for her. And as she answered my question — after plenty of Cantonese and a few Cuba Libres — I had an out-of-body experience, intellectually speaking. I saw the five of us — the writer and scholar from the States and the engineer, architect, and cardiologist from Cuba, all sitting there talking about the most mundane things. And I realized each of the Cubans had expressed a desire — could we say a demand? — for greater Internet access, not for some sinister or subversive reason, but for the most basic one: to communicate better with others.

That's why the fantasy that nothing will change in Cuba is simply not realistic. Changes are being thrust upon the island, whether it is ready for them or not, by the needs and thoughts and desires of its own people for things like more Internet access, more travel, more tourism and technology.

Cuba is not a "socialist paradise" and the people who live there know it. They welcome these changes, but they want them to come from within, and they want them less for ideological reasons than for reasons grounded in the basic desire of people everywhere to have a decent life and to communicate effectively with each other. That's what cell phones, satellites, the Internet, travel, tourism and technology all have in common: the facilitation of basic human communication.

At this point Arturo and I stress our belief that this inherent human desire for more and better communication will result in greater Internet access and more social networking in Cuba over time, but will *not* result in people taking to the streets as we have seen over the early months of 2011 in places ranging from Tehran to Tunis to Cairo. There are several reasons for this, but the two most prominent reasons are simple: First, as was stated in the Lugar Report, the Cuban system is institutionalized. The present Cuban government is not likely to be overthrown by force or internal revolution. And second, there are already many changes and reforms that have been initiated on the island, as we have described in previous chapters of this book, and as we further describe in our final two chapters. Like a valve, these reforms release pressure in a gradual, positive way.

So there will be change in Cuba. It is simply inevitable. Or, as Thomas Friedman might say, "It is inexorable." The question is this: What will it look like? I am reminded of another dinner in Havana, this one on my first trip to the island in 1998. My friend Dan — the same Dan who witnessed my discovery of Arturo a year later at Adath Israel — and I were eating at a fine *paladar* in Vedado. It was on the ground floor of a three-story mansion, every surface of which crumbled from lack of attention due to lack of building materials. All of the interior walls were covered with movie posters, most in Spanish. Tables were arranged to encourage conversation, like a salon.

We ate stewed chicken, roasted pork, rice and beans. Nothing exotic. But there was plenty of Havana Club being poured, and the cigars were real Cohibas. Voices were raised along with spirits. Conversation turned to the Special Period, which, our host said, "was still going on but was starting to wind down."

"What's the Special Period?" I interrupted.

Our host, the husband of the husband-wife team that ran the *paladar*, explained, "When the Soviets pulled out, they took all of their foreign aid with them. Many billions of dollars. Our economy plummeted. That was the beginning of the Special Period."

"The Special Period of Austerity," added his wife, frowning.

The conversation grew serious. Dan and I were both a little surprised that our hosts became as open as they did in their criticisms of their government. Soon all of the Cubans in the *paladar* were talking about politics and the future of Cuba.

I opened my mouth to comment. Dan kicked me into silence.

One of the Cubans said, "Most people here are hopeful that when things change, we will learn from our mistakes and the mistakes of others. We want capitalism with everything it offers: prosperity and hope and riches. And we want democracy with everything it offers: liberty and freedom. But we don't want the crime and corruption. And we want to keep what is best about the Revolution. Things like education, literacy, and universal health care.

"And solidarity," added another.

"Yes, and solidarity, too. We are looking for a third way."

It was the first time I had heard the phrase used in casual speech — usually it was used in scholarly writings — so I was intrigued.

I asked, "Are you talking about a blend of capitalism and socialism along the lines of the social democracies of Europe?"

"Yes."

"No."

"Not necessarily."

"Then what do you mean?" I asked.

Dan kicked me and hissed, "Listen!"

The husband shrugged and said, "Who knows? Maybe a blend. But maybe not. Maybe there really can be a totally different, totally new alternative."

"That is what Cuba is looking for," said his wife.

And that's how it was during my first trip to the island in 1998. I've returned many times and things have certainly changed. Now there are building cranes over Havana. Your taxi driver is as likely to drive a new blue Toyota as an ancient red Buick or Chevy. Changes have been made. More are coming. And no one talks about the "third way."

In *The Second Way: The Present and Future of Brazil*, Roberto Unger — Obama's law professor and the former minister of strategic planning in Brazil — writes that everyone in his native Brazil claims they have social concerns and social causes. The main political forces are, in some manner, social democratic. He is careful to define social democracy as a commitment to representative democracy together with a regulated market-based economy and social policies that "moderate inequalities and exclusion." The similarities to classic liberalism — or what this book calls market fundamentalism — create confusion. Unger calls that confusion the "third way" and takes great pains to distinguish it from what he argues is a practical and better alternative: the "second way."

The second way is the democratizing development to be achieved [through] the renovation of the institutions that define representative democracy, the market economy, and free civil society. It is not enough to transfer resources from the richer to the poorer; it is necessary to engage in a path of reorganization of political, economic, and social institutions. This path is not revolutionary in its method: It does not require an instantaneous and radical rupture with known solutions. It may advance, step by step and part by part, even though progress achieved in one area may condition the progress that might be expected in others.... *[But] what we can and must do is humanize market practices and globalization realities with social policies.*[16]

In other words, Professor Unger largely equates the first way (neoliberal capitalist-based democracy) with the third way (merely a softened version of the same). He calls for an alternative with deeper institutional content, some of which we have discussed in previous chapters. Typically, his descriptions are razor-sharp while his prescriptions border on fuzzy. Still, it is not difficult to agree with his basic conclusion: The third way, says Unger, "represents little more than the disguise of surrender."

Chapter Eight
A Detour to Russia?

In early 1953, Raúl Castro traveled to Romania, deep in the Soviet Bloc, for the Sixth Festival of the Youth and the Students, a celebration organized by the International Federation of the Democratic Youth, an organization affiliated with world communist groups. At that time, Fidel's connection with the communist movement was minimal. He had only joined the library and bookstore of the People's Socialist (Communist) Party, where he borrowed books by Marx and Lenin. In contrast, Raúl had become a member of the Young Communist League while studying social sciences in his college years, before the brothers' unsuccessful assault on the Moncada Barracks. The connections with Soviet political activists and agents that Raúl built during his trip to Romania strengthened when he met with Soviet agents in Mexico City while preparing to overthrow Batista in Cuba. Indeed, it was Raúl who initially went to Moscow to negotiate the importation of Soviet missiles to Cuba in 1962.

The crisis that followed is a watershed moment of history.

Only one thing could have brought my family of four together on the evening of October 25, 1962: WAR!—and rumors of war. My father had always obsessed over his years in the Army, fighting Rommel in North Africa and pushing the Germans from Italy. He could have been a poster boy for post–traumatic stress syndrome at a time when no one knew what it was. The Cuban Missile Crisis really got his juices going.

I sat next to my older brother on the floor of the living room of our duplex on North 38th in Omaha, glued to the black-and-white Zenith TV. Our father sat behind us. He was agitated and loud. His solution: "Nuke the Cubans, and the Soviets too!"

The drama was nearing its climax. Adlai Stevenson, the U.S. ambassador to the United Nations, was addressing the Security Council on live TV. Only the year before, he had been humiliated when he denied allegations that the Bay of Pigs fiasco had been financed by the CIA—and the truth had soon come out. He was now determined to recapture his credibility, the subject was again our pesky neighbor ninety miles across the Straits of Florida, and the stakes couldn't have been higher. The world stood on the brink of nuclear holocaust.

Bald and bespectacled, Stevenson was a respected lawyer who had twice run for the presidency. He appeared confident in his dark three-piece suit, white shirt, and dark narrow tie. Still, a hint of weariness tugged at his eyes. It had been an exhausting week and it was only Thursday. He was ripping into Valerian Zorin, his Soviet counterpart: "I don't have your talent for obfuscation, for distortion, for confusing language, and for doubletalk. And I must confess to you that I'm glad I don't. But if I understood what you said, you said that my position had changed, that today I was defensive because we didn't have the evidence to prove our assertions that your government had installed long-range missiles in Cuba. Well, let me say something to you, Mr. Ambassador — we do have the evidence. We have it, and it's clear and incontrovertible. And let me say something else — those weapons must be taken out of Cuba."[1]

We watched as Stevenson played his cards one by one.

Nuclear brinksmanship meant something special for everyone in Omaha, because only a few miles away the Strategic Air Command (SAC) was poised at DEFCON-2, the highest alert short of war. If the Soviets launched their missiles, the SAC would be the first target — even before Washington and New York — because it was where the War Room was. Remember *Dr. Strangelove* and *Fail-Safe*? Soviet ICBMs would rain down on Omaha. Everything would vaporize.

Those of us in the seventh grade at Saunders Elementary who understood the situation would taunt the girls and show off our bravado with that word: *vaporize*. "You know, it's a great way to go. Better than radiation sickness. There's just this flash of light and you're gone. You don't even know what hits you." We knew the drills that rushed us into the basement of the old brick school to duck-and-cover in its porcelain bathrooms were a joke. With so many direct hits, nothing near Omaha would survive.

Zorin wore a lighter three-piece suit than many in the Security Council that night. And while his hair was thin and he sported glasses like Stevenson, they projected very different images. The American was dark and somber; the Soviet was light and arrogant. The fuse had been lit on their historic confrontation.

Behind me, my father insisted, "Just nuke 'em and be done with it!"

From the kitchen, my mother hissed, a rarity: "Bill, let us listen!"

Stevenson escalated his rhetoric, real anger building in his voice: "All right sir, let me ask you one simple question. Do you, Ambassador Zorin, deny that the U.S.S.R. has placed and is placing medium and intermediate-range missiles and sites in Cuba?"

Then, without waiting a beat, the sharp Chicago lawyer demanded, "Yes or no? Don't wait for the translation, yes or no?"

A loud murmur swept through the Security Council. Stevenson had been reading most of his remarks, but now he whipped off his glasses, leaned forward over his notes, and glared across the chamber at Zorin. The TV lights bounced off his shiny forehead and the wire from his earpiece dangled loosely as a second ticked by.

Zorin started to speak in Russian, looking down. Then suddenly he looked up and an odd sort of smile broke upon his face. He chuckled. The murmur in the room turned to laughter.

The translator's words hit Stevenson's ear: "I am not in an American courtroom, sir, and therefore I do not wish to answer a question that is put to me in the fashion in which a prosecutor does. In due course, sir, you will have your reply. Do not worry."

Stevenson's hands were clasped in front of him, his fingers casually entwined. He looked less studious without his glasses. A bemused expression tweaked his lips. He'd scored a point on his counterpart. He said, "You are in the court of world opinion right now and you can answer yes or no. You have denied that they exist. I want to know if you — if this — if I've understood you correctly."

Zorin replied in Russian: "Sir, will you please continue your statement? You will have your answer in due course."

The chairman of the Security Council added, "Mr. Stevenson, would you continue your statement, please? You will receive the answer in due course."

The TV cameras cut back to Stevenson. His glasses were back on. He was shuffling his papers. He delivered these lines with precision, etching them into history: "I am prepared to wait for my answer until hell freezes over, if that's your decision. And I'm also prepared to present the evidence in this room."

Two hundred miles away, former Navy lieutenant John F. Kennedy, watching the confrontation, slapped the arm of his overstuffed chair and exclaimed, "Terrific!"

Two feet behind me, former Army lieutenant William S. Abrahams gripped the arms of his vinyl recliner so tightly his knuckles turned white. He gnashed his teeth. What was the White House waiting for?

On TV Stevenson stood up and strode across the chamber to a pair of easels that had been set up. On the easels were air reconnaissance photos taken by U-2 spy planes, greatly enlarged. In his cool Midwestern voice, Stevenson walked the world through the evidence that plainly showed the extent of Soviet duplicity. All his cards were shown. All his bets were in. He left the Security Council triumphant.

Still, the Soviet ship *Grozny* steamed toward Kennedy's quarantine line.

The world held its breath while Khrushchev decided how to play his hand.

And that's how things stood when I left for school the next morning. I walked there alone, eight blocks in the autumn sun, red and yellow leaves iridescent in the light. Nothing suggested that danger still lurked in the air — until shortly before the noon break, when the principal announced over the PA system that school would close early for the weekend and we should go home and stay there.

My neighbor Johnny Robinson — blond, crew-cut, and flabby — leaned across the aisle and whispered, "It must be getting worse. They're letting us go early so we can die with our families if the Russians launch."

No one joked about vaporizing. This was all too real. The bell rang and we left. I glanced around the gravel playground, searching for the pretty girl I had a crush on, thinking she might want me to walk her home. But she was nowhere to be seen, so I set off alone, taking the longer route home that avoided passing by her street. She had a real family that loved each other; she had a place to go.

I had a place, too, but not the family part. I knew no one would be home waiting for me. My father would be at his little cleaning plant in the seedy part of downtown, next to the bus station and down the street from the old Castle Hotel, letting off steam both literally and figuratively. My mother would have left her job at the counter to moonlight at Mutual of Omaha in the accounting department. My brother would be exercising the freedoms of high school to avoid the battleground that was our home.

I stood at the light at 42nd Street, waiting for it to turn. When it did, I decided to lengthen my trip by looping around an extra two blocks. I kept my eyes glued to the sky, and though a squad of jet fighters streaked across it to the south — silver bullets in the sun — that was not unusual. I saw no B-52s and somehow that made me feel better. I didn't realize the danger was precisely the opposite: a Stratofortress overhead could not be thousands of miles away, nearing its fail-safe coordinates.

More important, I saw no streaks of missiles falling to the ground: no writing in the sky that spelled, "vaporize." Yet behind the scenes, the crisis was hitting its peak, as the *Grozny* showed no signs of slowing in the water.

I arrived home and let myself in, glad to be alone. I flipped on the TV and turned to the news. But there was no news. Kennedy and Khrushchev were exchanging private letters behind the scenes. The president's were terse and direct. The chairman's were verbose and circuitous. They were locked in mortal combat, shedding words if not blood. Kennedy was surrounded by advisors — his own little brother Bobby; Adlai Stevenson, who had flown in from New York; and a crew of political, legal, and military experts.

I turned off the TV and went up the narrow stairs to the second floor. At the top was a small bookcase that held the family encyclopedia, a basic Funk & Wagnall's that my mother bought one at a time, volume by volume, each month at the grocery store. My parents never touched these books. And my brother used them only for his high school projects. But I sought refuge in their stories whenever I had a chance.

I would pick a figure from Greek mythology or world history and read the entry, then follow the cross references at the end to additional and related sources. In that way I taught myself how to research long before high school, college, or law school. Though I wasn't feeling especially afraid, nor obsessed like my father with the very thought of war, I didn't choose mythology or history that Friday afternoon.

I pulled out Volume III and read the entry on Cuba. It was current enough to reflect Fidel Castro and his Revolution. The Year Book for 1961 even had a modest report on the Bay of Pigs. But it would be years before this little detail would be added to that watershed moment of history: It was Raúl Castro who negotiated the bringing of Soviet missiles to Cuba. He did it when he visited Moscow in July 1962.

In January 2009, Raúl went to Moscow again. The *New York Times* reported:

> The presidents of Russia and Cuba signed a strategic partnership and several other documents on Friday aimed at rekindling an alliance that collapsed after the cold war. They pledged to expand cooperation in agriculture, manufacturing, science and tourism, but studiously avoided a public discussion of military ties....
> It is part of a larger Russian push into Latin America to secure new markets, and also to swipe at the United States.... "Your visit opens a new page in the history of Russian-Cuban relations," President Dmitri A. Medvedev said at a meeting with Mr. Castro at the Kremlin on Friday.... "Without a doubt," Mr. Castro said at the meeting, "this is a historical moment, an important milestone in the relations between Russia and Cuba...."
> At an informal gathering at Mr. Medvedev's country home on Thursday, Mr. Castro waxed nostalgic, recounting the time he and Soviet comrades sat around a campfire in the forest eating salo, the cured pig fat that is a staple chaser of Russian vodka. "I've desired this for 25 years," he said through a Russian translator. "I don't know if I'll get to eat any salo with black bread, but I'm here."
> A few hours later, Mr. Medvedev invited Mr. Castro to join him by a campfire in the forest around the presidential residence, and the two dined on the Russian delicacy.[2]

Strengthening trade ties is not the same, however, as adopting the Russian model of bankrupt communism replaced by capitalism overnight. In post-communist Russia, we witnessed privatization running amok, corruption rocketing to pandemic levels, party bureaucrats making alliances with select exiles to "drive without a map"[3] so they could steal everything in sight, and oligarchs riding in Bentleys while inflation soared. All of the dangers of overly rapid liberalization marched on display. It was the exact nightmare that prompts Arturo to counsel gradualism.

And he should know. Santa Clara was home to a lot of Soviets before their withdrawal in 1989. They came from a gigantic land, a nuclear super-power, far away, culturally and ethnically diverse. They were plainly different and they acted differently. It took roughly a decade from the time of Anastas Mikoyan's visit to Cuba in 1960 for the island's elite to understand the Russian leaders and build stable relations with them.

This relationship made Cuba a unique country in Latin America. Hundreds of thousands of Cubans learned to speak Russian, and in some cases gained a sophisticated knowledge of the national psychologies, literature, films, economics, and politics of the Soviet Union and its satellites. Part of the Cuban technical, political, and military elite received training and education in Soviet institutions. Special affinities emerged between the armed forces and security services of the two countries, since many of the Russian military upper echelons took vacations on the island, where they were lavishly welcomed by the FAR. That partially explains why the links between the two militaries were never broken and why Russian military support for the FAR remained strong until the late 1990s. There were also many Russian women who married Cuban men, though not so much the other way around. In short, the alliance between Cuba and the Soviet Union was not based on Cuban subordination, in contrast to the nations in Eastern Europe, but on subsidies, common goals, and strategies more than ideology (though ideology played a significant part).

Now, many years after the Special Period triggered by the Soviet with-drawal — those awful shortages suffered by Cubans when one-third of their economy simply evaporated — many on the island still harbor resentment toward their former benefactors. They feel they were abandoned. Their ways of life and their beliefs were gutted. The experience was also a lesson; Cubans today frequently say that never again will they put all their eggs in one basket, no matter how strong or appealing it looks. When people in Cuba think of their former Soviet sponsors, there's plenty of bitter to mix with the sweet. These bittersweet memories, plus the cultural differences and the poor per-formance of the Russian model over time makes the adoption of this model by Cuba unlikely.

The desire to avoid Russia's incredible levels of corruption should itself be enough to tip the scales against it, though certainly some corrupt officials and black-market tycoons would like to take that road. Still, the Russian model is no silly fantasy. Its alternative reality beckons with the allure of quick profits, more of a danger for Cuba than an opportunity. On balance, Arturo and I believe the Russian model is the least attractive alternative facing Cuba.

Fortunately, at this time most Cubans see it that way as well.

Chapter Nine

The Chinese Model, Europe and Brazil

In 1966 Arturo Lopez-Calleja was a tall, skinny young man — he had barely earned his engineering degree from the University of Santa Clara — when he approached Comandante Lussón for permission to marry Gilda Sara Fernandez-Levy. Today, Arturo Sr. is in his mid-sixties and comfortably settled in a cozy apartment in Nuevo Vedado with his second wife Vilna, the architect. He dotes on his Siberian Husky Tokker and longs for greater opportunities to travel to see his sons in Argentina and the States.

One afternoon he and I sat, with Tokker stretched out at our feet as usual, on the patio balcony off his living room, making small talk. He had served me a sweetened frozen confection of coconut and ice, with a generous slice of the round of cheese I had brought him from the country. I scratched Tokker behind the ear, his crystal blue eyes rolled up in his head, and I thought he was dreaming of doggie heaven.

Casually I said, "Tury tells me that you travel to China quite often to buy computer equipment?" I intoned the question mark at the end of the sentence to prompt Arturo Sr. to talk about his work.

"Well," he said, correcting me, "I actually go there to buy testing machines — calibration instruments. For things like metallurgical studies, yes? And it used to be quite often but now the money to send me there is very short because of the economy."

"Do you like going there?"

"Yes, very much. I get to see a lot and learn a lot. I go to the big universities and laboratories, that sort of thing. It is very interesting. I enjoy it very much."

"Where else have you traveled?"

"Oh, let's see. I have been to Spain, Argentina, France — and Russia when it was the Soviet Union. Now China, of course."

"Do you speak Chinese?"

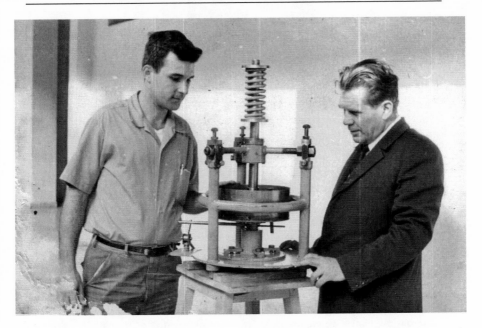

Arturo's father (left), as a young engineer, with a Soviet advisor (Arturo Lopez-Levy collection).

"Me? No. But when I am doing business in China, both sides speak English! Can you believe that?"

"So you don't use a translator?"

"Sometimes it is necessary, but not usually."

I wanted to ease him toward a discussion about the future of Cuba. He was obviously educated and well traveled. And he came from the generation immediately after the Revolution of 1959 — younger than both of the Castro brothers but older than his sons' more modern generation.

But Arturo Sr. was reluctant to respond to the direct approach. He and others had hinted vaguely that they had concerns about whether the older brother was still telling the younger brother what to do. He and others had stressed that changes were indeed coming to Cuba, but more in the future than the present — because the old guard still held the power and still clung tightly to its communist ideology.

So I became more abstract, hoping he'd feel more comfortable. "A lot of people say that Cuba will move in the direction of China. Opening up their markets to foreign investment and liberalizing the economy, while keeping the Communist Party in power. Do you think, with the changes that are coming to Cuba, it will take that route?"

"I don't know," said Arturo Sr. "It may go the Chinese way, but then again it may not. The younger people, when they get into power, may demand more change."

"What sorts of changes do you see now, directly, in your business?"

"Well, I work for the Ministry of Higher Education. Specifically, for the importing enterprise that goes out and buys supplies and things for our universities. Certainly the equipment I buy has changed with all the newer technology. And we have better engineers because we have better equipment. For me that is tangible change."

I thought perhaps I could get him to comment on China's continuing problem with counterfeiting products and labels. After all, to liberalize in the capitalist mode, countries must learn to respect property rights, and the most important forms of property rights in the future will involve intellectual property, the province of labels, trademarks, and patents — the things that pack so much into your iPhone.

"Counterfeiting is still a problem over there," said Arturo Sr. "But it is never as clear as some make it out to be. In some factories you will see the exact same thing being made with labels that say 'Made in the USA' or 'Made in Italy.' I have seen the exact same microscope but with different trademarks. One has a Chinese name and trademark, another down the same production line has a German or even American name and mark. So it's true. Over there intellectual property is not well respected."

To an author, copyrights are precious property. I paused to process.

Arturo Sr. finished his thought: "But you see, it is not so clear how much is right and how much is wrong. Some of it is wrong. But some of it is done through licenses with the companies that own the intellectual property. To the Chinese, it is not a lie — there is nothing wrong with what they are doing — because in many cases they are being asked to do it by American companies!"

The global recession of 2008–2009 prompted a lively debate among economists and policy experts over the future of capitalism. It was a debate that bears directly on the alternative realities facing Cuba in the future. On one side were those who were quick to declare the death or decline of capitalism, or market fundamentalism, or globalization, or democratization — or just about anything having to do with the West.

For example, Azar Gat, a professor of national security at Tel Aviv University, and author of *Victorious and Vulnerable: Why Democracy Won in the Twentieth Century and How It Is Still Imperiled,*[1] sparked controversy when he argued that it is not unthinkable that "authoritarian capitalist great powers" will arise to challenge the West. He pointed to China and Russia as examples. He also pointed at the weakness displayed by the West in the wake of the

Arturo's father on a business trip to China (Arturo Lopez-Levy collection).

global recession. In other words, Professor Gat attacked the "inevitability" of market-based capitalist economics — aka globalization — and their ability to drag the world into democracy. Capitalism could coexist with an authoritarian state.

Daniel Deudney and John Ikenberry, whose work was discussed in Chapter One, responded with a vengeance: "Gat's vision is remarkably devoid of reference to the myriad growing problems associated with globalization: rising interdependence, [the] growing mobility of labor, and environmental deterioration being just a few. Both theory and history suggest that liberal democratic states and the liberal international order are best equipped to grapple with these problems and seize the opportunities ahead."[2]

Still, the recession took the wind from the sails of the free-market ideologues.

By the middle of 2009 former deputy treasury secretary Roger Altman declared that globalization was in retreat and "the era of laissez-faire economics has ended. For 30 years the Anglo-Saxon model of free-market capitalism spread across the globe. The role of the state was diminishing, and deregulation, privatization, and the openness of borders to capital and trade were rising.... Now, a page has turned. The Anglo-Saxon financial system is seen as having failed.... The role of the state is expanding."[3]

Consider the case of Richard Posner, the conservative federal judge, who in 2009 published *A Failure of Capitalism: The Crisis of '08 and the Descent into Depression*.[4] His title says it all. As Jonathan Rauch wrote in the *New York Times Book Review*:

> It comes as something of a surprise that Posner, a doyen of the market-oriented law-and-economics movement, should deliver a roundhouse punch to the proposition that markets are self-correcting. It might also seem odd that a federal appellate judge ... would be among the first out of the gate with a comprehensive book on the financial crisis.... But Posner is the late Daniel Patrick Moynihan's successor as the country's most omnivorous and independent-minded public intellectual.... By the last page, not a single lazy generalization has survived Posner's merciless scrutiny, not one populist cliché remains standing.[5]

So, market fundamentalism — the version of capitalism that insisted markets were *always* better than governments at solving economic problems and that pushed deregulation, privatization and fantasies of riches trickling down to the poor — lay in ruins. The subprime bubble burst. The financial system melted down, and the U.S. government stepped in, before Obama became president, ideology be damned.

But does that mean each and every version of capitalism — every market-based system on the face of the Earth — is doomed to fail as well? Not if economists like the Nobel Prize winner Joseph Stiglitz have their way. In July 2009, Professor Stiglitz worried that people in the developing world would get the wrong message from seeing the flaws in America's social and economic system fully revealed.[6] The right message — that the roles of the government and market must be kept in balance through effective regulations, and the powers of special interests must be kept in check — would be lost.

Professor Stiglitz described how most communist countries turned to capitalism after the collapse of the Soviet Union, replacing Karl Marx with Milton Friedman as their new icon. But this simple sleight of hand didn't work. And so this fear arises:

> Many countries may conclude not simply that unfettered capitalism, American-style, has failed but that the very concept of a market economy has failed, and is indeed unworkable under any circumstances. Old-style Communism won't be back, but a variety of forms of excessive market intervention will return. And these will fail. The poor suffered under market fundamentalism — we had trickle-up economics, not trickle-down economics. But the poor will suffer again under these new regimes, which will not deliver growth. Without growth there cannot be sustainable poverty reduction. There has been no successful economy that has not relied heavily on markets. Poverty feeds disaffection. The inevitable downturns, hard to manage in any case, but especially so by governments brought to power on the basis of rage against American-style capitalism, will lead to more poverty.... Faith in democracy

is another victim. In the developing world, people look at Washington and see a system of government that allowed Wall Street to write self-serving rules which put at risk the entire global economy — and then, when the day of reckoning came, turned to Wall Street to manage the recovery. They see continued re-distributions of wealth to the top of the pyramid, transparently at the expense of ordinary citizens. They see, in short, a fundamental problem of political accountability in the American system of democracy. After they have seen all this, it is but a short step to conclude that something is fatally wrong, and inevitably so, with democracy itself.[7]

In other words, what is dead is the extreme version of market fundamentalism. What is not dead is the idea of capitalism itself. A market-based economy that is well balanced between freedoms for business and regulation by the government has become the paradigm for the future. Indeed, global markets kept operating throughout the crisis, however imperfectly. They are not going away. They are the very means by which the nations and multinationals of our world do business with each other. They buy and sell rice and beans, TVs and computers. But that does not mean there is no crisis.

In 2009, Fareed Zakaria, the editor of *Newsweek International*, published his "Capitalist Manifesto." It echoed many of the themes seen before. He wrote:

> [T]he fundamental crisis we face is of globalization itself. We have globalized the economies of nations. Trade, travel and tourism are bringing people together. Technology has created worldwide supply chains, companies, and customers. But our politics remains resolutely national. This tension is at the heart of the many crashes of this era — a mismatch between interconnected economies that are producing global problems but no matching political process that can effect global solutions. Without better international coordination, there will be more crashes, and eventually there may be a retreat from globalization toward the safety — and slow growth — of protected national economies.[8]

So what does this mean for Cuba, a nation emerging from the opposite extreme? There is little doubt, after all, that the island is moving, however gradually, away from its carefully controlled communist economy, the epitome of a "protected national" economy, to a more open system at the very time when the developed world is re-regulating both domestically and internationally.

Three "alternative realities" seem possible. Each is more likely than the fantasies discussed in Chapter Seven or the detour discussed in Chapter Eight.

Alternative Reality #1: The Chinese Model

In the late 1980s I practiced corporate and securities law with a firm in Denver. Late one wintry night in New York, I stood at a floor-to-ceiling window, thirty stories over Wall Street, gazing south at the lights of the ferries on the waters and the lit-up Statue of Liberty in the distance. Behind me legions of lawyers, accountants, and investment bankers haggled over the carcass of a once-mighty company, slicing and dicing its assets, debts, and equities into teeny-tiny little pieces. How many securities can be carved from a satellite in geosynchronous orbit, equipped with 24 transponders?

I thought, "Boy, those guys can commodify anything."

Soon after that I read one of the earliest articles written about the growing global markets for human transplant organs. I put the two together — the commodification of the body for life-saving organ transplants — and thus was born an obsession. Before I wrote and published *On the List: Fixing America's Failing Organ Transplant System* with Steve Farber, my former law partner, I wrote two unpublished novels using the organ markets as important plot points. By the mid–1990s I learned that China, which at the time executed more prisoners each year than all other countries combined, was selling the organs of executed prisoners to the elite and to foreign "transplant tourists."

I first traveled to Cuba — the forbidden island — in 1998 in search of an analog to the brutal Chinese practice in the Western Hemisphere. Why not start with Cuba, a sexy communist stronghold known in the United States for its repression?

I did not find the analog I was looking for in Cuba. First and foremost, there were very few executions in Cuba. And there was no evidence that the state had ever executed a prisoner and sold his organs. Plainly it wasn't enough to say that both Cuba and China were communist countries. There had to be more.

Why didn't they act the same way? I have asked the question of Cubans and the answer has almost always been the same. China's model — opening capitalist markets and foreign investments, and recognizing property rights, while keeping a one-party communist political system, despite local democratic openings and periodic flare-ups with pesky minorities and dissidents — may not be the best way to go.

Everyone talks about Cuba buying into the Chinese model, but few are certain it will occur. Or, if it does, that it will happen exactly in the Chinese way. Cubans harbor strong social democratic and nationalist sentiments, they are less ethnically diverse, and they have strong cultural, social and family ties to the West, especially Latin America.

Still, there is massive trade between China and Cuba. There are bound to be common interests. Their ideological ties cannot be minimized. And in the wake of the global recession of 2009, the Chinese model holds yet another attraction.

Former deputy treasury secretary Roger Altman explained in *Foreign*

Affairs that China was the one big winner because its unique political and economic system emerged from the recession relatively undamaged. Though China's growth had slowed, it remained at high levels. And when measured by its vast financial reserves, China is now the world's richest country. Its leadership is making major strategic investments that other nations cannot make, and its stature in the world is rising.[9]

Later, near the end of his article, Altman includes these ominous paragraphs:

> Only China has prevailed. China's growth did diminish but now may be picking up again. Recently, electricity consumption, freight shipments, and car sales in China have all increased. Its financial system is insulated and relatively unleveraged — and thus has been relatively unharmed. This has allowed China to direct a recent surge in lending for stimulus purposes. *Beijing's unique capitalist-communist model appears to be helping China through this crisis effectively. And measured by its estimated $2.3 trillion in foreign exchange reserves, no nation is wealthier.*
>
> All of this is enhancing China's geopolitical standing. The West is experiencing a severe economic crisis, seen as its own making, whereas China is not. The Chinese leadership is well aware of this relative advantage, even though its priorities are always domestic. Apart from its coal supplies, China is resource poor. But it has recently been making offshore investments in natural resources of a kind that others no longer can make — such as securing future oil supplies from Russia and Venezuela....
>
> This economic crisis is a seismic global event. Free-market capitalism, globalization, and deregulation have been rising across the globe for thirty years; that era has now ended, and a new one is at hand. Global economic and financial integration are reversing. The role of the state, together with financial and trade protectionism, is ascending.[10]

How should Cuba respond to this? No one doubts it is evaluating its alternatives. Adopting the Chinese model would do the least violence to its present ideology. It would keep the one-party system in power during a protracted period of economic liberalization. It would also channel Cuba's nationalist drive toward the goal of economic development, making political liberalization a secondary goal of the reforms. However, Cubans know all these reforms will come at a cost. They point to the dismantling of China's universal health care system as something they do not want to emulate. And Cuba lacks the sheer demographic weight of China, to say nothing of its financial reserves.

The lists of pros and cons — the similarities and differences between the evolution of the Chinese model at the end of the 20th century and the emergence of Cuba from strict communism at the beginning of the 21st century — could itself fill a book. I believe that in the next decade, Cuba will lean heavily in the direction of China, but it will not swallow the dragon whole. The cultural, social, geographic, and historical distinctions will see to that.

Arturo sees it this way: "On July 26, 2007 — the anniversary of Fidel's attack on the Moncada Barracks — Raúl stated that the Revolution must consider 'structural and conceptual changes,' especially in the economy. What has happened since then?

"Most of the changes prior to mid–2010 were moderate management adjustments, not structural ones. However, the removal of limits on salaries for government workers and the legalization of people having multiple jobs have prepared the ground for acceptance of a greater gap in equality in Cuban society. This seems to echo Deng Xiaoping's famous phrase, 'To be rich is glorious,' but in a softer Cuban tone.

"Following the Chinese and Vietnamese models, the Cuban government did not rush to full privatization. Instead, beginning in the early 1990s, Cuba began a gradual expansion of the role of the private sector in the economy. In the area of tourism, the construction of new hotels was conceived as part of a joint ventures strategy in which the Cuban government searched for partners among European corporations with experience in the business. This approach was later expanded to other key strategic firms, in some cases the most viable and the most profitable ones, such as the nickel mines in the northeast, the telephone companies, and the existing hotels on the beaches, which were transformed into new corporations of 'mixed property' held by the Cuban government and firms from Canada, Europe and Mexico.

"This sequence produced two distinct advantages from the nationalist perspective, both of which supported the idea of ruling for the benefit of the elite as a group, not as individualized officials connected directly to the assets. First, the firms were not privatized at a moment when their productive capacities were at their lowest, in the middle of a crisis, or during a transition. And second, by attracting owners in addition to the state, it would be more difficult to return the properties to their previous owners or to privatize them for corrupt officials without the consent of all involved parties.

"Another emulation of the Chinese model began with the development of the small private sector after 1993, despite Fidel Castro's ideology-driven attacks. This was probably the most popular reform among the Cuban population and one that many economists had advocated for decades, following the experience of communist Hungary where a small private sector provided around 10 percent of the industrial output by the mid–1980s.[11] The new self-employed and small businesses provided a buffer against the fall of the government-owned restaurants, cafeterias and reparation services, and the new unemployment. In the long run, the new private sector also created a demonstrative effect that helped the liberalization of prices since the government created stores in which it sold products at lower prices than the private sector, but far higher than those of the subsidized economy.

"The expansion of the private sector in Cuba was also accompanied by processes of de-politicization, including the increase of the role of religious communities and the relative liberalization regarding both the right to travel abroad and Cuban life in general. Although this transition to a post-totalitarian political regime has not yet reached the magnitude it has in China, let us not forget that as of this writing, Fidel Castro, the historical leader of Cuba — equivalent to Mao in China — is still alive, and the U.S. embargo is still in place. Note that American isolationist policies against China ended before Mao died. These are important factors to understand when considering change in the minds of many Cubans.

"The establishment of important institutions, before or in parallel to the economic openings to foreign investment and the creation of a small private sector, is an essential component of the gradualist approach. The need for a new tax authority is perhaps the best example. Some of these measures, as in China, have been unpopular because, due to the totalitarian features of the Cuban government, they have not been accompanied by competition and consumer protection laws. Still, in many cases the Cuban government has replaced command economy practices by state-connected capitalist monopolies.

"The hope of many is that the more the Cuban economy integrates into the world economy, the more competitive the domestic environment will become. Today the island is less isolated than ever. It has developed strong bonds with Brazil and Venezuela, the two nations competing for leadership in South America. It is less vulnerable to pressures from Europe and Canada, which have become important trading partners. It enjoys good relations with China, Venezuela, and Russia, which it uses as leverage when bargaining with the West.

"Moreover, a more market-oriented Cuban elite is emerging. Often associated with foreign investment, remittances, artists, and people who are related through business or family to foreigners and the Cuban community abroad, this proto–middle class is building aspirations for its children. Many of their sons and daughters receive extracurricular English lessons after school. They go to the beach and rent private homes or stay in hotels now open to Cubans with dollars and CUCs. They maintain legal or illegal connections to the Internet, they register on Facebook, they Twitter and they travel abroad more frequently than their revolutionary predecessors.

"Without question, Cuba will be more connected to the world in the next decade when the Internet cable between Cuba and Venezuela begins to work. Liberalizations — DVDs, cell phones, Internet, and travel — indicate more than consumer rights, however. When I was a child in Santa Clara, we had only one phone for half the block, located in the house of a militant member of the Committee for the Defense of the Revolution. Now it is completely different. Improvement of the phone system through a joint venture with an Italian phone company is making fixed lines available for even the average citizen.

"Access to information for average Cubans has risen dramatically. Foreign trade, investment, and work abroad by Cuban doctors, teachers, sports trainers, and others will also result in greater integration of the island with the outside world.

"So, can Cuba embrace a market economy, achieve economic development, and keep its one-party system? Yes, in the short term and maybe even the medium term, but not in the long run. And the 'long run' in Cuba will likely be less long than in China.

"Still, many reformers among the Cuban elite believe, as do their Chinese counterparts, that they can open their economy and continue to control the political process under one party. James Mann, a writer-in-residence at the Center for Strategic International Studies and the author of *The China Fantasy: Why Capitalism Will Not Bring Democracy to China*, describes it this way: 'As other authoritarian leaders around the world seek to stifle political opposition, they look to China.'

"Nevertheless, while the Chinese have been able to maintain a single-party system, the economic changes in that country have indeed forced important political reforms, even if they fall short of full democratization and free multiparty elections. In the same way that economic reform and openness have progressed, personal freedoms and social mobility have expanded. Even the limited experience in Cuba proves that much.

"What is happening in Cuba today has already happened to post-revolutionary systems in other countries. Once the revolutionary fervor passes, the party gradually becomes a tool of domination for the self-serving ruling elite. As a result, the earliest phases of the transition from a command economy become the most delicate, because many in power cover their actions with socialist rhetoric while using their control to appropriate parts of the society's wealth. The best example is Russia and the oligarchs. Theirs is not typical capitalism, where there are regulations and monitoring mechanisms embedded in the market economy.

"At the same time, it would be a mistake to assume that the party is only a tool of self-serving domination. The Communist Party in Cuba has a strong ideology of nationalism and social justice. It has built legitimacy on the idea of being the instrument of a revolution. Based on this legitimacy, Cuba has engendered a professional class, well educated and committed to national independence and economic development. Indeed, those in their thirties, forties and fifties seem more committed to this agenda.

"The optimal policy would be to use Cuba's nationalist culture to demand more transparency and to constrain theft by the 'big bosses,' who are the ones with greater opportunities to traffic influence and pocket money during the transition.

"Fidel has expressed admiration for the successes of China, but at the same time advises Cuban officials to be cautious in imitating the Chinese model. I believe he is right when he claims that the conditions are different in the two settings. China is a gigantic country with a strong Asian culture, located far from the United States. By contrast, Cuba is culturally and socially part of the West, close to the United States, where roughly 10 percent of its population now resides. In Cuba, religious communities, especially the Catholic Church and the evangelicals, are better organized and more independent than in China. Reforms of the magnitude implemented by the Chinese or Vietnamese might be destabilizing for Cuban communism, especially if there is no embargo.

"More importantly, Fidel has stated his rejection of the Chinese model in terms of ideological coherence. For decades, he has presented the elimination of private property as a necessary step of progress. A friend told me that he even said to an official who came with a report after a visit to China, 'You can choose the box in which you want to hide the report. Wait until I die, I don't want to make any concessions to capitalism.'

"This Cold War attitude is likely the central reason for Cuba's refusal to open its economy to direct investments from its population living abroad, as has been done in all the successful experiences of economic growth in East Asia. I have advocated for such a policy among my relatives and friends on the island. I have also written about this issue in publications of the Cuban Catholic Church and the exile community. In addition to the resistance of some right-wing exiles who called my position a betrayal of their interests — something I couldn't care less about — I have also encountered some legitimate negative reactions from people on the island. Some insist that it is important to take these steps after the country is opened to investment by those who actually live there. Others rightly point out that some incentives for joint ventures between Cubans living in Cuba and Cubans living abroad could help the political processes of national reconciliation.

"Raúl, for his part, spent all of November in 1997 touring China to study its economic reforms. He seems more open to the use of market mechanisms to revive the Cuban economy, but will resist reforms he perceives as 'too speedy.' Still, for years before Raúl became president, Cuba had already been intensifying its links with China.

"Today academic exchanges are increasing and tourism is growing. The last two presidents of China have visited the island. China is advising Cuba on how to reform — and how to control its reforms. There is considerable cooperation, for example, between Cuba and China on policing Internet access and use. Most importantly, with $2.6 billion in trade in 2007, plus significant investments in nickel, oil exploration, and joint ventures in biotechnology, China has become Cuba's second largest trading partner.

"Still, given the Western character of Cuban society, especially its ties to Spain, and its social connections with the rest of the world, it is hard to believe that Cuba can replicate the Chinese model for long. Cuban reforms may go slower than many predict, but eventually, when the tensions become unmanageable under its single-party regime, the island will begin to open its political system. At first it will probably diffuse protests by allowing the opposition to participate in the process without wielding major amounts of real power. But over time the reforms will continue and the island will open itself to even greater economic and political liberalization.

"Already Cuban political culture contains important elements of social democratic and Christian democratic values. Many reform-minded Cubans who have visited China criticize the increase of inequality and corruption in that country. In particular, many economists, politicians, and others have criticized the deterioration of universal health coverage in China as a grave mistake. This will become a major problem if anyone tries to change the universal access to health care — or quality education — in Cuba.

"Ironically, the China that should be inspiring Cuba is not the People's Republic, but rather Taiwan. That China has transitioned to an efficient welfare state. It has expanded substantive freedoms and economic growth, implemented wealth and education guarantees, and opened its political system in ways that reward economic performance.

"I believe that in the long run Cuba, much like Taiwan, will evolve into a welfare state. It will preserve basic health care and education for all in ways closer to the Taiwanese, European or Canadian models than the current U.S. model. Alternative reality #1 — the so-called Chinese model — may well carry the short term, but alternative reality #2 — the Northern European model — eventually will carry the longer term."

Alternative Reality #2: The Northern European Model

Arturo has been a fan of social democracy for decades. It wasn't only his vocal criticism of the Soviets that got him into trouble during the 1980s and 1990s but also his well-considered preference for the flexibilities of social democracy over the rigidities of Marxist-Leninist communism. So it comes as no surprise that Arturo would like to see his native Cuba evolve into a welfare state, or social democracy, even if it adopts the Chinese model in the short term.

Most definitions of "social democracy" are politically loaded. The dictionary, perhaps, says it most plainly: It is "a political movement advocating a gradual and peaceful transition from capitalism to socialism by democratic means" or a "democratic welfare state that incorporates both capitalist and socialist practices."[12] That doesn't sound too scary. After all, the United States incorporates both capitalist and socialist practices, ranging from Social Security and Medicare programs to the sweeping bailouts of banks and financial institutions during the recent recession. Isn't it all just a matter of degree?

Still, most Americans shun the label. They criticize social democracy for its inefficiencies, over-regulation of labor and business, and high unemployment rates. And, indeed, most European social democracies — and that means most European countries — do suffer from these ills. What they achieve, of course, is universal education, universal health care, wider social and economic safety nets, and greater income equality.

According to most of these measures, like the Human Development Index of the U.N. Development Program, the Northern European social democracies and Canada generally fare better than the Southern European social democracies and even the United States. And among the Northern European versions, the model adopted by Denmark — often called the "Copenhagen Consensus" — has gained the admiration of many. Journalist and author Robert Kuttner explained the essence of this model in *Foreign Affairs* in 2008:

> Denmark's social compact is the result of a century of political conflict and accommodation that produced a consensual style of problem solving that is uniquely Danish. It cannot be understood merely as a technical policy fix to be swallowed whole in a different cultural or political context....
>
> *At the center of the current Danish model is a labor-market strategy known as flexicurity.* The idea is to reconcile job flexibility with employment security. The welfare state is often associated with rigid job protections: laws and union contracts making it illegal or prohibitively expensive to lay off workers.... It is here that Denmark offers its most ingenious blend of free markets and social democracy: despite heavy unionization, there are no regulations against laying off workers other than the requirement of advance notice.
>
> In fact, Denmark has Europe's highest rate of labor turnover.... And with employers free to deploy workers as they wish and all Danes eligible for generous social benefits, there is no inferior "temp" industry.... Where most other [social democratic] nations have a knot of middle-aged people stuck in long-term unemployment, in Denmark, the vast majority of the unemployed return to work within six months, and the number of long-term unemployed is vanishingly small.
>
> What makes the flexicurity model both attractive to workers and dynamic for society are five key features: full employment; strong unions recognized as social partners; fairly equal wages among different sectors, so that a shift from manufacturing

to service-sector work does not typically entail a pay cut; a comprehensive income floor; and a set of labor-market programs that spend an astonishing 4.5 percent of Danish GDP on initiatives such as transitional unemployment assistance, wage subsidies, and highly customized retraining.

In return for such spending, the unions actively support both employer flexibility and a set of tough rules to weed out welfare chiselers; workers are understood to have duties as well as rights.... [T]he income security guaranteed by the Danish state, as well as the good prospects for reemployment, enables Danes to comfortably take risks with new jobs.[13]

It sounds too good to be true. And it is. Kuttner also emphasizes the difficulties in transposing the Copenhagen Consensus onto other nations. He points out that Denmark is a small country with a homogenous population roughly half the size of Cuba's. And already the Copenhagen Consensus is showing strains from the influx of immigrants into the country, especially from Muslim nations. Their cultural and ethnic diversity are new to Denmark and the accommodations Danes have made among themselves are not as forthcoming when it comes to "the other."

Still, of the two presently existing, fully developed alternatives facing Cuba, social democracy likely does, as Arturo argues, present the best choice. But there is a third alternative brewing. It is not yet as fully developed as the other two, but in the long run it could become the most dynamic, most constructive, and most attractive alternative of all.

Alternative Reality #3: The Brazilian Model

Despite its challenges — poverty, illiteracy, crime, environmental degradation — Brazil is the rising hegemon of Latin America. Analyst Nathan Gill has written, "From a socio-economic point of view, Brazil represents about half of South America ... it is the home of more than half of the population and produces slightly less than half the total gross domestic product of South America. Internationally, Brazil is also a global power. It is one of the ten largest economies in the world, and has served on the UN Security Council as a non-permanent member more than any other country except Japan."[14]

Brazil's foreign policy recognizes that its "position as a global actor is fully consistent with the emphasis that we put on regional integration."[15] It combines a vibrant capitalist economy with a fully functional democracy. Perhaps most importantly, the rule of law is gaining strength in Brazil, a country with a long history of crime and corruption.

The Brazilian model differs from the Northern European model in subtle but important respects. As Roberto Unger explains in *The Second Way*, traditional European social democracy is "useless to Brazil." This is due to its content rather than its execution.

Until recently, the idea of a contrast between two styles of capitalism exerted great influence. There would be American capitalism, characterized by economic flexibility and efficiency as much as by low social protection. There would also be European or "Rhinish" capitalism — that is, [social democracy]. One of the features of this other capitalism would be the effort to safeguard against market instability [with] a basic set of rights and social benefits. Another characteristic would be the ability of governments of negotiating, alongside labor unions and employers associations, agreements destined to reconcile salary improvement with currency stability.... The history of the last decades ... is the history of the practical and ideological weakening of this so-called ... alternative. Its techniques of social and economic stabilization ended up being seen as the sacrifice of the collective interest in growth and employment [to the] benefit of a powerful minority of organized workers and protected enterprises. Its generosity in social spending [became] incompatible with realism and responsibility in public finances. And its defense of acquired labor rights is an onus on innovation and efficiency that impoverished many in order to benefit a few....

Since [social democracy, or what some call the third way] was empty of institutional content, it was poor in practical results....

[Several] commitments guide the second way.... The first guideline is the building of an active, enriched, and able state that counts on a high level of tax revenue and national savings. Without high tax revenues, national problems remain unsolved since private initiative is insufficient.[16]

Let's pierce the fog of Unger's language. While social democracy smacks of compromise, accommodation, and the "blending" of old ideologies, the "second way" envisions reform at the deepest institutional levels. Such reform could include the redefinition of basic property rights and the creation of new institutions — the very organs of government — that respond more readily to the needs of the people. It could include a reformulation of the social contract itself, bringing health care, education, and social justice within the realm of legally protected rights. The re-thinking of fundamental concepts animates the spirit of the "second way." It is more experimental.

Indeed, Unger's native Brazil has become the most self-consciously experimental democratic capitalist state in the world today. We have already reviewed the wildly successful efforts that shattered its dependence on foreign oil by using its vast sugarcane industry to produce ethanol, making it the world's leader in biodiesel fuel. Given the prominence of sugarcane in Cuba's economy, the opportunity to follow a similar path appears open to the island. Yet Brazil's experimentation has not stopped with agriculture and energy. To reduce poverty, the country has initiated a program —*Bolsa Família*—that gives direct money subsidies to poor families so long as they keep their children in school and take them for regular health checks. The need to create opportunities — not to give charity — motivates this program.[17]

As a result of its grand experiments in agriculture, energy, poverty reduction, and lately the prevention of crime and corruption, Brazil has not only weathered the global economic crisis of 2008–2010 better than most countries but it has also lifted millions out of poverty and created a vibrant middle class. It is the emergence of this new middle class that has given Brazil such great weight on the global stage.

Whether the rising hegemon of Latin America will, over the long haul, live up to the aspirations of its former "minister of ideas" remains to be seen. Grand strategies often get lost in the rhetoric. But if there really is a "second way," as Professor Unger advocates, then it would behoove Cuba to take a good hard look at it. The attraction goes beyond the natural affinity Cuba might show for the leader of its region — it goes to the very design of its future.

Assuming the economic, political, and legal reforms in Cuba proceed as Arturo predicts and prefers, I fear its resort to social democracy will block its willingness to learn from the Brazilian alternative. I see the former as a remnant of the 20th century. And I hope the latter becomes the model for the 21st century.

Only time will tell which of us is right.

PART IV

THE NEW CONVERGENCE

Chapter Ten

Making Space

Battles raged in 2009 over the future of capitalism. A "wise Latina woman" fought her way onto the Supreme Court. And the McClatchy-Tribune News Service offered a curious point-and-counterpoint on lifting the Cuban embargo to allow oil drilling off the island's north coast by U.S. oil companies.

Mark Perry, a professor of economics and finance at the University of Michigan, wrote the "point," headlined "Yes; Oil Is Too Important." His conclusion:

> With the global economy in recession, we should not place U.S. energy companies at a disadvantage in the international marketplace ... Congress should lift the trade embargo against Cuba. It is a failed economic policy.... Preventing U.S. companies from drilling in Cuban waters within 45 miles of U.S. shores, when foreign firms are allowed to, is ludicrous. Since the drilling will take place, it may as well be by U.S. energy companies.[1]

The "counterpoint" was written by John Quigley, a professor of law at Ohio State. It appeared under the headline "Don't Do It Just for the Oil." His conclusion:

> Oil may soon trump politics in our relations with Cuba.... The idea behind our trade embargo was to bring down the Cuban government. Half a century later, that hasn't happened. We are the only country that blocks trade with Cuba. Oil is far from the only reason to end the trade embargo with Cuba. The embargo hurts us while it has done little good for the people of Cuba. The Obama administration is, wisely, taking a hard look at our Cuba policy. It is time for a change.[2]

The problem is obvious: The exchange was no point and counterpoint. It was point and same point — arrived at from different angles. I call that *the new convergence*.

Now this does not mean "convergence" in the older, more technical sense used by many economists and scholars in international relations. To them, "convergence" means the so-called catch-up effect, which signifies that economies in poor developing nations grow faster than economies in rich industrialized nations, so eventually the developing economies will converge with or catch up to the developed economies. The Economist.com website says, "This, at least, is the traditional economic theory. In recent years, there has been considerable debate about the extent and speed of convergence in reality."[3]

To the extent the theory does hold true, convergence often connotes a political as well as economic catch-up effect. The inescapable attraction of market-based capitalism, magnetic and seductive, eventually drags authoritarian systems out of their tyranny and into the enlightenment of democracy. Capitalism does, after all, encourage pluralism, which encourages democracy and the republican institutions that check and balance it.

Since the recession of 2009, however, "convergence" means something different — something glimpsed in the faux-debate between Professors Perry and Quigley, and that reflects the demise of market fundamentalism. Countries that embraced the "hard right-wing" version of unregulated free-market capitalism are re-regulating their economies. Countries that tried to preserve their single-party "hard left-wing" socialist systems are embracing limited market-based economic openings and limited democratic reforms. Their styles are creeping — for very different reasons — toward a pragmatic, progressive, broad middle ground not envisioned in the 20th century.

The changes that have begun in Cuba under Raúl Castro are consistent with this emerging style of creeping convergence. We have seen changes that started out quickly but then slowed down. And, as we will discuss in the next chapter, there have now been additional changes that started up again, in relatively spectacular fashion, in 2010. There have been, and there will continue to be, changes out in the open and changes taking place behind the scenes — and in the corridors of power — that have yet to be fully revealed.

But one thing is certain: Change is always relative. Often it is measurable. Sometimes it is controversial. People with different perspectives, who start from very different positions, often arrive at the same result from different angles — like Professors Perry and Quigley. And often it is more a matter of necessity than ideology.

In 2007 Judge Richard Posner was not hoping for a global financial meltdown to challenge the economic and legal beliefs he had proselytized for decades. The financial, environmental, energy, health care, and other sectors now being re-regulated in the United States are not accepting their fates gracefully. But the failure of the most extreme form of free-market capitalism proved itself in unemployment numbers and personal tragedies.

The West did not reject market fundamentalism because it had an epiphany. Communist countries have not opened their markets to capitalist intrusions because they welcome ideological dilution. They've done it because the events of today — the histories of tomorrow — drive people to act in real time and in multiple dimensions. That is why, when measuring change, it's important to do it in multiple dimensions — not just economically, politically, and legally, but over time as well.

After one of our trips to Cuba, Arturo and I flew directly to Toronto, where we rented a Ford Fusion and drove three hours northeast to Kingston, Ontario. This was going to be one of those trips where we didn't agree on everything — or much of anything. Eventually it caused Arturo some embarrassment, for which I was completely to blame. But it also revealed something deeply important about the changes going on in Cuba.

The highway skirted the shores of Lake Ontario. Occasionally we could glimpse sparkling waters through the trees. The cool, cloudy weather came as a welcome break from the heat and humidity of Havana. We arrived in Kingston late in the morning and found the dormitory at Queens University where we would stay for the next few days. We were attending a conference titled "The Measure of a Revolution: Cuba 1959–2009."

The website for the conference implied there would be a balanced evaluation of both the successes and failures of the past 50 years.

> The Cuban Revolution was one of the most important hemispheric events of the twentieth century, with both a regional and a global impact; and the country had to re-imagine itself. The conference ... will assess the Cuban Revolution on its 50th Anniversary through a variety of lenses: international relations, culture, gender, the economy, environment, sexuality, politics, migration, race, education, health and religion. The Conference provides a superb opportunity to encourage critical thought on the Revolution, what it has and has not accomplished, and on its future prospects. This forum is important in that it will bring together scholars from different disciplines, as well as writers, artists, film makers and government officials — past and incumbent — to present and debate issues arising from the subjects of their expertise.[4]

I knew the conference was meant to celebrate the anniversary of the Revolution. Those attending — nearly half from the United States and the other half a mixture of Canadians and Cubans — would be overwhelmingly against the U.S. embargo. Since there are the many reasons for the failure of the embargo, and few rational arguments to support it, this is typical of academic conferences about Cuba, with the exception of some that are held in Florida. And that was fine with me.

What I didn't foresee was how I would react to my three days in Kingston. I wasn't looking for a cable news throwdown of talking heads, nor "equal time" for the sort of right-wing fanatics that gave Arturo a hard time at his conference in Miami. I was looking for a multi-disciplined, deeply nuanced, intellectually honest approach.

The setting was certainly conducive. The campus of Queens University reminded me of Harvard and other Eastern Seaboard institutes of higher learning: classic limestone office and classroom buildings, stately grounds turned green and lush by the late spring sun and rain, serious thoughts hanging heavy in the air. The shores of Lake Ontario were just around the corner from our dormitory and whenever the clouds broke, we could see, far in the distance, rows of giant white wind turbines. They hovered over the waters, their blades turning slowly, proudly proclaiming Canadian progressivism.

I admit I wasn't a good team player. This type of academic conference bores me. The panels — 4 speakers, 15 minutes each, followed by Q&A — do not lend themselves to in-depth debate. And every professor seeks to graft his or her personal agenda onto every other professor's presentation. So I did what came naturally: I played hooky and treated myself, after 10 days in Havana, to an afternoon matinee of the new *Star Trek* movie.

True, I did not attend much of the conference, but I attended enough to see that any hope of balance was lost. Of the 44 sessions, only one dealt with legal issues. On the panel for that session, there were only two lawyers. The words "rule of law" were not uttered. Throughout, two themes were encouraged: the achievements of the Revolution, including the strides Cuba was currently making, and the failure of U.S. foreign policy toward the island. And, it appeared to me, one theme was strictly taboo: the very real shortcomings and failures of the Revolution, including the human rights problems that plague the nation.

We missed one of the earliest speeches, where the human rights issue was raised, and the speaker, Robert Pastor, was soundly criticized by the audience. So by the time Saturday morning arrived, and I headed for my panel presentation, I had mixed feelings. I was flattered to be on the same panel as a well-known journalist from Havana; a well-known academic from the University of North Carolina; and Dan Erikson, the author of *The Cuba Wars*. And I expected a decent reception, since the paper I wrote with Arturo argued that the embargo should not be seen as a policy that legitimately promotes human rights. Still, I harbored nagging concerns that something would go wrong.

The medium-sized class auditorium filled to standing room only as I settled in next to Arturo at the end of the long table at the front. I scanned the spectators, looking for Mariela Castro, the daughter of Raúl, who had come to the conference to speak on gay rights, and Ricardo Alarcón, the president of Cuba's National Assembly, who had come to deliver the closing remarks that night. Both had attended the session that discussed legal issues the prior day. Neither attended my panel.

The first two speakers went over their allotted time, so the moderator held my feet to the fire. I quickly hit the high points of our paper, pitched my three-part analysis that added the legal dimension to the economic and political dimensions, and ended with a prediction that greater Internet access, more travel opportunities, and the rise of the younger generation in Cuba would hasten the changes happening there.

During the truncated Q&A that followed, an Associated Press reporter named Nestor Ikeda — bright eyes behind gold spectacles, with a crumpled tweedy sports coat — addressed me pointedly: "You said the Internet would bring down the regime —"

"No," I insisted, interrupting him, "that's not at all what I said."

The audience loudly murmured its agreement with me. Ikeda wiped a smirk from his face — as an experienced journalist, he had known exactly what he was doing — and rephrased his question. I answered by repeating what I had said about the impact of the Internet, travel, and the youth on the changes happening on the island. Later, after the session broke, I approached Ikeda and told him, "I don't mind being quoted, but I do mind it when words are put in my mouth. Please be accurate."

He responded in a conciliatory manner, assuring me that any quote he used would be accurate. And that's all I thought about the matter until later that evening. I spent the afternoon reading *Sherlock Holmes* and walking along the lakeshore. At about 6 o'clock I joined Arturo and a few hundred others for the closing ceremonies of the conference: cocktails, remarks by Ricardo Alarcón, dinner, and self-congratulation.

I strolled to the bar and ordered a Diet Cuba Libre. The bartender, an attractive young blond woman, replied, "I'm sorry, sir, but we don't have any rum tonight."

"Why not?" I asked.

I was curious, since I had ordered the exact same drink the night before at the exact same spot and had been served with no trouble. At the time I had noticed the bar was serving Bacardi — once a proud Cuban label but now forever claimed by an exile family that gives major financial support to the pro-embargo lobby — not Havana Club, the popular Cuban brand, which is easily available in Canada.

The bartender said, "Because our guests" — meaning the Cubans — "objected to the brand we were serving. Can I get you something else?"

"No, thanks." I smiled and walked away. Arturo was twenty paces away, sitting down at a well-placed table for the closing speeches and dinner. I took a seat next to him.

The emcee from Queens University made a few remarks, garnered enthusiastic applause, and introduced Ricardo Alarcón, a lifelong servant of the Revolution, trim and dapper in his seventies, with a high forehead and sandy-silver hair. He had been a key player in securing the return of Elián González to his father in Cuba a decade before, and he was highly articulate, fluent in English. I had been looking forward to his speech.

The first third was what you'd expect: a review of the great accomplishments made by the Revolution over the past half-century, warm words for his Canadian hosts, nothing earth-shattering or noteworthy. Then the president of Cuba's National Assembly launched into a bitter and impassioned denunciation of U.S. foreign policy toward Cuba. While I didn't particularly care for the rhetoric Alarcón deployed, I could hardly protest, since I too have always been against the embargo.

Finally, the last third of his remarks came. They transitioned from a denunciation of U.S. policy toward Cuba to a denunciation of the United States itself. Quoting freely from the *Federalist Papers*, Alarcón attacked everything from the structure of America's government to its democratic ideals to its way of life. The tone and manner of delivery were careful and studious, but the message was anything but conciliatory.

I was taken aback. I was angry. I was insulted. I took it personally. As a man who has spent much of his career teaching American constitutional law, I will put our system of government up against any in the world. It is imperfect. It blunders. And yet our system has one thing that trumps anything remotely contemplated in Cuba today or in the past: the capacity to self-correct. The system we enjoy in the United States — periodic free elections feeding branches of government that not only are separated but also check and balance each other — continues to be, I believe, the best on Earth.

Admittedly, I am attracted to Roberto Unger's ideas about the need for deep institutional reform. And yes, I believe there are many things we can do to improve our existing system. But I do not know of a better system of government that exists in the here and now on the face of the planet. Just one guy's opinion.

And that one guy voted with his feet. I excused myself, not wanting to expose my anger over polite dinner conversation. It was more an impulse than a deliberate decision. As I left the grand dining hall in the grand old university building, I passed Nestor Ikeda.

"What did you think?" I asked him.

He shrugged. "It's his usual spiel. I've heard it all before. What did you think?"

I opened my mouth to answer and he whipped out a small voice recorder from the inside pocket of his sports coat. I consciously slowed my mind and chose my words very carefully. This is what I said, reconstructed almost verbatim: "I find it interesting that a conference that's supposed to be about the pros and cons of the Revolution — the accomplishments and failures, the benefits and burdens — should be so unbalanced. It seems any time the discussion gets anywhere close to a criticism of the present regime, the discussion degenerates into a condemnation of the United States."

Ikeda thanked me for the quote and I finally took my leave. The lovely campus of Queens University beckoned, so I crossed it under a gentle rain, and ate some barbecue at a quaint Texas-themed saloon in downtown Kingston.

Later, at the dormitory, Arturo said to me, "You know, Harlan, a few people overheard what you said to that reporter, and they weren't very happy about it. What you said wasn't really fair to many of the sessions at the conference. There were, in fact, critical discussions about race, economic reform, literature, and other topics in which nobody blamed the embargo or the United States."

"Well," I replied stubbornly, "I stand by what I said. What did *you* think of Alarcón's remarks?"

"I did not agree with them," he said. "In fact, I also found them to be insulting. And they were counterproductive. He missed an opportunity to send a conciliatory message to Obama and the United States. Also, he was discourteous to the Canadians by not recognizing Canadian aid to Cuba. However, rather than speaking about it to a reporter like Ikeda, I think it would be more effective to write to those who organized the conference to state my concerns."

"Fair enough," I responded, "but like I said, I stand by what I told that reporter. I was not speaking for you and me. I was speaking in my own capacity. And by any reasonably objective standard, this conference has been unbalanced. There has been very little criticism of the present regime. What little there has been, has been drowned out by the rest. The sessions were structured that way. What was especially lacking was any real consideration of human rights and political freedoms in Cuba. That's my opinion."

The cabin of our Ford Fusion was frosty on the return from Kingston to Toronto.

We flew to Chicago and connected to Denver, talking little along the way. I knew Arturo was hoping my statement to the AP reporter would not come back to haunt us. But the next day it did. The quote got picked up by a couple of Spanish-speaking media outlets, including the Spanish edition of the *Miami Herald*. I could not, however, find it anywhere in English, which I found to be ironic.

In any event, I continue to stand by my remarks. And for me they have morphed into something more: a renewed commitment to those institutions — a well-regulated economic marketplace, a political democracy with free elections and real checks and balances, and an independent judiciary that maintains the rule of law — that make our system self-correcting.

If there is one thing I have learned from my trips to Cuba and my weekend in Canada, it's this: There is precious little willingness to engage in genuine self-evaluation at the institutional level when it comes to the Revolution. It's all black and white, us and them, polarized and stubborn.

"This is a tragedy," Arturo has said, while looking at Cuba from his American perspective. "One of the American expressions that I like the most is 'I can live with it.' It shows a willingness to compromise — to meet in the middle of the road — that has helped this country avoid great catastrophes. I have noticed that you even have a prestigious prize, the Profile in Courage Award, which is given by the Kennedy Center to those who have the courage to compromise. We don't have anything like that in Cuba or Miami. Cubans on both sides have too much reverence for militancy and intransigence. And that is sad."

So, despite our disagreement about the conference, Arturo and I do agree there is often little willingness to entertain the competing truths — indeed, the competing realities — that characterize the "problem of Cuba." And without that willingness, there can be no meaningful change. Recall what Che himself insisted, as Arturo once boldly reminded Captain Olga: "Our minds should never become slaves of the official thinking."

Self-evaluation, the ability to self-correct, can be institutionalized. It can be built into the system. Americans and Cubans alike must start *making space* for each other's competing realities. The ideologies of the 20th century are dying. They're being replaced with more flexible, progressive, pragmatic techniques of problem-solving.

The changes initiated between Havana and Washington from 2008 to 2010 should be magnified and quickened. The process of dismantling the embargo — piece by piece and step by step in that elaborate dance between Raúl Castro and Barack Obama — should reach its climax and free the people on both sides of the Straits to get on with their lives.

Carlos Batista started out as an economics professor at the University of Havana. He was a card-carrying member of the Communist Party, climbing the ladder of success. He later became a professor of international relations and served as the vice director of the Center for U.S. and Hemispheric Studies before Carlos Alzugaray.

Then, in 1996, Cuban Air Force jets shot down two planes flown by the radical exile group, Brothers to the Rescue. That was the final straw for Carlos Batista. He was no fan of the radical group, but he realized the Cuban government was not doing its share to keep tempers calm. It was spoiling the possibility of an end to the embargo. So he decided to leave Cuba. He took a fellowship in Japan, wrote a book, and eventually landed in Virginia, teaching math to high school students.

He likes Virginia; he gets to live close to one of his two sons. He misses being a university professor; high school students are just not as challenging. And he's very open about his negative views of the current regime in Cuba. I got to hear those views over lunch at a shiny new proto–American grill in the Cherry Creek neighborhood of Denver.

Carlos was in town visiting his second son and agreed to talk with me and Arturo. They were old friends and arrived together, both dressed in shorts and casual pullovers. Carlos had a high forehead, silver hair, and a silver goatee. His eyes were very bright and he was plainly pleased to be living in the States and able to travel freely to see his sons.

I sat between the two of them, listening to them debate their visions for the future of their native island. Carlos was insisting that there weren't any real, genuine changes happening in Cuba — it was all just cosmetic. And Arturo was arguing that greater Internet access, and more travel opportunities, and the rise of the youth were indeed changing Cuba faster than many expected. The ironies didn't escape me.

But I wasn't in a talkative mood that day, so mostly I just listened. Occasionally, I would interject something. I would turn to Carlos and say, "Tury tells me..." And he would respond without missing a beat.

At these times I would notice I had taken to calling Arturo by his Cuban nickname even though we weren't in Cuba and he had never given me permission. It was something that just came naturally. Later, I pulled him aside in the parking lot and said, "I hope you don't mind that I called you Tury back there. I guess it's become a habit."

He just laughed and winked at me. "Of course not," he said, "it's what all my Cuban friends call me."

At the time of our talk in that parking lot in Denver, nickel prices were dropping. The global recession was hitting Cuba very hard. Storm clouds were gathering over the seas of change. They were gathering so fast, in fact, a lot people never saw them coming.

These were the ones who had been looking forward to the Sixth Congress of the Communist Party — the first congress since 1997 — slated, finally, after so many delays, for the end of 2009. There was speculation that Fidel would formally step aside as head of the Communist Party, a post he still held, making the transition to Raúl even more complete. There was also speculation that bigger economic reforms loomed on the horizon.

But on July 31, 2009, *Granma*— the official newspaper in Cuba — announced that, due to the serious economic crisis, the Sixth Congress of the Communist Party had been postponed indefinitely.[5] Did this mean Raúl had stepped off the dance floor?

Chapter Eleven
Fits and Starts

When General Arnaldo Ochoa faced the firing squad in July 1989, he knew the full extent of Raúl's loyalty to Fidel. I first heard of the "Ochoa Affair" from an elderly anesthesiologist, the mother of an interpreter whom I had met on an early visit to Cuba. We were dining in the back room at La Bodequita del Medio in Old Havana, for while there were many private restaurants — *paladares* — that served much better food, she was a strict member of the party and preferred restaurants run by the state.

Still, she was angry that night. Over pork with *morros y cristianos*, she vented her frustration. She was an internationally recognized physician who had traveled abroad to speak many times, yet her Internet access was being filtered like everyone else's, so she couldn't get past the home page of some Swedish medical website.

"I'm certainly not subversive," she said, and it sounded funny coming from this elderly matron. "I have family — a sister and a brother — in Florida. They have always wanted me to join them there. They even sent a boat for me during the Mariel Boatlift. But I have stayed — through it all — and I have stayed because I do believe in the system. We have some of the best education and health care in Latin America. Our economy is getting better. True, we have political problems, but these days that is mostly a matter of one question: When will you Americans drop the Bloqueo? Me? I am starting to get older now and yet I believe many things will change here in Cuba while I still am alive."

"Wasn't there any time," I asked, "when you felt disillusioned?" I didn't need to recite the various reasons why an ordinary Cuban might feel disillusion: an autocratic single-party government that suppresses individual, political, and economic freedoms, and so forth.

"Of course," she said. And then she told me about the execution of Ochoa after he was convicted of charges of corruption, drug trafficking, and — therefore — treason.

"It was a very difficult time for us," said the anesthesiologist. She finished her *morros y cristianos* and wiped her mouth with her napkin, then continued her thought: "Nobody felt good about it. If Ochoa was being made a scapegoat over some petty political squabble, then it was terrible. If he was truly guilty of the charges brought against him, then how could such a high-ranking general, a hero of the Revolution, fall so low? Where did all that greed and corruption come from? Many of us worried the truth lay somewhere in between the rumors. We worried about the system. For me it was so disillusioning because Ochoa was one of Raúl's best friends. Think about it. Raúl had to have one of his best friends executed to prove his loyalty to his brother."

This version of the Ochoa Affair is consistent with others. Raúl appears not only as the ideologue and military man but also as the little brother fiercely devoted to Fidel. Throughout 2009 and 2010, as Raúl continued his own presidency and Fidel continued, generally, to stay out of public view, people wondered whether that loyalty would endure. Still, soon after the Sixth Party Congress was canceled in mid–2009, Raúl made it clear: "I was not elected president to return capitalism to Cuba!"[1]

Will the ideologues of yesteryear triumph over the youth of tomorrow?

Two months after Raúl declared his allegiance to the past, the wildly popular Colombian rock star Juanes cast his lot with the future. He led an international roster of performers through a 4-hour "Peace Without Borders" concert that drew a million fans to the Plaza de la Revolución—the place where Arturo and I had marched on May Day only five months before.[2]

The concert caused quite a stir on both sides of the Straits of Florida. In an article that was published by the digital newspaper *Cubaencuentro*, Arturo said the attacks from the right-wing exile community brought to mind the story of the woman who called her husband, worried about the report on the radio that a crazy person was driving against the traffic. He responded it was not one person but rather thousands, and that he had spent hours on the freeway avoiding all those cars coming toward him.

These exiles—many with justified complaints against the communist system—haven't noticed the Cold War is over, nor do they understand that policies of engagement are what brought about its end. They don't even notice that free elections in a democracy like America have consequences. President Obama won after declaring clearly that he planned to engage in dialogue and communication with our adversaries. He will do it, over time, with Cuba. Yet despite the failure of the embargo, the right-wing ideologues continue to drive in the opposite direction, against the entire world. They are oblivious.

When the press focuses only on the right wing's side of the equation, it distorts reality. The majority of Cubans, both on the island and in Miami, supported the peace concert. In Miami most of them never questioned Juanes' decision to perform, and a significant number of the youngest residents traveled to Cuba to attend the concert. A more tolerant viewpoint is gaining ground, even among the exiles. Or, as Arturo says, "The intransigents have the clocks. But the new generations have the time."

Juanes staged his concert in Cuba with the blessing of the U.S. government. Before he went, he met with Secretary of State Hillary Clinton, who stated that U.S. policy encourages such contacts. And "Peace Without Borders" was just the beginning. The New York Philharmonic Orchestra, which traveled to Pyongyang in 2008 to play a concert for peace, plans several concerts in Cuba. The American Ballet Theater has traveled to the Havana International Ballet Festival, participating in two special functions dedicated to José Manuel Carreño and Carlos Acosta, two Cuban dancers in the company who were students of Alicia Alonso in the Cuban National Ballet but have danced for ABT in the last fifteen years. And Wynton Marsalis flew to Cuba in the autumn of 2010 to give jazz concerts and lessons to young musicians.

These cultural exchanges have also included many Cuban artists and performers coming to the United States. Chucho Valdés, a Grammy-winning jazz pianist, has played several times in New York and San Francisco. Los Van Van, an important Cuban salsa band, has twice toured cities like Washington, New York, Los Angeles, San Francisco, Miami, and Philadelphia. Even Silvio Rodriguez, whose visa was denied for the Pete Seeger concert at Madison Square Garden in early 2009, came to New York, Washington, and San Juan in the summer of 2010, dedicating some of his songs to the "Cuban Five" in his concerts at Carnegie Hall. Indeed, between 2009 and 2010, social exchanges between Cuba and the United States slowly returned to the "happy days" of the Clinton era, when the number of cultural, religious, humanitarian, and academic licenses to travel to Cuba multiplied.

But more accurately, Obama has picked up where Clinton left off. Early in 2009, Obama dismantled most of the regulations Bush imposed on Cuban Americans' travel and remittances to the island. And in January 2011, Obama began a new policy of promoting academic, cultural, and religious exchanges that licensed significant amounts of purposeful travel to Cuba.[3]

Nongovernmental actors have heard from the State Department that a further increase in cultural, sports, and scientific exchanges is on its way. The rigidity and obstacles inherent in government-to-government negotiations will be softened, if not removed, by greater people-to-people contact. Still, concerts and exchanges can do only so much. There must be political will, economic determination, and legal institutionalization behind the push for change.

At the climax of his set in Havana, Juanes appealed to people on both sides of the Straits of Florida, chanting, *"Cuba libre! Cuba libre!"* — Free Cuba! — before ending with a second chant: "One Cuban family! One Cuban family!"[4]

The question becomes obvious: Did the cancellation of the Sixth Party Congress in July 2009, and the subsequent declarations by Raúl that he was not elected president to bring capitalism back to Cuba, signal the end of the reforms that would be introduced on the island?

The answer is clearly no. Progress seldom follows a linear path. More often it occurs in fits and starts. By the second half of 2010, Cuba was back on the dance floor. At least four major developments announced its return to reform.

The first outward sign of renewed change came in July, when the Cuban government announced that it would release, over the next few months, the 52 prisoners still incarcerated who were among the 75 dissidents arrested in March 2003.[5] The deal was brokered by the Catholic Church — increasingly, as we have seen, the voice of moderation on the island — in response to demands made by Spain and the European Union. At first 39 of the prisoners were released and sent into exile in Spain. The remaining 13 refused exile and stayed in prison; the following November, two more were let go, one of whom finally accepted exile while the other remained "free under parole" in Cuba.[6] The release of these dissidents seemed to indicate to most analysts of the Cuban situation that the island was open for business politically. The winds of change had started blowing again.

A second major development signaled Cuba was open for business economically as well as politically. In September 2010, a plan was announced to fire between 500,000 and one million state workers while dramatically expanding the categories of allowable private and self-employment.[7] The plan occupied three full pages of *Granma* and no one on or off the island doubted that, if fully implemented, it would constitute monumental change. The plan was endorsed by Fidel himself in November,[8] and became the subject of open public debate in December.[9]

Also in September, in a third major development, Fidel launched a surprise charm offensive. He summoned journalist Jeffrey Goldberg of *The Atlantic* to Havana for a personal interview. Goldberg took with him Julia Sweig, an expert on Latin American and Cuban affairs from the Council on Foreign Relations. His report on the visit ran as a two-part series on the *Atlantic* website.[10]

In the first segment, Castro sent a stern message to Mahmoud Ahmadinejad, the president of Iran: "He criticized Ahmadinejad for denying the Holocaust and explained why the Iranian government would better serve the cause of peace by acknowledging the 'unique' history of anti–Semitism and trying to understand why Israelis fear for their existence." This was an unusual statement from one "bad boy" to another.

After their first meeting with him, Julia Sweig commented, "Fidel is at an early stage of reinventing himself as a senior statesman, not as head of state, on the domestic stage, but primarily on the international stage, which has always been a priority for him."

In the second segment of the report, Fidel "let slip" that he didn't think the Cuban system was working any longer, and Sweig later suggested "that one effect of such a sentiment might be to create space for his brother, Raúl, who is now president, to enact the necessary reforms in the face of what will surely be push-back from orthodox communists within the Party and the bureaucracy. Raúl Castro is already loosening the state's hold on the economy. He recently announced, in fact, that small businesses can now operate and that foreign investors could now buy Cuban real estate."

Fidel even treated his guests, including Adela Dworin, the president of Cuba's Jewish community, to the famous dolphin show at Havana's aquarium. A photograph included in Goldberg's second segment shows the merry group. Fidel is wearing a red plaid shirt, looking old and frail but very much alive. The caption reads in part, "Fidel is the guy who looks like Fidel if Fidel shopped at L.L. Bean."

And finally, in November 2010, Raúl took the space created for him and rescheduled the long-overdue Sixth Congress of the Communist Party. It would be held in April 2011, after the period of public debate that began in December 2010.[11] Indeed, in this fourth major development, Raúl didn't just take the space — he took the stage.

One report said that he "encouraged Cubans to express themselves freely in the public debate now underway about economic changes for the communist-ruled island.... At a Jewish community event in Havana aired on state television, Castro asked Cubans not to worry about expressing [themselves] publicly.... 'That is what we want to defend: permanent differences in all ideas, which, in my modest experience, is where the best solutions come from,' he said.... The Cuban president expressed these considerations while taking part in a Hanukkah celebration [at the Patronato] of the Jewish Community of Cuba ... where he gave a brief speech wearing the traditional Jewish 'kippah' cap. Castro said he was satisfied because 'the train has started rolling,' referring to the debate over the plan for economic reform."[12]

So, whether taken individually or as a cumulative blitz over a six-month period, these four developments — the release of the prisoners, the new economic plan, the Fidel charm offensive, and the scheduling of the next party congress — clearly signal a new ferocity in the dance between Havana and

Washington, not to mention a new ferocity in the dance among Raúl, his beloved Communist Party, and his restive people.

Did the autumn of 2010 — maybe sometime around the dolphin show — mark the shift when people really did stop waiting for Fidel to die, and started thinking more about Raúl and his agenda for the New Cuba?

The artist Adrián Pellegrini arrived in Denver for a six-day visit with Carolyn and me in October 2010. He had come to the United States on a cultural exchange, after some dicey time waiting for a visa. As part of a two-man show at the Hahn Ross Gallery in Santa Fe, he was breaking into the American gallery system. After staying a few weeks with his father in Florida, he called and said he would love to see the Rocky Mountains.

When I picked him up at Denver International Airport, I asked him if he wanted lunch and he requested, "A fill-a-steak."

Now that sounded a bit rich for a casual lunch, but I figured "what the heck?" and took him to a steakhouse in Cherry Creek where he could get a nice fillet. He almost choked when he saw the prices on the menu and quickly realized I had made a mistake. "No, no," he said, "not a steak fillet. Just a sandwich. You know, a fill-a-steak."

I laughed and said, "Oh, you mean a Philly cheesesteak!"

"Yes," he said, and we were off to grungy little joint in Capitol Hill where he could satisfy his craving for a fraction of the price we had nearly spent.

This episode, so full of humor and good will, made me understand just how fragile communication can be with someone from another country. Over the next couple of days, I drove Adrián to Breckenridge, though the snow he longed to see wouldn't blanket the little ski town for another month. I gave him a tour of Boulder, where he could ogle the coeds on the Pearl Street Mall. And Carolyn and I hosted a small reception for him at our home.

For Adrián, however, the high point came when he asked me to take him to Golden to visit the Colorado Railroad Museum. There, on a beautiful clear morning at the base of Table Mountain, we wandered the 15-acre spread and studied most of the 100 engines, cabooses and coaches that were on display. Little did I know my guest was a train freak! He knew all about the various drive mechanisms and could easily talk exotic train talk with the attendants, who were greatly taken with their guest from Cuba.

As we walked from engine to engine, I commented on how the elaborate locomotives reminded me of the *Alien*-like drawings Adrián made with different colored inks on solid black paper. There was a "steam-punk" quality to both that was intricate and fascinating. That led to a discussion about what kind of artist he was trying to be. We bandied about the word "apolitical," and I argued that nothing can be truly without political content. Indeed,

Both photographs: The Cuban artist Adrián Pellegrini at the Colorado Railroad Museum, October 2010 (photographs by Harlan Abrahams; courtesy Adrián Pellegrini del Riego).

by his very "apolitical" nature, Adrián was making a political statement of sorts.

Finally we settled on a label that attracted him more: "post-political." That one seemed to fit him better. And in fact he reluctantly admitted that perhaps one reason why he was given a visa to leave Cuba, when so many other artists had been denied, was because he presented himself as a "post-political" person. He was a perfect calling card for the Cuban government, a young professional who came to the United States to do something other than bitch about conditions on the island.

As our conversation eased toward politics and economics, Adrián repeated his contention, which he made when I first met him at his art deco home in Havana, that for him freedom was not really an issue in Cuba. He was perfectly free to do and say whatever he wanted. I challenged him and pointed out that the state was still blocking and filtering the Internet, so he really wasn't as free as he thought he was. He could not easily access controversial websites and blogs, like Yoani Sánchez's *Generación Y.*

Adrián scoffed and said, "Anyone clever enough to use the Internet can, in fact, easily find *Generación Y* and other sensitive materials on the Internet merely with a few extra strokes of the keypad." It was just a matter of knowing what shadow or "mirrored" websites to look for. If, for example, you used a Spanish search engine, you could get to *Generación Y* without any filtering or blocking. He later showed me exactly what he was talking about on my home computer.

That really made an impression on me. It was less about the ineffectiveness of the Cuban government's efforts to filter the Internet and more an affirmation that, here in the guise of a single person, was the complete embodiment of the new Holy Trinity: travel, the Internet, and the youth. These would be engines of change in Cuba as well as in many other developing nations.

Near the end of his visit, I took Adrián to a store on South Broadway that claims it is the largest model train store in the country. He must have shopped there for two hours. Finally he bought a small electric train set that he immediately set up in our lower level recreation room, deriving as much pleasure from it as a kid on Christmas morning.

But during Adrián's visit to the store something else happened. Chatting up one of the older salesmen, he told the man — grey haired with a plaid shirt, glasses, and stubble — that he was from Cuba. And the man told Adrián that he had been stationed at Guantánamo before the Revolution. Somewhere in the middle of their discussion, the older man started ranting about those "socialists in Washington who are trying to ruin our country."

I held my tongue and, wisely, so did Adrián. But when we left the store, and he was putting his purchases in the trunk of my car, he remarked, "That guy back there wouldn't know a real socialist if he was hit over the head with one."

I realized then just how much misunderstanding still has to be swept away before Cubans and Americans can truly move beyond their past and into their brave new future.

Chapter Twelve
The Path to Reform

Looking back at the first years of Raúl's presidency, and forward to the alternatives facing the island, Arturo should have the last word. After all, it's his nation of birth — his country of origin — and it's the future of his people.

So Arturo sees it this way: "On February 24, 2008, Raúl Castro was elected president of the Council of State and Council of Ministers by the Cuban National Assembly. This was a turning point in the succession of leadership that began in June 2006. At that time, anticipating the possibility of Fidel Castro's absence in the future, the Central Committee of the Cuban Communist Party — the PCC — reinstated the Secretariat and discussed a collective party leadership as the only possible substitute for Fidel's charisma.

"Only two months later, on July 31, 2006, the Central Committee's prescience proved itself. Fidel fell ill and 'temporarily' ceded his state responsibilities, not to Raúl exclusively, but to a select group of members of the Politburo and Council of Ministers. Included in this group were Francisco Soberón, the president of Cuba's Central Bank; José Luis Rodríguez, the minister of the economy; Carlos Lage, the executive secretary of the Council of Ministers; and Felipe Pérez Roque, the minister of foreign relations. As it became increasingly clear that Fidel would not return to the helm of the Cuban state, Raúl began to consolidate his role as the new leader of the government and began to promote his own team of ministries and party leaders. In a move that signaled Raúl's distrust of Lage and the others, the National Assembly elected José Ramón Machado Ventura, the face of the orthodox wing of the PCC, as Raúl's first vice president.

"Raúl finally had his own Council of Ministers, which replaced two-thirds of his brother's Cabinet, including the key portfolios of the economy and the president of the Central Bank. In the Armed Forces — the FAR — there was not only a new minister but all regional commanders of the Eastern, Central, and Western Armies were also replaced by generals in their early fifties. The old chiefs were promoted to permanent members of the Politburo, guaranteeing unity of leadership between the PCC and the FAR.

"Did the transfer of power from Fidel to Raúl on February 24, 2008, imply a substantive shift in Cuba's politics beyond a change of faces? Has the evolution of Cuban politics under Raúl's presidency since February 2008 increased the probability of liberalization in the future? Does the new situation in Cuba create opportunities for the reintegration of Cuba into a world order led by the United States? And if so, then what is the optimal American policy at this point in time?

"These questions require a review of some ideas we have discussed previously in this book: First, the Cuban Revolution has a dual character. In addition to the Leninist project embodied in the PCC, the triumph of January 1, 1959, represented the victory of a nationalist revolution. This perspective envisions Cuba not as a surviving outlier of the Eastern European communist regimes but as closer to the communist regimes of East Asia, where the Communist Party presented itself as the embodiment of nationalism. While the communist project has failed in Cuba, the politics of the last five decades consolidated a nationalist narrative as the last reservoir of legitimacy for Cuba's rulers to tap. Only by building a narrative of nationalist authenticity can the opposition or other groups within the current elite propose an alternative course from the one proposed by the PCC.

"Second, the succession from Fidel to Raúl completed a regime change from totalitarianism to post-totalitarianism.[1] The current Cuban political regime admittedly retains some of the repressive features of its totalitarian predecessor, but since the 1980s significant trends toward social, cultural, and even economic pluralism have emerged. Communist ideology has weakened within the limits of the single-party system, driving a shift toward more pragmatic decision-making. Examples of this de-totalitarianism include the existence of a 'second culture' in Cuba in which artists, intellectuals, and social activists now operate outside the ideological apparatus,[2] and the expansion of the social space occupied by the religious communities, which defeated the atheist policies of the communist project even before the beginning of the Special Period.

"Third, Cuba's transition features three different but intertwined processes: openness, marketization, and political liberalization. Economic reforms trigger social and political consequences, like the growth of a technocratic managerial middle class. Openness increases contacts with the outside world, creating more access and cross-pollination of new ideas and opportunities for the people and the different elites.

"Finally, there are foreign policy implications to the reformist acceptance that Cuba's inability to develop has stemmed fundamentally from its own flaws, and not from foreign interference. If the government takes responsibility for its own problems, improves the performance of the public sector, and opens space to a significant private sector, as it is beginning to do, then the last defenses of the embargo will be undermined.

"In situations of post-totalitarianism, legitimacy is not a unitary concept that is associated with the periodic celebration of multiparty elections, but rather an aggregation of 'different zones'[3] in which the party builds acquiescence by responding to the demands of the population it rules. A short but not exclusive list of 'zones of legitimacy' includes: charisma of the leaders; economic performance in terms of growth and distribution; state-civil society relations, particularly the responsiveness of the state to claims by religious communities and the various professional and fraternal nonpolitical groups; and the defense of the national and public interest in foreign relations.

"It is also important to take the revolutionary cycle seriously. The revolutionary impulse in Cuba is now exhausted. For most of the current elites, 'The business of the revolution is business.' Opposing economic reforms would only wound themselves. Taking an experimental approach, however, these elites prefer a gradual and piecemeal march to reform, beginning in selected sectors and provinces, with the less controversial and easier topics first. The purpose of these nonliberal reformers is not to dismantle single-party rule but to create a developmental state that preserves their own privileges, takes the country out of its current economic debacle, and shapes a national consensus that emphasizes economic growth and political stability under the PCC.

"So, when I ask, 'Did the transfer of power to Raúl imply substantive changes in Cuba's politics?' I ask it in the way it is often asked in the United States.[4] But this is the wrong way to ask it. It focuses on the American perspective, not the Cuban perspective.

"The Cuban regime, up to the transfer of power, rested on three significant pillars: the extraordinary charisma of the historic leader of the Revolution, Fidel Castro; the FAR complex[5] as the central military, political, and economic defense of the regime; and the PCC as the central tool for political mobilization, promotion of the elite, and ideological indoctrination. Each pillar was shaped by Fidel's virtues and flaws.

"The change from the charismatic rule of Fidel to institutionalized rule is a fundamental shift in the Cuban power structure. The contrast between the most charismatic figure in Cuban history and his younger brother — or anybody else — shows how the Cuban regime is losing the charisma of its maximum leader as a source of legitimacy. Fidel's charisma can only be replaced by showing the capacity to keep order, improve the economic performance of the nation, and play some redistributive role through the preservation of a minimal welfare state.

"This reality anticipates a regime shift to the FAR and the PCC.[6] The first years of Raúl's presidency were marked by changes within the PCC and leadership renewal within the FAR. But these actions were accompanied by key initiatives of dialogue and cooperation with well-organized segments of civil society, such as religious groups (particularly the Catholic Church). These strategic steps promoted a friendly environment for the most important challenge the regime now faces: enhancing its political legitimacy by showing positive economic performance, and increasing the non-state sector of the economy while reducing the excessive labor force on the government payroll.

"Since taking power, Raúl has prepared the institutional platform for the reforms announced as the 'updating' of the Cuban system and the Sixth Congress of the PCC. These processes were seen in the renewal of the FAR and the PCC, which included the non-traumatic purge of those out of line with Raúl's programs. Similar processes have occurred in other dependencies of the FAR, like MININT and GAESA. The latest generations of officer-managers might lack the globalized mentality of the economic and political elites of other countries, who may have lived for long periods in the West, but they are nevertheless well informed, with modern educations and orientations. These are not leaders promoted 'by helicopter,' but military men who developed a professional career on the institutional ladder.

"To train these people to rule the country, the FAR has established CODEN (the Colegio de Defensa Nacional). At CODEN, FAR officers interact with cadres from all of the sectors of the government and the PCC, and have been discussing for years different courses and sequences of reform. CODEN promotes a vision of national security based on 'the war of the whole people' doctrine against an American invasion, but it includes a less well-known dimension of internal security that extends to economic reforms, political institutionalization, anti-riot monitoring and policing, the experience of the collapse of communism elsewhere, and the challenges and opportunities of globalization for Cuban political stability.

"If the purpose is to institutionalize PCC rule, the management of civil-military PCC-FAR relations will be a decisive factor for the political stability of the country and the possibility of future liberalization or democratization from within the system. The current juncture under Raúl's rule is optimal for establishing the principle of civilian control of the Armed Forces, as well as the habituation to it. Something to watch at the next National Party Conference, discussed below, will be the election of new leaders for the party and the government. Will Raúl promote more civilians to the Politburo from the ranks of the party, albeit ones undoubtedly in good relations with the military?

"The role of the FAR 'as a state within the state' will be hard to sustain in a more institutionalized setting. It is not clear whether Raúl intends to leave the FAR as an equal partner of the PCC, to guarantee civilian supremacy over the military, or to insulate the military from civilian interference. For now, the purpose seems to be unity of leadership among the PCC, FAR, and the government. The PCC has promoted several members of the FAR High Command to the Buro Politico and Generals Alvaro Lopez Miera and Leopoldo Cintras to the Council of State.

"In this marriage between the FAR and the PCC, the party has not historically been the minor partner. The structure of the Cuban state is constitutionally and ideologically based on the premise that the party, not the armed forces, is the guiding force of society. This is what generations of Cubans have learned in their political education.

"In March 2011, after postponing the Sixth Party Congress since 1997, the Central Committee is scheduled to finally convene the event next month, in April. Economic reforms will be widely discussed, with considerable input encouraged from the population. Then, in January 2012, internal party and political matters will be handled more restrictively by a National Party Conference, with less input from the population.

"The writing is on the wall. The Cuban elites know that to smooth the political challenges of an economic transition and social liberalization, these two events need to renew and reinvigorate the PCC.

"In the last four years, Raúl has acted on the premise that only the party can replace Fidel. That is why the Raúlistas began by strengthening and consolidating a unified and coordinated PCC leadership. The drive to institutionalize single-party rule did not begin with the temporary transfer of power, however, but with Fidel's announcement at the University of Havana in November 2005 that in his absence, without greater institutionalization, the Revolution could destroy itself.

"Despite Fidel's warning, it was extremely difficult to institutionalize rule by the party as long as he remained the minimal winning coalition of Cuba's politics in and of himself. But Fidel never destroyed the party as Mao did during the Chinese Cultural Revolution. Outside Havana, in provinces such as Santiago de Cuba, Villa Clara, Cienfuegos, Guantánamo, Holguín, and Pinar del Río, the party remains the power center in both reality and perception. Throughout the country — in universities, factories, municipalities and the armed forces — the party has preserved a significant reservoir of power.

"Thus, Raúl and his loyalist José Ramón Machado Ventura used their first three years in power to speed up the process of party revitalization. Since Raúl wants not a transition to democracy, but economic reform managed by the PCC, the adopted political sequence is logical: first, to strengthen the party; second, to prepare the people for the adjustments and collateral dislocations, such as an increase in inequality and corruption; and third, to implement the economic changes.

"How is this institutionalization taking place?

"Remember, it started in 2006, when the Central Committee reinstated the Secretariat to monitor and implement party policies in sectors like health, education, culture, organization, and ideology. Today Raúl is at the top, but the execution of the party's policies is not micromanaged by him or assigned to ad hoc groups. Party policies are guided by professional cadres, either from the central apparatus or from the provinces.

"Another component is the renewal of the PCC among the bases, trying to recruit ambitious young people, particularly from the military, educational, and health sectors, with prestige and managerial training. Most new ministers and vice ministers who are not from the military are coming from the party or from the middle cadres of the same agencies they are promoted to lead. The local and provincial party structures and governments are becoming the institutionalized training ground for the promotion of the political elite of the country. Young communist or student leaders do not go directly to ministries or work for the president, as was the case under Fidel.

"The importance given by Raúl to the party was seen clearly in the designation of José Ramón Machado Ventura as his vice president. "Machadito" is the quintessential party man, a civilian member of the Politburo with close relations to the FAR. He was a founding member of the Second Front with Raúl in the Sierra Cristal and later served as the chief of medical military services. Given Machado's age — one year older than Raúl — it is hard to imagine that he will succeed Raúl. Rather, his rise to the vice presidency and the dismissal of Carlos Lage and Felipe Pérez Roque suggested that Raúl and the military command distrusted those of the younger generation who topped the list of candidates available for the position at the time.

"According to the narrative of the PCC, the major cause of what Fidel Castro called *desmerengamiento* (the cake-melting) of the Soviet Union was the lack of leadership unity, due to factional divisions and the absence of an institutionalized promotion of the cadres. Thus, Raúl will likely try to select as his successor somebody with a proven trajectory and the approval of the upper echelons of the PCC and FAR.

"So, the question becomes this: Has the evolution of Cuban politics under Raúl's presidency increased the probability of liberalization in the short or medium term? What should we expect, in other words, from the Sixth Congress?

"Confronting in 2010 the worst economic crisis since 1959, Raúl's government is speeding up the most serious reform effort since the collapse of the Soviet Union. The purposes of the changes are twofold: to provide stabilization to the leadership transition, without any traumatic fracture of the current elite, and to enhance the zones of legitimacy of rule by the PCC through improving the performance of the Cuban economy and the order and predictability of Cuban life.

"The lesson learned from Eastern Europe is that reforms, if they are mismanaged, can destroy reformist politicians, particularly if there are significant divisions among the party leaders. The PCC leadership now feels more confident beginning more significant economic reforms after the advances in party institutionalization and the renewal of the regional commanders of the FAR and more than half the Council of Ministers. Raúl is following a gradualist piecemeal approach, beginning with the most urgent (and easier) field of agriculture, but extending to almost all sectors of the economy with the release of 500,000 workers — and eventually more — from the government payroll.

"It is very important to note, in this context, that the economic crisis has not translated into a crisis of governability in Cuba, since the opposition does not have the capacity to mobilize a challenge to those in power.

"Different from governments in countries like Egypt, the government in Cuba has the nationalist narrative on its side. The nature of the population — due to the Revolution's changes in education, health care, and the access of women to economic life — does not support the conditions for a revolt. The Cuban average age is 35.1 and only 22 percent of its population is below 15 years. In Egypt that percentage is 33 percent. The most desperate forms of poverty have been avoided through a heavily subsidized sector, today totally unsustainable, that reaches everybody. And there is always the chance to immigrate to the United States as an escape valve for the frustration and discontent of the middle classes and most urban poor.

"Still, the future doesn't look rosy, especially during the transition from the current economic system to the proposed 'mixed economy.' The government is facing a crisis of confidence, especially among the younger generations who harbor serious doubts about the capacity of those in power to make the necessary reforms. Adjustment is particularly hard because Cuba doesn't enjoy the support of the international financial institutions. Also, the current rise in food prices could create tensions and shortages before the agricultural reforms begin to achieve their results.

"There is also the growing inequality gap due to the role of the double economy. Most Cubans living abroad are white, from the cities (mainly Havana), and represent the upper classes or those well connected with the outside world. In Cuba, dependence on remittances and connections to the dollar economy for a large segment of the population have created disadvantages in which sometimes region of origin, class, and race overlap. The government and the social organizations affiliated with its political projects, such as the UNEAC (the Artists and Writers Union), the ANEC (the Economists Association), and the CTC (the trade unions), have recognized this reality but fall short of solutions.

"By September 2010 — just three months after the government announced its plan to cut more than a million workers from the state sector — it became clear that this action would require a triplication of the non-state sector, creating new small and medium-sized private businesses alongside the 178 existing categories and allowing the private sector to hire some of the unemployed. The process gained momentum in November 2010, with the call for the Sixth Party Congress in April 2011. The congress process, strictly limited to economic issues, began with the distribution and discussion of a document titled 'Lineamientos de la política económica y social.'

"The document presents a plan of transition from the current command economy to a model closer to the market economies of China or Vietnam. Several parts of the existing Cuban social contract — things like major subsidies and gratuities — would be eliminated. Significant markets, like those for second-hand cars and real estate, would be liberalized, including the possibility of residential and commercial leasing. At the same time, the document proclaims a continued commitment to economic planning and socialist guarantees of health care and education.

"Bottom line: The central challenge on the path to Cuba's economic reform is to develop a market-oriented developmental state rather than a predatory one. And just as the Sixth Party Congress takes its economic cues from the experiences of China and Vietnam, the National Party Conference, with its focus on renewal of the single party, will take its political inspiration from those same two countries.

"Nobody should expect an outright abandonment of socialism or a repudiation of Fidel's legacy. On the contrary, even if the model is radically changed, the rhetoric will still be one of continuity and reverence for the previous stages.

"Integral elements of the strategy of adjustment and reform are the redesign of state-society relations and the quest for a national and international environment friendly to the economic reforms. As part of the first component, the government has engaged in high-level dialogue with the Cuban Roman Catholic Church in the person of Cardinal Jaime Ortega to reduce social and political tensions. This dialogue is part of a general increase in communications and recognizes the social space conquered by the Church and the rest of the religious communities, which remain the most active, independent, and relevant organizations of civil society.

"The dialogue between the state and the religious communities continues policies approved by Fidel, who by the mid–1980s saw that the congregations of faith had defeated the atheistic policies of his totalitarian project. The conquest of major social space by the religious communities — through their own education networks, recreation for the youth, social press and communication, and humanitarian support for vulnerable groups — not only opened a significant civil, economic, and cultural pluralism but also made the use of massive repression against these sectors less politically feasible or justifiable.

"Under these post-totalitarian conditions, the state's dialogue with the Church serves the reform interests of the nonliberal moderates within the government. Some of these groups recognize that many of the hopes and energies initially associated with the Revolution have languished. Now, due to their fundamental nationalist identity (as opposed to their defeated communist vision), and because they recognize that their legitimacy relies more on performance than on ideology, these groups are in favor of a transition to a market economy and the recognition of a significant pluralism in civil and economic society.

"The Church and many of the intellectuals associated with it have been thinking and promoting such reforms for quite a long time, while emphasizing their rejection of foreign interference in Cuban affairs. The stated goal of the religious leadership among the main Jewish, Protestant, and Catholic communities is to push for the pending reforms while preserving the social order, with a strong preference for gradualism.

"The acceptance of more cultural, economic, and civil pluralism by the nonliberal reformers inside the government does not equal tolerance of political opposition or representative democracy. In the instrumentalist view, for example, the state's release into exile of opposition activists and their relatives exports a segment incommodious for the government at this particular juncture of adjustment and reform. This way the state reduces frictions with foreign actors such as the United States and the European Union.

"So part of this context of renewal is the release of the political prisoners discussed in the last chapter, as well as another large group of prisoners connected to violent acts against the state. In what amounts to a partial amnesty, the government has astutely mixed people who have engaged in serious violent activities with the mainly peaceful activists arrested in the Black Spring of 2003 — people condemned to draconian penalties in fast-track trials without the minimal guarantees of due process.

"Meanwhile, the Church accepts the asymmetric nature of its dialogue with the state because this dialogue advances its corporatist, humanitarian, and pastoral interests — and it is consistent with the Church's support for gradual and peaceful solutions. The religious communities, and most other relevant actors in Cuba today, operate in a nationalist environment that promotes a peaceful transition and opposes any heavy-handed foreign intervention in the internal affairs of their country. In the view of most Cuban religious leaders, and a significant segment of the intellectuals who are pushing for reform, the antidote to totalitarian nationalism is not foreign intervention but democratic nationalism."

In March 2011, earthquakes, tsunamis, and a nuclear disaster ravaged Japan, sending shockwaves throughout Asia and the Pacific. Twitter-fueled revolutions swept the Middle East. Instability threatened a fragile global recovery from the biggest economic recession since the Great Depression. And Cuba prepared for the first congress of the PCC since 1997.

Finally, on the morning of April 18, the anniversary of Cuba's victory at the Bay of Pigs, a great parade led to Havana's Plaza of the Revolution. Raúl addressed the crowd and later that day the proceedings of the Sixth Congress convened. One thousand delegates gathered to approve more than 300 guidelines as a blueprint for economic and social reform. Everything from the continued availability of ration books to the ability of people to buy and sell houses was put on the table. Some observers, both on the island and off, remained aloof, skeptical that real change was afoot. Others followed the congress closely, parsing every word.

In actuality, the Sixth Congress began in November 2010, when the organizing commission published its "Social and Economic Guidelines" and opened discussion on them in assemblies within both the party and the general population. For the first time, nonpartisan organizations of Cuban civil society, like the religious communities, debated the document in their publications and published articles and editorials about the proposed reforms. In the end, the organizing commission rewrote the document, which was discussed again by the different provincial delegations to the congress and then on the floor of the Sixth Congress itself.

The suggested amendments to the guidelines were separated by the PCC into the acceptable and the unacceptable. For example, the party drew the line on the issue of concentration of property, rejecting 45 proposals that would have allowed more concentration as necessary for development. The final version of the document is now considered a blueprint for reform.

Economically, the most important shift was the declaration that the government and PCC must build a new type of socialism, one in which private property and markets are not stigmatized but promoted by authorities. According to the minister of the economy, almost 35 percent of the Cuban labor force must be employed by the non-state sector by 2015. The congress also created a commission led by former minister of the economy Marino Murillo to develop and implement the various reforms. Murillo responded positively to the demand from delegates to create credit and wholesale market mechanisms to promote the new non-state sector. And answering a long-held hope of the population, the government finally allowed for the sale of houses and cars, creating a market of collateral assets that people can now use to secure credit from banks.

Showing the importance of gradualism, Raúl acknowledged widespread concern about the proposed elimination of the ration cards; he said the ration cards would not go immediately, but only upon an economic recovery and in an orderly manner. In the same vein, he announced that decentralization would speed up in ways that will create a more efficient separation of powers among the central government, the provinces, and the municipalities. The Sixth Congress also approved a separation between the government's functions of running the country and the party's role as the political custodian of socialism and order. And the PCC is expected to recommend to the National Assembly a change in Article 74 of the Cuban Constitution to separate the first secretary of the PCC and the president of the council of state from the prime minister.

Politically, the most important development came in the form of term limits. The idea of limiting the term of the president to two five-year terms signaled a continued shift away from a leadership based on personality toward a leadership based on periodic elections. This is not a subtle change. The adoption of term limits for the party and all top positions of the state would be welcomed by many younger party and FAR members because: 1) it would create a promotion system based more on merit and education; 2) it would create space for more predictable upward mobility and intergenerational transition; and 3) it would soften the transition to a leadership with a more pragmatic and market-oriented approach. Paradoxically, however, the congress elected a very conservative and old Politburo, with an average age of 68.7 years and only four members younger than 60. And the congress also elected 80-year-old José Machado Ventura, who is associated with the most conservative approach to the reforms, as second secretary of the PCC.

On the last day of the Sixth Congress, Fidel made an appearance, clad in a plaid shirt and blue jogging suit, lately his standard uniform. He sat next to his little brother and approved of what Raúl was doing. The boat was being rocked, all right, but not too much.

Later Fidel called the Sixth Congress a success and said Raúl had explained to him that some old people would have to remain on the Central Committee even though they would not be effective leaders due to their age. Raúl didn't want to treat them rudely. Fidel then declared that he had not taken any position in the party and encouraged others of the "historical generation" to do the same. In his final speech to the congress, Raúl further explained that the PCC would go through a process of leadership renewal in the next five years, and it was possible that new members would be added to the Politburo and Central Committee before or during the Party Conference to be held in January 2012.

The Central Report to the Congress said clearly that the PCC is planning an intergenerational transition. This makes Raúl and Machado the launchers of the reforms and the caretakers of the succession, but not the long-term solution to the party's new leadership. Machado will play a key role in choosing not only the successors but also the structure of separation of powers destined to replace, both within the party and between the party and government, the current model of "Castro in command." The PCC eventually will choose its presidential successor as a business corporation chooses its new CEO. The successor will be a person with wide experience and a vast network in different sectors of the government, the party, and the regions.

It would be a mistake to focus too much on the generation of appointees to the Politburo who are in their forties and fifties. Miguel Díaz Canel is probably the only one who fits the requirements. He is a minister and became a member of the Politburo after he was a leader of the party in two strategic provinces. He is also a civilian. This is better for the image of the elite, though it might create some distrust in the high military command.

So, overall, the Sixth Congress came and went, reinforcing the process of gradual change. Still, many questions remain unanswered. The reforms have yet to be implemented. Over the long term, the biggest question facing Cuba seems increasingly clear: Will its path to reform stop halfway with the Chinese model, or will it forge ahead to create a brave new model, perhaps neither European nor Brazilian, but one uniquely Cuban?

And the biggest issue facing the United States seems equally clear: How soon and how fast will it finally "tear down this wall" that we call the embargo?

Chapter Notes

Chapter One

1. D. Deudney and J. Ikenberry, "The Myth of the Autocratic Revival," *Foreign Affairs* 88, no. 1 (January/February 2009): 83–84.
2. See "Ocho Leones Feroces," *Granma*, http://www.granma.cubaweb.cu/secciones/50_granma-80_fidel/secretos_de_generales/art09.html.
3. In Spanish, the song goes like this: "Alla en la Siria, hay una mora, que tiene los ojos tan lindos, y un lucero encantador..."
4. Thomas Friedman, *The Lexus and the Olive Tree* (New York: Anchor Books, 2000), 9 ("globalization ... is the inexorable integration of markets").
5. D. Sanger, "Beyond the Trade Pact Collapse," *New York Times*, August 3, 2008 (online) (emphasis added).
6. T. Friedman, "Living Hand to Mouth," *New York Times*, October 26, 2005 (online) (emphasis added).
7. The word is adapted from the book by Thomas Friedman, *The World Is Flat* (New York: Farrar, Strauss and Giroux, 2005).
8. See Maryann Cusimano Love, *Beyond Sovereignty: Issues for a Global Agenda*, 2nd edition (South Melbourne: Thomson Wadsworth, 2003), 3.

Chapter Two

1. See, for instance, "Fidel Castro Praises Barack Obama as 'Absolutely Sincere,'" *Sunday Times*, January 22, 2009 (online).
2. For a discussion of so-called rogue states and the pertinence of using that label, see T. H. Henriksen, "The Rise and Decline of the Rogue States," *Journal of International Affairs* 54, no. 2 (Spring 2001): 349–73; see also R. S. Litwak, "What's in a Name? The Changing Foreign Policy Lexicon," *Journal of International Affairs* 54, no. 2 (Spring 2001): 375–92.
3. Roberto Unger, *Democracy Realized: The Progressive Alternative* (London/New York: Verso, 1998), 269.
4. *Ibid.*, 277 (emphasis added).
5. The following paragraphs present a narrative synthesis of information gathered from the authors' interview of Miguel Sanchez on September 1, 2008, in Denver, Colorado, and from pages 161–74 and page 184 of the definitive biography of Ernesto "Che" Guevara written by Jon Lee Anderson (*Che Guevara: A Revolutionary Life* [New York: Grove Press, 1997]). Direct quotes from the Anderson biography will be duly noted.
6. *Ibid.*, 173.
7. *Ibid.*
8. *Ibid.*, 184.
9. *Ibid.*, 190.

Chapter Three

1. For a discussion of the operation known by the names "Candela" or "Patty-Candela," see Aleksandr Fursenko and Timothy Naftali, *One Hell of a Gamble: Khrushchev, Kennedy and Castro* (New York: W.W. Norton, 1997). Another well-documented review of the operation from the Cuban revolutionary perspective appears in Fabian Escalante, *The Secret War: CIA Covert Operations Against Cuba, 1959–1962* (Melbourne, Australia: Ocean Press, 2004). Fursenko and Naftali studied not only the Cuban reaction but also the Soviet reaction after learning about the plan.

2. See Tomas Diez Acosta, *October 1962: The "Missile" Crisis as Seen from Cuba* (New York: Pathfinder, 2002).

3. J. Hansen, "Soviet Deception in the Cuban Missile Crisis," https://www.cia.gov/library/center-for-the-study-of-intelligence/csi-publications/csi-studies/studies/vol46no1/article06.html.

4. *Ibid.*

5. Anderson, *Che Guevara*, 526.

6. *Ibid.*, 526–30.

7. See James Blight, Bruce Allyn, and Daniel Welch, *Cuba on the Brink: Castro, the Missile Crisis and the Soviet Collapse* (Lanham, MD: Rowman & Littlefield, 2002), 345; James Blight and Phillip Brenner, *Sad and Luminous: Cuba's Struggle with the Superpowers After the Missile Crisis Days* (Lanham, MD: Rowman & Littlefield, 2002).

8. Hansen, "Soviet Deception in the Cuban Missile Crisis."

9. Anderson, *Che Guevara*, 527.

10. *Ibid.*, 530.

11. Ernest May and Phillip Zelikow, *The Kennedy Tapes: Inside the White House During the Cuban Missile Crisis* (Cambridge, MA: Belknap Press/Harvard Press, 1997).

12. Brian Latell, *After Fidel: Raul Castro and the Future of Cuba's Revolution* (Basingstoke/New York: Palgrave Macmillan, 2005).

13. Robert Woodward, *Veil: The Secret Wars of the CIA* (New York: Simon & Schuster, 1987), 334–35.

14. Daniel Erikson, *The Cuba Wars: Fidel Castro, the United States, and the Next Revolution* (New York: Bloomsbury Press, 2008).

15. The Cuban Liberty and Democratic Solidarity (Libertad) Act of 1996 ("Helms-Burton Act"), Public Law 104–114, 110 Stat. 785, 22 U.S. Code §§ 6021–6091.

16. William Jefferson Clinton, *My Life: The Presidential Years* (New York: Random House, 2004), 310–11.

17. See, for instance, M. Laffey and J. Weldes, "Decolonizing the Cuban Missile Crisis," *International Studies Quarterly* 52, no. 3 (September 2008): 555–77.

Chapter Four

1. Johanna Tablada is today the assistant director of the Department of Relations with the United States at the Cuban Ministry of Foreign Relations.

2. For Professor Stiglitz's discussion of competition, see Joseph Stiglitz, *Wither Socialism?* (Cambridge, MA: MIT Press, 1994), at chapter 7.

3. For a discussion of the convergence of opinions on the issue of American policy when it comes to exploiting the island's north coast oil fields, see the opening pages of Chapter Ten.

4. The 2000 Trade Sanctions Reform Act also created exceptions in the embargo for the sale of medical products to Cuba, but the restrictions and monitoring conditions are so intrusive on Cuban sovereignty that no major trade has happened in this field. However, agricultural products are commonly purchased from the United States.

5. See Hernando De Soto, *The Mystery of Capital: Why Capitalism Triumphs in the West and Fails Everywhere Else* (New York: Basic Books, 2000).

6. See, for instance, M. Fineman, "Little Known Biotech Industry Vital to Cuba's Future," *Miami Herald*, August 14, 1998, http://www2.fiu.edu/~fcf/biotech81498.html.

7. See, for instance, J. Randal, "License to Test Cancer Vaccines in U.S. a Victory for Cuban Biotechnology," *Journal of the National Cancer Institute* 96, no. 23 (2004): 1740–42, http://jnci.oxfordjournals.org/content/96/23/1740.full.

8. "Cuba Continuing to Develop Innovative Biotechnology Products," *Granma International*, November 18, 2009, http://www.granma.cu/ingles/2009/noviembre/mier18/Cuba.html.

9. "Russia to Drill for Oil Off Cuba," *BBC News*, July 29, 2009 (online), http://news.bbc.co.uk/2/hi/8175704.stm.

10. See A. Lopez-Levy, "Not Your Father's Cuba," *Foreign Policy*, November 5, 2010, http://www.foreignpolicy.com/articles/2010/11/05/not_your_fathers_cuba.

11. The definitive work on the subject is Gary Hufbauer, Jeffrey Schott, and Kimberley Elliott, *Economic Sanctions Reconsidered*, 3rd edition (Washington, D.C.: Peterson Institute for International Economics, 2009), which reflects over 200 case studies.

12. "Changing Cuba Policy — In the United States National Interest," Staff Trip Report to the Committee on Foreign Relations, U.S. Senate, 111th Congress, 1st Session, February 23, 2009, http://www.fas.org/irp/congress/2009_rpt/cuba.html (hereafter referred to as "Lugar Report").

13. R. Inglehart and C. Welzel, "How Development Leads to Democracy," *Foreign Affairs* 88, no. 2 (March-April 2009): 33, 42, 47. Professors Inglehart and Welzel are also the coauthors of *Modernization, Cultural Change, and Democracy: The Human Development Sequence* (Cambridge: Cambridge University Press, 2005).

14. See Lugar Report, 7–10.

15. *Ibid.*, 10, 12.

Chapter Five

1. See "25 Best Blogs 2009," *Time*, http://www.time.com/time/specials/packages/complete list/0,,1879276,00.html.

2. See *Generacion Y* at http://www.desdecuba.com/generationy/.

3. See Yoani Sánchez, "My Profile," *Generacion Y*, http://www.desdecuba.com/generationy/?page_id=108.

4. See Yoani Sánchez, "The Shredder," *Generacion Y*, http://www.desdecuba.com/generationy/?m=200903.

5. See Yoani Sánchez, "Third Time Is Not a Charm," *Generacion Y*, http://www.desdecuba.com/generationy/?m=200903.

6. See Yoani Sánchez, "And They Gave Us the Microphones," *Generacion Y*, http://www.desdecuba.com/generationy/?m=200903.

7. Between 2002 and 2004, the *New York Times* ran 18 articles about the Varela Project. They are collected and available at "Varela Project," *New York Times* (article collection), http://www.nytimes.com/keyword/varela-project. The description that appears in the next several paragraphs is based on these articles and other sources, including the personal experiences of coauthor Arturo Lopez-Levy.

8. See "Wives of Political Prisoners March in Cuba," Associated Press, March 18, 2006; "Ladies in White March in Cuba, Pay Price for Disobedience," *Chicago Tribune*, March 3, 2006; "Dissidents' Wives Hit Castro, Seek Release," *Washington Times*, December 27, 2005; "Ladies in White Stopped from Collecting EU Award," Associated Press, December 15, 2005.

9. In Chapter Eleven, we discuss the eventual release of the dissidents arrested in 2003, which occurred in the second half of 2010. See "Cuban Government Vows to Release 52 Prisoners," *New York Times*, July 7, 2010, http://www.nytimes.com/2010/07/08/world/americas/08 cuba.html?. While causation is a tough thing to prove, in or out of a court of law, most people view the release of these prisoners as less of a response to the Ladies in White and more of a step in the continuing dance of liberalization described throughout this book.

10. C. Gershman and O. Gutierrez, "Ferment in Civil Society: Can Cuba Change?" *Journal of Democracy* 20, no. 1 (January 2009): 36–54, http://www.journalofdemocracy.org/articles/gratis/Gutierrez-20-1.pdf.

11. See Freedom House Report, *Change in Cuba: How Citizens View Their Country's Future*, http://www.freedomhouse.org/template.cfm?page=383&report=69.

12. See R. Mackey, "Fidel Castro Blogs about the 'Honey of Power,'" *New York Times*, March 3, 2009, http://thelede.blogs.nytimes.com/2009/03/03/fidel-castro-blogs-about-the-honey-of-power/.

13. See, for instance, "Congressional Black Caucus Meets with Castro Brothers," NPR.org, April 9, 2009, http://www.npr.org/templates/story/story.php?storyId=102903658.

14. See, for instance, "Obama to Free Cuba Family Travel, Remittances," Reuters.com, April 3, 2009, http://www.reuters.com/article/idustre5326hv20090403.

15. *White House Fact Sheet: Reaching Out to the Cuban People* (April 13, 2009), http://www.whitehouse.gov/the_press_office/Fact-Sheet-Reaching-out-to-the-Cuban-people/.

16. See W. Smith, R. Muse, and G. Baker, *Center for International Policy Report*, "Cuba Should Not Be on the Terrorist List," http://www.scarletnotes.com/downloads/CubaonTerroristList_.pdf.

17. *Ibid.*; see also Robert Muse's email to Arturo Lopez-Levy, January 25, 2011.

18. P. Baker, "Building Coalitions, One Issue at a Time," *New York Times*, March 14, 2009, http://www.nytimes.com/2009/03/15/us/politics/15obama.html.

19. Unger, *Democracy Realized*, 243.

20. See Cusimano Love, *Beyond Sovereignty*, 3.

21. Harlan Abrahams and Steve Farber, *On the List: Fixing America's Failing Organ Transplant System* (New York: Rodale, 2009), 32.

22. See Yoani Sánchez, "At the Meliá Cohiba," *Generacion Y*, http://www.desdecuba.com/generationy/?m=200905&paged=2.

Chapter Six

1. *Kent v. Dulles*, 357 U.S. 116, 125–26 (1958) (majority opinion).

2. *Aptheker v. Secretary of State*, 378 U.S. 500, 519–20 (1964) (concurring opinion).

3. *Aptheker v. Secretary of State*, 378 U.S. 500, 507–8 (1964) (majority opinion).

4. *Zemel v. Rusk*, 381 U.S. 1, 15–16 (1965) (majority opinion).

5. *Regan v. Wald*, 468 U.S. 222, 242 (1984) (5–4 majority opinion).

6. See H. Fontova, "Hollywood Loves Fidel — But Why?" *Canada Free Press*, May 9, 2009, http://www.canadafreepress.com/index.php/site/article/hollywood-loves-fidel-but-why/. Arturo says he knows that Mr. Fernandez used to work for the Cuban government, but Arturo considers him a charlatan. Mr. Fernandez is paid for appearing on Miami TV to describe the lifestyle of the Cuban elite. According to Arturo, he has spoken some truths but frequently fantasizes, even creating fake characters. On one occasion, speaking about Arturo's cousin Luís, Mr. Fernandez told the host that Luís has a secret account in the Netherlands through "Luís's oldest brother Rigoberto," who lives and works in that country. But Arturo says that he knows his own family: his cousin Luís doesn't have any brother by that name, and nobody in the family is living in the Netherlands.

7. See Lon Fuller, *The Morality of Law* (Storrs Lecture Series) (New Haven, CT: Yale University Press, revised edition 1969).

8. See "Supreme Court: Miami School Can Ban Book on Cuba," *Christian Science Monitor*, November 16, 2009, http://www.instablogs.com/outer_permalink.php?p=supreme-court-miami-school-can-ban-book-on-cuba. The ACLU'S 2006 background statement on the litigation can be found at "News and Alerts," American Civil Liberties Union of Florida, http://www.aclufl.org/news_events/?action=viewRelease&emailAlertID=1949. The press release that was issued by the ACLU when it lost the case can be found at "U.S. Supreme Court Denies ACLU's Petition to Hear *Vamos a Cuba* Book Censorship Case," American Civil Liberties Union, http://www.aclu.org/free-speech/us-supreme-court-denies-aclus-petition-hear-vamos-cuba-book-censorship-case. The press release is subtitled "Decision a Blow to the First Amendment; Clears Path for Removal of Books."

9. The Constitution of the Republic of Cuba (1992) can be found online at http://

www.cubanet.org/ref/dis/const_92_e.htm. In December 1991, in the wake of the collapse of the Soviet Union, the constitution was amended to allow for limited forms of foreign investment and private property. Today's economic reforms can be traced to these amendments. The next amendments came in 2002, when the Cuban Constitution was again changed to make it clear that socialism was permanent and irrevocable on the island. The dualistic signals sent by the amendments of 1991 and 2002 are entirely consistent with the contradictions that plague the island as described throughout this book. They are not, however, entirely different from the inconsistent signals sent by parts of the U.S. Constitution.

    10. Cuban Constitution, Chapter I, Article 3.
    11. *Ibid.*, Chapter VII, Article 53.
    12. *Ibid.*, Chapter I, Article 1.
    13. *Ibid.*, Chapter I, Article 5 (emphasis added).

Chapter Seven

    1. See A. Ferguson, "Gary Hart Comes Out," CNN.com, January 17, 2000, http://edition.cnn.com/Allpolitics/time/2000/01/17/hart.html.
    2. See, for instance, Dan Simmons, *The Crook Factory* (New York: Avon, 1999); H. Mitgang, "Publishing the FBI File on Hemingway," *New York Times*, March 11, 1983, http://www.nytimes.com/books/99/07/04/specials/hemingway-fbi.html.
    3. See Martin Cruz Smith, *Havana Bay* (New York: Random House, 1999).
    4. Department of Justice, Office of Public Affairs, "Former State Department Official and Wife Arrested for Serving as Illegal Agents of Cuba for Nearly 30 Years," June 5, 2009, http://www.justice.gov/opa/pr/2009/June/09-nsd-554.html.
    5. See S. Hsu, "Walter Myers, State Dept. Analyst Who Spied for Cuba, Gets Life; Wife 6 Years," *Washington Post*, July 17, 2010, http://www.washingtonpost.com/wp-dyn/content/article/2010/07/16/AR2010071600684.html.
    6. See "Arturo López-Levy at UM Cuba Conference April 4, 2009 Pt. 2," YouTube, http://www.youtube.com/watch?v=DotzkLI8C4Y.
    7. Lugar Report, 2–3.
    8. See Lopez-Levy, "Not Your Father's Cuba."
    9. "Executive Summary," *2007 FIU/Cuba Poll*, http://www2.fiu.edu/~ipor/cuba8/ExecutiveSummary.htm.
    10. Bendixen & Amandi, *National Poll of Cuban & Cuban Americans on Changes to Cuba Policy*, http://www.bendixenandassociates.com/Cuba_Flash_Poll_Executive_Summary.html.
    11. "Poll Shows Strong Cuban American Support for Obama," Reuters.com, April 21, 2009, http://www.reuters.com/article/idustre53K5cs20090421.
    12. D. Cave, "U.S. Overtures Find Support Among Cuban-Americans," *New York Times*, April 20, 2009, http://www.nytimes.com/2009/04/21/us/21miami.html?scp=1&sq=a%20stunning%20change%20of%20heart%20now%20shared%20by%20a%20wide%20majority%20of%20Cuban-Americans&st=cse.
    13. See A. Lopez-Levy, "Cuban Americans Vote with Their Feet," *Havana Note*, November 23, 2010, http://www.thehavananote.com/node/822.
    14. See T. Barnett, "The Next Five States," *Esquire* (September 19, 2007), http://www.esquire.com/features/esquire-100/fivestates1007.
    15. Constitution of the Republic of Cuba, Article 12.
    16. See R. Unger, "Introduction to *The Second Way: The Present and Future of Brazil*" (São Paolo: Boitempo, 2001).

Chapter Eight

    1. The historic confrontation between Adlai Stevenson and Valerian Zorin at the United Nations is available on many websites. One of the most useful is the Online Speech Bank, which

includes both a video and transcript; see "Adlai Stevenson: United Nations Security Council Address on Soviet Missiles in Cuba," American Rhetoric, http://www.americanrhetoric.com/speeches/adlaistevensonunitednationscuba.html.

2. M. Schwirtz, "Russia and Cuba Sign Strategic Partnership," *New York Times*, January 30, 2009, http://www.nytimes.com/2009/01/31/world/europe/31russia.html?_r=1&scp=1&sq=The%20presidents%20of%20Russia%20and%20Cuba%20signed%20a%20strategic%20partnership%20&st=cse.

3. This is an obvious reference to the archetypical defense of "shock therapy reform" in Russia. See Andrei Shleifer and Daniel Treisman, *Without a Map: Political Tactics and Economic Reform in Russia* (Cambridge, MA: MIT Press, 2000). Shleifer, then a Harvard professor, was later found liable for conspiracy to defraud the U.S. government while making considerable profits from advising the Russian government's economic reforms; see "'Tawdry Shleifer Affair' Stokes Faculty Anger Toward Summers," *Harvard Crimson*, February 10, 2006, http://www.the crimson.com/article/2006/2/10/tawdry-shleifer-affair-stokes-faculty-anger/.

Chapter Nine

1. Azar Gat, *Victorious and Vulnerable: Why Democracy Won in the Twentieth Century and How It Is Still Imperiled* (Lanham, MD: Rowman & Littlefield, 2009).

2. See A. Gat, D. Deudney, J. Ikenberry, R. Inglehart, and C. Welzel, "Which Way Is History Marching?" *Foreign Affairs* (July-August 2009), http://www.foreignaffairs.com/articles/65162/azar-gat-daniel-deudney-and-g-john-ikenberry-and-ronald-inglehar/which-way-is-history-marching?page=show.

3. R. Altman, "Globalization in Retreat," *Foreign Affairs* 88, no. 4 (July-August 2009), http://www.foreignaffairs.com/articles/65153/roger-c-altman/globalization-in-retreat.

4. Richard Posner, *A Failure of Capitalism: The Crisis of '08 and the Descent into Depression* (Cambridge, MA: Harvard University Press, 2009).

5. J. Rauch, "Capitalism's Fault Lines," *New York Times Sunday Book Review*, May 14, 2009, http://www.nytimes.com/2009/05/17/books/review/Rauch-t.html.

6. J. Stiglitz, "Wall Street's Toxic Message," *Vanity Fair* (July 2009).

7. *Ibid.*

8. F. Zakaria, "The Capitalist Manifesto: Greed Is Good (to a Point)," *Newsweek* (June 13, 2009), http://www.newsweek.com/2009/06/12/the-capitalist-manifesto-greed-is-good.html.

9. See Altman, "Globalization in Retreat."

10. *Ibid.* (emphasis added).

11. See P. Hare and T. Revesz, "Hungary's Transition to a Market Economy: The Case Against a 'Big Bang,'" *Economic Policy* 14 (1992), 227–64.

12. See *Merriam-Webster Dictionary* definition of "social democracy," http://www.merriam-webster.com/dictionary/social+democracy.

13. R. Kuttner, "The Copenhagen Consensus," *Foreign Affairs* (March-April 2008), http://www.foreignaffairs.com/articles/63223/robert-kuttner/the-copenhagen-consensus (emphasis added).

14. N. Gill, "Historiography: Brazilian Hegemony in South America," *Southern Affairs*, March 31, 2008, http://www.southernaffairs.org/2008/03/historiography-iii-brazilian-hegemony.html.

15. Ibid.

16. See Unger, "Introduction to *The Second Way*"; see also note 11, chapter six and accompanying text of this book.

17. For a description of the program, see "Bolsa Família: Changing the Lives of Millions in Brazil," available on the website of the World Bank at http://web.worldbank.org/Wbsite/External/Countries/Lacext/Brazilextn/0,,contentMDK:21447054~pagePK:141137~piPK:141127~theSitePK:322341,00.html: "The Bolsa Família Program, which has technical and financial support from the World Bank, is cited as one of the key factors behind the positive social outcomes achieved by Brazil in recent years. The Program is an innovative social initiative taken by the

Brazilian Government. It reaches 11 million families, more than 46 million people, a major portion of the country's low-income population. The model emerged in Brazil more than a decade ago and has been refined since then. Poor families with children receive an average of R$70.00 (about U.S. $35) in direct transfers. In return, they commit to keeping their children in school and taking them for regular health checks. And so Bolsa Família has two important results: helping to reduce current poverty, and getting families to invest in their children, thus breaking the cycle of intergenerational transmission and reducing future poverty."

Chapter Ten

1. The article ran under different headlines in different newspapers. See M. Perry, "End Embargo Before China Taps Oil 45 Miles Off U.S. Coast," *Billings Gazette*, July 16, 2009, http://billingsgazette.com/news/opinion/guest/article_98b56854-71b2-11de-976d-001cc4c002e0.html.

2. Again, the article ran under various guises. See J. Quigley, "Opinion," *Cleveland Plain Dealer*, July 11, 2009 (online).

3. See "Convergence" in "Economics A–Z," Economist.com, http://www.economist.com/research/economics/alphabetic.cfm?term=catchupeffect&CFID=150606091&CFTOKEN=89214014.

4. Queens University, Department of Sociology, "The Measure of a Revolution" (May 7–9, 2009), http://www.queensu.ca/sociology/?q=themeasureofarevolution09.

5. See "Cuba Suspends Communist Party Congress," *Guardian*, July 31, 2009, http://www.guardian.co.uk/world/2009/jul/31/cuba-communist-party-economy.

Chapter Eleven

1. Speech given by Raúl Castro Ruz, President of the Council of State and Ministers, at the 3rd Regular Session of the Seventh Legislature of the National Assembly of People's Power, Havana Convention Center, August 1, 2009, "Year of the 50th Anniversary of the Revolutionary Triumph," http://www.cubanembassy.net/documents/314AA7388FD0f31a56279a59b5f4784034c1923d.html.

2. See T. Padgett, "Cuba's Mega-Rock Concert: A Win-Win for Juanes," *Time* (September 21, 2009), http://www.time.com/time/world/article/0,8599,1925283,00.html.

3. See A. Lopez-Levy, "Strait Talk," *Foreign Policy*, January 31, 2011, http://www.foreignpolicy.com/articles/2011/01/31/strait_talk.

4. See "Colombian Rocker Juanes Makes Cuba Concert Political After All," *Examiner*, September 21, 2009, http://www.examiner.com/international-travel-in-chicago/colombian-rocker-juanes-makes-cuba-concert-political-after-all. In Miami, roughly 73 percent of the Cuban American households watched the concert. Cultural exchanges were clearly building bridges and shifting attitudes among the exiles. After the concert, a Bendixen & Amandi poll found that support for the concert had leaped from 27 percent to 53 percent. The biggest shift came from older exiles, a group that went from only 17 percent in favor before the concert to 48 percent afterward.

5. See "Cuban Government Vows to Release 52 Prisoners." See also note 9 and accompanying text in Chapter Five.

6. See "Cuba Frees Political Prisoner Who Refused Exile Deal," *BBC News*, November 14, 2010, http://www.bbc.co.uk/news/world-latin-america-11752157; "Cuba to Free Two More Political Prisoners," Reuters.com, November 13, 2010, http://www.reuters.com/article/2010/11/14/us-cuba-prisoners-idustre6ac2fp20101114.

7. See "Cuba Maps Out Economic Reforms," *CBC News*, September 24, 2010, http://www.cbc.ca/world/story/2010/09/24/cuba-economic-reforms024.html.

8. See "Fidel Castro Appears to Support Cuban Economic Reforms," *McClatchy*, November 19, 2010, http://www.mcclatchydc.com/2010/11/19/104019/fidel-castro-appears-to-support.html.

9. See "Cuba Begins Public Debate on Economic Reforms," *BBC News*, December 1, 2010, http://www.bbc.co.uk/news/world-latin-america-11894593.

10. J. Goldberg, "Castro: 'No One Has Been Slandered More than the Jews,'" The atlantic.com, September 7, 2010, http://www.theatlantic.com/international/archive/2010/09/castro-no-one-has-been-slandered-more-than-the-jews/62566/; and J. Goldberg, "Fidel: 'Cuban Model Doesn't Even Work for Us Anymore,'" Theatlantic.com, September 8, 2010, http://www.theatlantic.com/-international/archive/2010/09/fidel-cuban-model-doesnt-even-work-for-us-anymore/62602/. The brief quotations in the next four paragraphs come from these two articles.

11. See "Sixth Congress of the Communist Party of Cuba to be Held Next Year," *Cuba Journal* (November 9, 2010), http://cubajournal.blogspot.com/2010/11/sixth-congress-of-communist-party-of.html.

12. "Raul Castro: Open Debate Best Way to Solve Problems," *Fox News Latino*, December 6, 2010, http://latino.foxnews.com/latino/politics/2010/12/06/raul-castro-open-debate-best-way-solve-problems/.

Chapter Twelve

1. This classification of regime type comes from the seminal work of Juan Linz and Alfred Stepan, who differentiated non-democratic regimes in terms of their pluralism, leadership, mobilization, and ideology. See Juan Linz and Alfred Stepan, *Problems of Democratic Transitions and Consolidation* (Baltimore: John Hopkins University Press, 1996), 42–51.

2. The list of tolerated intellectuals, singers, and painters who project views dissenting from the official discourse is too long to recite fully. Here are but a few examples: Tania Bruguera, Carlos Garaicoa, Carlos Varela, Los Aldeanos, and Pablo Milanés.

3. See G. Schubert, "One Party Rule and the Question of Legitimacy in Contemporary China," *Journal of Contemporary China* 17, no. 54 (2008), 191–204. Schubert bases his theoretical framework on David Easton, *A System Analysis of Political Life* (Chicago: University of Chicago Press, 1979), 282–86.

4. Dr. Cynthia Arnson formulated the question in those terms at the seminar titled "Engaging Cuba: Policy Options for the United States, Europe and the Western Hemisphere," at the Woodrow Wilson Center in Washington, D.C., where she is the director of the Latin American Program, on November 16, 2009.

5. The FAR complex goes beyond the strict military tasks of the FAR. Although it is centered on the Ministry of the Armed Forces, it includes other political, economic, and social spaces. Politically, it includes several ministries such as those of the interior, transportation, communication, and tourism. Economically, in addition to the other ministries, the FAR complex controls the Grupo de Administración Empresarial (GAESA), which in turn controls a significant sector of tourism and the most dynamic sectors of the Cuban economy. Socially, the FAR complex includes groups like the Association of Veterans of the Cuban Revolution, which serve as channels of communication, distribution of favors, and mobilization between the leaders and the most militant bases. In terms of social services, the FAR has a network of hospitals and agricultural companies associated with the Ejército Juvenil del Trabajo, which provide cheap food and medical services to significant segments of the population. It also has a very effective system of hurricane relief and evacuation, the Defensa Civil, much appreciated by the population. Cadres of the FAR, or those closely related to it, are in charge of important departments of the PCC, such as ideology and organization.

6. Both Fidel and Raúl Castro have insisted that the Communist Party, and not the Armed Forces, is the political vanguard of the country. Military dictatorship is an anathema in Cuba leftist history and indoctrination, but there is a long advocacy in favor of military autonomy in the Cuban state, insulated from civilian intervention.

Bibliography

Books

Acosta, Tomas Diez. *October 1962: The "Missile" Crisis as Seen from Cuba.* New York: Pathfinder, 2002.

Anderson, Jon Lee. *Che Guevara: A Revolutionary Life.* New York: Grove Press, 1997.

Blight, James, Bruce Allyn, and Daniel Welch. *Cuba on the Brink: Castro, the Missile Crisis and the Soviet Collapse.* Lanham, MD: Rowman & Littlefield, 2002.

Blight, James, and Phillip Brenner. *Sad and Luminous Days: Cuba's Struggle with the Superpowers After the Missile Crisis.* Lanham, MD: Rowman & Littlefield, 2002.

Clinton, William Jefferson. *My Life: The Presidential Years.* New York: Random House, 2004.

Cusimano Love, Maryann. *Beyond Sovereignty: Issues for a Global Agenda.* 2nd edition. South Melbourne: Thomson Wadsworth, 2003.

De Soto, Hernando. *The Mystery of Capital: Why Capitalism Triumphs in the West and Fails Everywhere Else.* New York: Basic Books, 2000.

Easton, David. *A System Analysis of Political Life.* Chicago: University of Chicago Press, 1979.

Erikson, Daniel. *The Cuba Wars: Fidel Castro, the United States, and the Next Revolution.* New York: Bloomsbury Press, 2008.

Escalante, Fabian. *The Secret War: CIA Covert Operations Against Cuba, 1959–1962.* Melbourne, Australia: Ocean Press, 2004.

Farber, Steve, and Harlan Abrahams. *On the List: Fixing America's Failing Organ Transplant System.* New York: Rodale, 2009

Filkins, Dexter. *The Forever War.* New York: Knopf, 2008.

Friedman, Thomas. *The Lexus and the Olive Tree.* New York: Anchor Books, 2000.

_____. *The World Is Flat.* New York: Farrar, Strauss and Giroux, 2005.

Fuller, Lon. *The Morality of Law* (Storrs Lecture Series). New Haven, CT: Yale University Press, revised edition 1969.

Fursenko, Aleksandr, and Timothy Naftali. *One Hell of a Gamble: Khrushchev, Kennedy and Castro* (New York: W.W. Norton, 1997.

Gat, Azar. *Victorious and Vulnerable: Why Democracy Won in the Twentieth Century and How It Is Still Imperiled.* Lanham, MD: Rowman & Littlefield, 2009.

Hufbauer, Gary, Jeffrey Schott, and Kimberley Elliott. *Economic Sanctions Reconsidered.* 3rd edition. Washington, DC: Peterson Institute for International Economics, 2009.

Inglehart, Ronald, and Christian Welzel. *Modernization, Cultural Change, and Democracy: The Human Development Sequence.* Cambridge: Cambridge University Press, 2005.

Latell, Brian. *After Fidel: Raul Castro and the Future of Cuba's Revolution.* Basingstoke/New York: Palgrave Macmillan, 2005)

Linz, Juan, and Alfred Stepan. *Problems of Democratic Transitions and Consolidation.* Baltimore: John Hopkins University Press, 1996.

May, Ernest, and Phillip Zelikow. *The Kennedy Tapes: Inside the White House During the Cuban Missile Crisis.* Cambridge, MA: Belknap Press/Harvard Press, 1997.

Posner, Richard. *A Failure of Capitalism: The Crisis of '08 and the Descent into Depression*. Cambridge, MA: Harvard University Press, 2009.
Shleifer, Andrei, and Daniel Treisman. *Without a Map: Political Tactics and Economic Reform in Russia*. Cambridge, MA: MIT Press 2000.
Simmons, Dan. *The Crook Factory*. New York: Avon, 1999.
Smith, Martin Cruz. *Havana Bay*. New York: Random House, 1999.
Stiglitz, Joseph. *Wither Socialism?* Cambridge, MA: MIT Press, 1994.
Unger, Roberto. *Democracy Realized: The Progressive Alternative*. London/New York: Verso, 1998.
_____. *The Second Way: The Present and Future of Brazil*. São Paolo: Boitempo, 2001.
Woodward, Robert. *Veil: The Secret Wars of the CIA*. New York: Simon & Schuster, 1987.

Statutes, Court Cases, and Other Governmental Sources

Aptheker v. Secretary of State. 378 U.S. 500 (1964).
"Changing Cuba Policy — In the United States National Interest." Staff Trip Report to the Committee on Foreign Relations, U.S. Senate, 111th Congress, 1st Session, February 23, 2009. http://www.fas.org/irp/congress/2009_rpt/cuba.html.
The Constitution of the Republic of Cuba, 1992 (amended).
The Cuban Liberty and Democratic Solidarity (Libertad) Act of 1996 ("Helms-Burton Act"). Public Law 104–114, 110 Stat. 785, 22 U.S. Code §§ 6021–6091.
Department of Justice, Office of Public Affairs. "Former State Department Official and Wife Arrested for Serving as Illegal Agents of Cuba for Nearly 30 Years." June 5, 2009. http://www.justice.gov/opa/pr/2009/June/09-nsd-554.html.
Hansen, J. "Soviet Deception in the Cuban Missile Crisis." https://www.cia.gov/library/center-for-the-study-of-intelligence/csi-publications/csi-studies/studies/vol46no1/article06.html.
Kent v. Dulles. 357 U.S. 116 (1958).
Regan v. Wald. 468 U.S. 222 (1984).
Speech given by Raúl Castro Ruz. 3rd Regular Session of the Seventh Legislature of the National Assembly of People's Power, Havana, August 1, 2009, "Year of the 50th Anniversary of the Revolutionary Triumph." http://www.cubanembassy.net/documents/314A A7388FD0f31a 56279a59b5f4784034c1923d.html.
Zemel v. Rusk. 381 U.S. 1 (1965).

Articles and Online Resources

"25 Best Blogs 2009." *Time*. http://www.time.com/time/specials/packages/completelist/0,,1879276,00.html.
"Adlai Stevenson: United Nations Security Council Address on Soviet Missiles in Cuba." American Rhetoric. http://www.americanrhetoric.com/speeches/adlaistevensonunitednation scuba.html.
Altman, R. "Globalization in Retreat." *Foreign Affairs* 88, no. 4 (July–August 2009). http://www.foreignaffairs.com/articles/65153/roger-c-altman/globalization-in-retreat.
"Arturo López-Levy at UM Cuba Conference April 4, 2009 Pt. 2." YouTube. http://www.you tube.com/watch?v=DotzkLI8C4Y.
Baker, P. "Building Coalitions, One Issue at a Time." *New York Times*, March 14, 2009. http://www.nytimes.com/2009/03/15/us/politics/15obama.html.
Barnett, T. "The Next Five States." *Esquire* (September 19, 2007). http://www.esquire.com/fea tures/esquire-100/fivestates1007.
Bendixen & Amandi. *National Poll of Cuban & Cuban Americans on Changes to Cuba Policy*. http://www.bendixenandassociates.com/Cuba_ Flash_Poll_Executive_Summary.html.
"Bolsa Família: Changing the Lives of Millions in Brazil." WorldBank.org. http://web.world-

bank.org/Wbsite/External/Countries/Lacext/Brazilextn/0,,contentmdk:21447054~pagepk:
141137~pipk:141127~theSitepk:322341,00.html.

Cave, D. "U.S. Overtures Find Support Among Cuban-Americans." *New York Times*, April 20,
2009. http://www.nytimes.com/2009/04/21/us/21miami.html?scp=1&sq=a%20stunning
%20change%20of%20heart%20now%20shared%20by%20a%20wide%20majority%20of
%20Cuban-Americans&st=cse.

"Colombian Rocker Juanes Makes Cuba Concert Political After All." *Examiner*, September 21,
2009. http://www.examiner.com/international-travel-in-chicago/colombian-rocker-juanes-
makes-cuba-concert-political-after-all.

"Congressional Black Caucus Meets with Castro Brothers." NPR.org, April 9, 2009. http://
www.npr.org/templates/story/story.php?storyId=102903658.

"Convergence" in "Economics A–Z." Economist.com. http://www.economist.com/research/eco-
nomics/alphabetic.cfm?term=catchupeffect&CFID=150606091&CFTOKEN=89214014.

"Cuba Begins Public Debate on Economic Reforms." *BBC News*, December 1, 2010. http://www.
bbc.co.uk/news/world-latin-america-11894593.

"Cuba Continuing to Develop Innovative Biotechnology Products." *Granma International*,
November 18, 2009. http://www.granma.cu/ingles/2009/noviembre/mier18/Cuba.html.

"Cuba Frees Political Prisoner Who Refused Exile Deal." *BBC News*, November 14, 2010. http://
www.bbc.co.uk/news/world-latin-america-11752157.

"Cuba Maps Out Economic Reforms." *CBC News*, September 24, 2010. http://www.cbc.ca/
world/story/2010/09/24/cuba-economic-reforms024.html.

"Cuban Government Vows to Release 52 Prisoners." *New York Times*, July 7, 2010. http://www.
nytimes.com/2010/07/08/world/americas/08cuba.html?.

"Cuba Suspends Communist Party Congress." *Guardian*, July 31, 2009. http://www.guardian.
co.uk/world/2009/jul/31/cuba-communist-party-economy.

"Cuba to Free Two More Political Prisoners." Reuters.com, November 13, 2010. http://www.
reuters.com/article/2010/11/14/us-cuba-prisoners-idustre6ac2fp20101114.

Deudney, D., and J. Ikenberry. "The Myth of the Autocratic Revival." *Foreign Affairs* 88, no.
1 (January/February 2009).

"Dissidents' Wives Hit Castro, Seek Release." *Washington Times*, December 27, 2005.

"Engaging Cuba: Policy Options for the United States, Europe and the Western Hemisphere"
(seminar). Woodrow Wilson Center in Washington, DC (November 16, 2009).

"Executive Summary." *2007 FIU/Cuba Poll*. http://www2.fiu.edu/~ipor/cuba8/ExecutiveSum
mary.htm.

Ferguson, A. "Gary Hart Comes Out." CNN.com, January 17, 2000. http://edition.cnn.com/
Allpolitics/time/2000/01/17/hart.html.

"Fidel Castro Appears to Support Cuban Economic Reforms." *McClatchy*, November 19, 2010.
http://www.mcclatchydc.com/2010/11/19/104019/fidel-castro-appears-to-support.html.

"Fidel Castro Praises Barack Obama as 'Absolutely Sincere.'" *Sunday Times*, January 22, 2009
(online).

Fineman, M. "Little Known Biotech Industry Vital to Cuba's Future." *Miami Herald*, August
14, 1998. http://www2.fiu.edu/~fcf/biotech81498.html.

Fontova, H. "Hollywood Loves Fidel—But Why?" *Canada Free Press*, May 9, 2009. http://
www.canadafreepress.com/index.php/site/article/hollywood-loves-fidel-but-why/.

Freedom House Report. *Change in Cuba: How Citizens View Their Country's Future*. http://
www.freedomhouse.org/template.cfm?page=383&report=69.

Friedman, T. "Living Hand to Mouth." *New York Times*, October 26, 2005 (online).

Gat, A., D. Deudney, J. Ikenberry, R. Inglehart, and C. Welzel. "Which Way Is History Marching?" *Foreign Affairs* (July–August 2009). http://www.foreignaffairs.com /articles/65162/
azar-gat-daniel-deudney-and-g-john-ikenberry-and-ronald-inglehar/which-way-is-history-
marching?page=show.

Gershman, C., and O. Gutierrez. "Ferment in Civil Society: Can Cuba Change?" *Journal of
Democracy* 20, no. 1 (January 2009): 36–54. http://www.journalofdemocracy.org/articles/
gratis/Gutierrez-20-1.pdf.

Gill, N. "Historiography: Brazilian Hegemony in South America." *Southern Affairs*, March 31,
2008. http://www.southernaffairs.org/2008/03/historiography-iii-brazilian-hegemony.html.

Goldberg, J. "Castro: 'No One Has Been Slandered More Than the Jews.'" Theatlantic.com, September 7, 2010. http://www.theatlantic.com/international/archive/2010/09/castro-no-one-has-been-slandered-more–than-the-jews/62566/.
_____. "Fidel: 'Cuban Model Doesn't Even Work for Us Anymore.'" Theatlantic.com, September 8, 2010. http://www.theatlantic.com/-international/archive/2010/09/fidel-cuban-model-doesnt-even-work-for-us-anymore/62602/.
Hare, P., and T. Revesz. "Hungary's Transition to a Market Economy: The Case Against a 'Big Bang.'" Economic Policy 14 (1992).
Henriksen, T. H. "The Rise and Decline of the Rogue States." Journal of International Affairs 54, no. 2 (Spring 2001).
Hsu, S. "Walter Myers, State Dept. Analyst Who Spied for Cuba, Gets Life; Wife 6 Years." Washington Post, July 17, 2010. http://www.washingtonpost.com/wp-dyn/content/article/2010/07/16/AR2010071600684.html.
Inglehart, R., and C. Welzel. "How Development Leads to Democracy." Foreign Affairs 88, no. 2 (March–April 2009).
Kuttner, R. "The Copenhagen Consensus." Foreign Affairs (March–April 2008). http://www.foreignaffairs.com/articles/63223/robert-kuttner/the-copenhagen-consensus.
"Ladies in White March in Cuba, Pay Price for Disobedience." Chicago Tribune, March 3, 2006.
"Ladies in White Stopped from Collecting EU Award." Associated Press, December 15, 2005.
Laffey, M., and J. Weldes. "Decolonizing the Cuban Missile Crisis." International Studies Quarterly 52, no. 3 (September 2008): 555–77.
Litwak, R. S. "What's in a Name? The Changing Foreign Policy Lexicon." Journal of International Affairs 54, no. 2 (Spring 2001): 375–92.
Lopez-Levy, A. "Cuban Americans Vote with Their Feet." Havana Note, November 23, 2010. http://www.thehavananote.com/node/822.
_____. "Not Your Father's Cuba." Foreign Policy, November 5, 2010. http://www.foreignpolicy.com/articles/2010/11/05/not_your_fathers_cuba.
_____. "Strait Talk." Foreign Policy, January 31, 2011. http://www.foreignpolicy.com/articles/2011/01/31/strait_talk.
Mackey, R. "Fidel Castro Blogs About the 'Honey of Power.'" New York Times, March 3, 2009. http://thelede.blogs.nytimes.com/2009/03/03/fidel-castro-blogs-about-the-honey-of-power/.
Mitgang, H. "Publishing the FBI File on Hemingway." New York Times, March 11, 1983. http://www.nytimes.com/books/99/07/04/specials/hemingway-fbi.html.
"News and Alerts." American Civil Liberties Union of Florida. http://www.aclufl.org/news_events/?action=viewRelease&emailAlertID=1949.
"Obama to Free Cuba Family Travel, Remittances." Reuters.com, April 3, 2009. http://www.reuters.com/article/idustre5326hv20090403.
"Ocho Leones Feroces." Granma. http://www.granma.cubaweb.cu/secciones/50_granma-80_fidel/secretos_de_generales/art09.html.
Padgett, T. "Cuba's Mega-Rock Concert: A Win-Win for Juanes." Time (September 21, 2009). http://www.time.com/time/world/article/0,8599,1925283,00.html.
Perry, M. "End Embargo Before China Taps Oil 45 Miles Off U.S. Coast." Billings Gazette, July 16, 2009. http://billingsgazette.com/news/opinion/guest/article_98b56854–71b2–11de-976d-001cc4c002e0.html.
"Poll Shows Strong Cuban American Support for Obama." Reuters.com, April 21, 2009. http://www.reuters.com/article/idustre53K5cs20090421.
Queens University, Department of Sociology. "The Measure of a Revolution" (May 7–9, 2009). http://www.queensu.ca/sociology/?q=themeasureofarevolution09.
Quigley, J. "Opinion." Cleveland Plain Dealer, July 11, 2009 (online).
Randal, J. "License to Test Cancer Vaccines in U.S. a Victory for Cuban Biotechnology." Journal of the National Cancer Institute 96, no. 23 (2004): 1740–42. http://jnci.oxfordjournals.org/content/96/23/1740.full.
Rauch, J. "Capitalism's Fault Lines." New York Times Sunday Book Review, May 14, 2009. http://www.nytimes.com/2009/05/17/books/review/Rauch-t.html.
"Raul Castro: Open Debate Best Way to Solve Problems." Fox News Latino, December 6, 2010.

http://latino.foxnews.com/latino/politics/2010/12/06/raul-castro-open-debate-best-way-solve-problems/.

"Russia to Drill for Oil Off Cuba." *BBC News*, July 29, 2009 (online). http://news.bbc.co.uk/2/hi/8175704.stm.

Sánchez, Yoani. "And They Gave Us the Microphones." *Generacion Y*. http://www.desdecuba.com/generationy/?m=200903.

_____. "At the Meliá Cohiba." *Generacion Y*. http://www.desdecuba.com/generationy/?m=200905&paged=2.

_____. "My Profile." *Generacion Y*. http://www.desdecuba.com/generationy/?page_id=108.

_____. "The Shredder." *Generacion Y*. http://www.desdecuba.com/generationy/?m=200903.

_____. "Third Time Is Not a Charm." *Generacion Y*. http://www.desdecuba.com/generationy/?m=200903.

Sanger, D. "Beyond the Trade Pact Collapse." *New York Times*, August 3, 2008 (online).

Schubert, G. "One Party Rule and the Question of Legitimacy in Contemporary China." *Journal of Contemporary China* 17, no. 54 (2008): 191–204.

Schwirtz, M. "Russia and Cuba Sign Strategic Partnership." *New York Times*, January 30, 2009. http://www.nytimes.com/2009/01/31/world/europe/31russia.html?_r=1&scp=1&sq=The%20presidents%20of%20Russia%20and%20Cuba%20signed%20a%20strategic%20partnership%20&st=cse.

"Sixth Congress of the Communist Party of Cuba to be Held Next Year." *Cuba Journal*, November 9, 2010. http://cubajournal.blogspot.com/2010/11/sixth-congress-of-communist-party-of.html.

Smith, W., R. Muse, and G. Baker. "Center for International Policy Report, Cuba Should Not Be on the Terrorist List." http://www.scarletnotes.com/downloads /CubaonTerroristList_.pdf.

Stiglitz, J. "Wall Street's Toxic Message." *Vanity Fair* (July 2009).

"Supreme Court: Miami School Can Ban Book on Cuba." *Christian Science Monitor*, November 16, 2009. http://www.instablogs.com/outer_permalink.php?p=supreme-court-miami-school-can-ban-book-on-cuba.

"'Tawdry Shleifer Affair' Stokes Faculty Anger Toward Summers." *Harvard Crimson*, February 10, 2006. http://www.thecrimson.com/article/2006/2/10/tawdry-shleifer-affair-stokes-faculty-anger/.

"U.S. Supreme Court Denies ACLU's Petition to Hear *Vamos a Cuba* Book Censorship Case." American Civil Liberties Union. http://www.aclu.org/free-speech/us-supreme-court-denies-aclus-petition-hear-vamos-cuba-book-censorship-case.

"Varela Project." *New York Times* (article collection). http://www.nytimes.com/keyword/varela-project.

"Wives of Political Prisoners March in Cuba." Associated Press, March 18, 2006.

Zakaria, F. "The Capitalist Manifesto: Greed Is Good (to a Point)." *Newsweek* (June 13, 2009). http://www.newsweek.com/2009/06/12/the-capitalist-manifesto-greed-is-good.html.

Index

Numbers in **_bold italics_** indicate pages with photographs.